DANCING LONGER
DANCING STRONGER

A Dancer's Guide to Conditioning,
Improving Technique, and Preventing Injury

Second Edition

DANCING LONGER DANCING STRONGER

A Dancer's Guide to Conditioning,
Improving Technique, and Preventing Injury

Second Edition

Robin Kish & Jennie Morton

Illustrations by David A. Gabriel

A DANCE HORIZONS BOOK
PRINCETON BOOK COMPANY, PUBLISHERS

Dancing Longer, Dancing Stronger is not intended as medical advice. Its intention is solely informational and educational. Please consult a medical or health professional should the need for one be indicated; if possible, try to find one who has expertise in dance medicine. Princeton Book Company, Publishers, and the authors disclaim responsibility and liability for any damages, including consequential and special damages, arising out of or in connection with your use of *Dancing Longer, Dancing Stronger,* whether based on contract or tort.

Published in the United States by Dance Horizons,
an imprint of Princeton Book Company, Publishers
www.dancehorizons.com

Book design and composition by Mulberry Tree Press
Cover design by Alessia Arregui
and Mulberry Tree Press
Cover photograph of Backhausdance in *Hive,* courtesy of Jennifer Backhaus
Interior photographs by Emily Duncan

Library of Congress Cataloging-In-Publication Data

Names: Kish, Robin, author. | Morton, Jennie, author. | Gabriel, David A., illustrator.
Dancing longer dancing stronger.
Title: Dancing longer, dancing stronger : a dancer's guide to conditioning, improving technique and preventing injury / Robin Kish and Jennie Morton
Description: Second edition. | Trenton, NJ : Princeton Book Company, Publishers, [2019] | First edition, by Andrea Watkins and Pricilla M. Clarkson, published in 1990. | "A Dance Horizons Book." | Includes bibliographical references and index.
Identifiers: ISBN 978 087127 3970
Subjects: LCSH: Dance. | Physical conditioning. | Dance--Physiological aspects. | Dancing--preventing injuries. | Dance--Safety measures.
Classification: LCC GV1588 .K57 2019 | DDC 792.8--dc23

CONTENTS

Foreword *xi*

Preface *xiii*

Acknowledgments *xv*

PART I: FOUNDATIONS FOR SUCCESSFUL TRAINING 1

1 Integration of Physical Requirements for
    Performance 3
       The dancing body 3
       Why conditioning is a dancer's secret weapon 3
       Using this book to your advantage 4

2 The Purpose of Conditioning 6
       Recognizing the benefits 6
       Defining your needs and goals 7
       Past ideas vs. current knowledge 8

3 Basic Anatomical Information 10
       Body orientation 10
       Body movements 10
       Body tissues 11
       Types of muscle action 13
       Neutral alignment 13

4 Conditioning for Strength 16
       The overload principle 16
       The specificity principle 18
       The reversibility principle 19
       Periodization 19

5   Conditioning for Flexibility   21
    Hypermobility   21
    The relationship between strength and flexibility   22
    When to stretch   23

6   Additional Training Protocols   24
    Cardiovascular fitness   24
    Balance and proprioception   24

7   The Strength Conditioning Exercises   26
    Introduction to the exercises   26
    Determining the number of repetitions   27
    Timing patterns and tempos   29
    Variety in your exercise program   30
    Finding the time   31
    Top priorities   31

8   The Flexibility Exercises   34
    Timing the stretch   34
    Intensity of the stretch   35
    Use of breath   35
    Exercise sessions per week   35
    Other flexibility exercises   36

9   Equipment and Setup   37
    Required equipment   37
    Selecting your exercise space   38

PART II: THE FOOT, ANKLE, AND LOWER LEG   39

10   Structural Anatomy   41
    Movements of the foot and ankle   43
    Muscles of the foot and ankle   43
    Neutral alignment   52

11   Questions and Answers: The Foot, Ankle,
   and Lower Leg   53

12   Strength and Flexibility Exercises: The Foot, Ankle, and Lower Leg   70

Foot articulation   71

Dorsiflexion   76

Plantar flexion   80

Eversion   84

Inversion   88

Pointing without the calf   90

PART III: THE KNEE AND HIP   93

13   Structural Anatomy   95

Movements of the knee joint   96

The structure of the hip joint   100

Movements of the hip joint   102

Neutral alignment for the knees and hip   110

14   Questions and Answers: The Knee and Hip   112

15   Strength and Flexibility Exercises: The Knee and Hip   128

Knee flexion   129

Knee extension   133

Hip flexion   135

Hip extension   142

Hip abduction   148

Hip adduction   153

External rotation with abduction   157

Internal rotation with abduction   165

Functional knee stability   166

PART IV: THE TRUNK AND NECK   169

16   Structural Anatomy   171

Movements of the trunk and neck   172

Neutral alignment   183

17   Questions and Answers: The Trunk and Neck   185

18   Strength and Flexibility Exercises: The Trunk
     and Neck   199

    Trunk flexors   200

    Trunk extensors   209

    Rotating the trunk   214

    Trunk side-bending   218

    The neck   221

    Spinal articulation   229

PART V: THE SHOULDER AND ARM   233

19   Structural Anatomy   235

    Movements of the shoulder joint   236

    Movements of the shoulder girdle   237

    Structure of the elbow joint   248

    Movements of the elbow joint   249

    Structure and movements of the wrist joint   253

    Neutral alignment of the shoulder and arm   256

20   Questions and Answers: The Shoulder and Arm   257

21   Strength and Flexibility Exercises: The Shoulder
     and Arm   263

    Scapular stabilization   263

    Shoulder flexion   268

    Shoulder extension   270

    Shoulder abduction   273

    Shoulder adduction   274

    External rotation   275

    Internal rotation   277

    Combined movements of the *scapulae* and *glenohumeral joint*   279

    Elbow flexion   283

    Elbow extension   285

    Elbow pronation and supination   288

    Wrist flexion   289

    Wrist extension   291

PART VI: PUTTING IT ALL TOGETHER   293

22   Training the Entire Dancer   295

    Cardiovascular fitness   295

    Balance and proprioceptive training   300

    Psychological health   301

    Rest   302

23   Conditioning Programs   305

    Section I—Specific aims   305

        Exercise combinations: Foot and ankle   *306*

        Exercise combinations: Knee and hip   *307*

        Exercise combinations: Trunk and neck   *308*

        Exercise combinations: Shoulder and arm   *309*

    Section II—Comprehensive conditioning   310

        Quick warm-up for class, rehearsal, or performance   *310*

        Full-body training—beginning, intermediate/advanced   *312*

24   Moving Beyond and Next Steps   316

    Personal trainers   317

    Alternative training modalities   317

    Cooling down and wrapping up   319

Appendix: Interviews with Dancers   *321*

References   *330*

Resources   *333*

Index   *339*

FOREWORD

THIS BOOK WILL BE USEFUL for dancers and teachers, and those involved in concert and commercial dance, from students to professionals. Dancers today are expected to have more agility, technical versatility, and range of motion than dancers of a generation ago. Choreographic demands for todays' dancers include higher side extensions, arabesques, and more rotations in turns; and may require aerial and acrobatic work, and a variety of footwear.

Although we have better understanding of dance injuries and contributing factors, the injury rates among dancers remains unacceptably high. This is in part because a typical dance technique class does not adequately prepare the dancer for the variety of demands placed on them in performance. Dancers today must be proactive in adding supplemental conditioning, strengthening and flexibility training. This book should be their guide.

I am honored the authors asked me to write a foreword for this new edition of *Dancing Longer, Dancing Stronger*. I have a well-worn copy of the original I have owned and used for many years in both my dance medicine practice and when teaching dance; this updated version is timely indeed. While maintaining the relevance to dancers and ease of understanding of the original, this book has incorporated new scientific evidence, training, and conditioning principles from sport science. The authors have successfully translated these principles into dancer friendly combinations of exercises while maintaining the integrity and purpose of cross-training and supplemental conditioning so critical for developing a healthy, balanced dancer.

This revised edition retains the original clarity of definitions and descriptions of anatomy and conditioning principles for strength and flexibility, while adding important newer concepts. Interviews with dancers from a variety of genres have been added, giving their personal insights into how supplemental conditioning has helped them in their daily dancing lives. Clear and insightful discussions of neutral alignment, periodization, hypermobility, the importance of core stabilization, and the use of breath are enhancing additions. New sections on cardiovascular fitness, balance and proprioception, warm-up and cool down, and a discussion on the importance of rest (so often overlooked by the dedicated dancer) are some highlights for me. I was happy to see "pointing without the calf" added to the foot and ankle section as I have used this concept in my practice when treating dancers with posterior ankle impingement and Achilles tendon problems.

This book is appropriate for dancers and dance educators of any style, genre, or level. Dancers with professional aspirations or those simply using dance as exercise could benefit from the principles presented here. *Dancing Longer, Dancing Stronger* will give any dancer or teacher the tools for enhancing their strength, flexibility, and health.

Dancers who embrace the concepts of supplemental cross-training and conditioning will be better prepared to face the challenges ahead in their dance career. Stronger, fitter, and balanced dancers are better dancers—freer to develop their artistry within challenging choreographic demands.

Nancy J. Kadel, M.D.
Orthopaedic Surgeon, Foot & Ankle, Dance Medicine
Seattle Clinic for Performing Artists
Past President, Performing Arts Medicine Association (PAMA)

PREFACE

THE FIRST EDITION OF THIS BOOK was published in 1990, when the field of dance medicine and science was very young. It was one of the first books that used this new scientific information to create evidence-based practice protocols and delivered this information in a usable way to dancers and dance educators. In the intervening years, the field of dance medicine and science has grown exponentially and there is now a wealth of information available, much of which is accessible via the Internet. However, searching the available data circulating in online form can be overwhelming for the individual who is looking for specific protocols for managing his or her technical and artistic development as a dancer. This book represents a comprehensive yet concise guide to supplemental training for dancers that places much of the latest scientifically recommended information into one text. It provides a roadmap for the implementation of dance science "best practice" into the studio, rehearsal space, or performance environments. Whether you want to enhance your anatomical knowledge, have your technique questions answered, address specific body or injury challenges, or build your own personalized supplemental training routine, this book is a portable companion that you can carry with you on whichever path or in whichever direction your dance career may take.

Whether you are a dancer who is finding it hard to move forward with your technique, or a teacher who is frustrated by the lack of response to your technical cues, the cause may lie not in the dancer's lack of desire to change, nor in the teacher's ability to communicate a correction. Instead, it may be that the dancer lacks the requisite strength or flexibility to bring about a change. It may also be that either the dancer or the teacher lacks the appropriate anatomical information to safely effect a change. It is also key to note that any changes made to underlying technique require time to be absorbed and implemented by the body: so-called "quick fixes" are rarely sustainable. In the case of injuries, whether they be from overuse or from a traumatic onset, the root cause is often related to issues such as a lack of strength and flexibility, compromised coordination, or an over-optimistic training, rehearsal, or performance schedule. This book will highlight such issues and offer solutions for optimal training practices and scheduling.

The reality is that a dance career in the 21st century typically places very high demands on the body, and standard dance technique classes do not provide all the components that our bodies require for a long and healthy career. It is therefore imperative that dancers undertake supplemental training to provide the additional strength and flexibility requirements, as well as addressing the cardiovascular, proprioceptive, and psychological components of fitness. When the body is finely tuned for all that it may face in a dance career, it will provide a dynamically stable foundation from which the true essence of dance performance—artistic expression—can emerge.

Dancers today need to be proficient in a wide range of dance styles, so this book is designed to target all the requirements of the dancing body. Once a dynamically stable foundation has been created, it provides the roots from which any style of movement can grow. Whether you are a beginner or a seasoned professional, you must continue to evaluate and assess your ever-changing needs as a dancer. Just as a dancer is always in motion, the body is also on an ever-moving trajectory of growth and transition. By becoming aware of your ever-changing needs in the context of the challenges of your current working environment, you can define your own personal training requirements at any given time. This book is designed for you to be able to devise your own personal "prescription" to meet these needs, and to shape and refine them to particular episodes in your career.

We, the authors, consider it an honor and privilege to have been asked to create this new edition of *Dancing Longer, Dancing Stronger*. We are grateful for the opportunity to support dancers and dance educators on their journey to discovering, through safe and effective practice, the wonders of the dancing body and to play a role in their creating a path to a long and healthy dance career.

ACKNOWLEDGMENTS

OUR INITIAL THANKS go to Andrea Watkins and Priscilla Clarkson, the authors of the first edition of this book, whose shoulders we stand upon in writing this updated version. Special thanks go to Jan Dunn, founder of the *Journal of Dance Medicine and Science*, who created the opportunity for us to rewrite this book. For the photography in the book, we thank Emily Duncan for her work behind the camera. We thank the following dancers for allowing us to use their images: Harmony Adams, Jonah Almanzar, Sam Cantoria, Alexis Difilippo, Aika Donne, Morgan Goodfellow, Anna Reed Grass, Sophia Lang, McKell Lemon, Karli Jo List, Sean McElaney, Dani Mullan, Elijah Richardson, Maddie Robertson, Eugenia Rodriguez, Megan Seagren, Ashley Sims, Tiffany Theodore, Samantha Waugh, and Rachel Yuter. Thank you, as well, to Backhausdance for providing the cover photograph.

DANCING LONGER DANCING STRONGER

A Dancer's Guide to Conditioning,
Improving Technique, and Preventing Injury

Second Edition

Part I

FOUNDATIONS for SUCCESSFUL TRAINING

The field of Dance Medicine and Science, or Dance Wellness (the two terms are synonymous) started in the late 1970s. However, after several decades, the concept of supplemental training in addition to dance class is still not common practice, and the purpose of such training is still unclear to many dancers. Consequently, many do not realize the benefits of a good conditioning program with respect to improving dance technique—whether it is ballet, modern, contemporary, jazz, Spanish, Bollywood, tap, or any other style. In today's world, dancers are expected to be able to master many forms of dance, regardless of the style of their basic training. Classical ballet companies often include modern works in their repertoire; Broadway shows can include a diversity of styles—classical, jazz, hip hop, tap, circus, and even Bollywood; and freelance dancers need to be proficient in as many styles as possible in order not to exclude themselves from job opportunities.

Those dancers who embrace the concept of supplemental conditioning will find that they have an advantage in safely meeting the many physical challenges that are demanded by these varying dance forms. The key to a long and healthy career lies in recognizing where there are gaps in your training needs and in creating a supplemental training program to bridge those gaps. This book is designed to help you navigate this process and to support your journey to a long and fulfilling career.

1

INTEGRATION of PHYSICAL REQUIREMENTS for PERFORMANCE

The dancing body

Dancing requires a wonderfully rich and complex interaction between numerous body systems. While our bodies may be seen as being comprised of many components, such as bones, muscles, fascia, nerves, organs, and so forth, it is the harmonious integration of these structures into movement that makes dance a fulfilling experience for both the dancer and the audience. In order to achieve this integration, the dancer must first have a basic understanding of the role of all the body systems utilized in movement to ensure that they are being used efficiently and to their full potential. The soft tissues (muscles, tendons, fascia, etc.) need to be both supple and powerful to create flexible, but dynamic, movement. We then need a power source to fuel this system, and this comes in the form of our cardiovascular and respiratory systems. Finally, to coordinate all these instruments into a cohesive whole, we need a conductor. This comes in the form of our brain and nervous system that provide our coordination, balance, and sensory feedback, allowing us to constantly monitor and adjust our movements in response to the environment. Dance training needs to address all these systems to ensure that they are functioning optimally and to our best advantage. Only then can we meet the technical demands of the various dance genres, reduce the risk of injury, and free ourselves for expressive movement.

Why conditioning is a dancer's secret weapon

While dance is a highly technically demanding art form, a skilled dancer makes it appear effortless. A dancer's technique is the scaffolding upon which

3

an artistic performance can be built, but it should not be the visible part of the process. When we begin training, the technical aspects of movement often appear very obvious as we strive to grasp the intricacies of the steps. However, through repetition and fine tuning we are able to turn these conscious processes into subliminal patterns, freeing us up for artistic expression. In order to achieve this transition, we must hone all the aforementioned body systems into a highly integrated and highly skilled unit that works in the background to facilitate our performance. This is achieved through specific conditioning protocols. We can all recognize the distinction between those dancers who appear in complete control of their bodies and those whose bodies appear to be controlling them! Those who are in control have managed to harness all the body systems and exploit them to their full potential, and this can represent a "secret weapon" when it comes to booking that job.

With the competition for professional work being very high, the dancer who has optimal physical fitness and fewer injuries has a clear advantage. A conditioning program is not only an essential part of pre-professional training, but it is also a vital part of a dancer's regular routine—whether they are currently employed or not. The dancer who is fit and ready to attend that last minute audition is more likely to book the job. Injured dancers also represent a financial burden to an employer, so the dancer who is able to fulfill their contractual obligations fully is more likely to be rehired than someone who has been consistently out of performance with an injury. So here again, the dancer who is able to maintain his or her physical fitness and reduce the risk of injury also has a secret weapon that provides an advantage in the professional world.

While we are talking here of secret weapons, a dance career should not be seen as a battlefield for which we need to arm ourselves to gain an advantage. In an ideal world, all dancers would be undertaking supplemental conditioning programs, giving everyone an equal opportunity to have a long and productive career and thus benefiting the profession as a whole.

Using this book to your advantage

This book has been designed to address the conditioning needs of any dancer. Regardless of the genre, all dancers' bodies have the same muscular structure and the same requirement for balanced training. This book is designed to focus on the fundamentals of movement that cross all dance styles. The exercises are grouped by body area, allowing you to easily navigate from foot to head. While some exercises may form your core conditioning program, you may choose to select others for specific repertoire needs. For instance, if you are currently working on choreography that requires weight-bearing on the arms, you may want to visit the upper-body section for supplemental training ideas.

There are no quick fixes or shortcuts to optimum health and performance, and there are no magic tricks for developing, overnight, the necessary flexibility for a beautiful leg extension. However, by educating yourself about the fundamentals of conditioning you will be able to create a plan to optimize your training. **Part I** of this book lays the groundwork for understanding basic anatomy, the purpose of conditioning, the principles of strength training, and the science of flexibility. It also establishes safe and effective practices for dancers' supplementary conditioning. To help to guide you in your practice, the components of strength conditioning are discussed, including repetitions, resistance choices, timing, and programing. Techniques for achieving flexibility, including timing and intensity, are also covered in this section with a view to supporting healthy training practices. Take the time to read through **Part I** so you have a clearer understanding of how the body works and what is needed to assemble an effective conditioning program. **Parts II through V** focus on specific areas of the body and provide information on basic anatomy, exercises, and interviews from artists. As you progress through to **Part VI**, it is important to keep in mind that your body works as a complete system. An effective conditioning program may need to have a narrow focus on specific areas of concern, but should also maintain a global context that addresses the whole dancer.

2
The PURPOSE of CONDITIONING

Recognizing the benefits

Historically, a supplemental conditioning program has not been a regular feature of most forms of dance training. Dance class was seen as the sole requirement for the development of technique and fitness levels. We now know that the traditional dance class format does not necessarily prepare dancers for all aspects of performance, and while the physical demands of the profession have increased over recent years, dance training has not notably altered to accommodate these changes. For instance, traditional ballet and modern classes, with their stop/start nature, do not allow for optimal development of aerobic fitness. However, performance choreography often involves long, continuous dance sequences that require cardiovascular endurance for which a dancer may be unprepared. Therefore a supplemental aerobic fitness program would be a useful addition. Conditioning the whole body to find the balance between strength and mobility is key to preventing further injury and improving performance.

Dance requires repetitive training that, unfortunately, can lead to muscular imbalances and overuse injuries. Take a moment to think of the percentage of time you work in turn-out versus a turned-in position of the hip joint. Some dancers work in turn-out so extensively that finding a parallel stance for their jazz or modern class is nearly impossible. A conditioning program allows dancers to work outside the realm of dance class where they can focus on strengthening any underworked or neglected muscle groups. It can help to increase joint range of motion and reduce muscle tension when it is not always possible to fully address such things in class. If you find yourself on a plateau and are struggling to improve your technique, it may be that you are lacking the appropriate strength or flexibility. If so, a supplemental conditioning program, in addition to your dance classes, may help you in this regard.

Have you ever had an injury? Dancers are notorious for not fully completing their physical rehabilitation programs after injury, and some do not even seek help to begin with. The healing phase of an injury provides an opportunity to learn more about the body and to come back better and stronger than before. Chronic injuries and lingering pain are frequently caused by weak and imbalanced musculature. A good dance conditioning program will complement the work in technique class, and as strength and flexibility improve, technical skill will also improve. By making moderate and consistent efforts toward overall health, you can both increase the longevity of, and improve the quality of, your dance career.

Defining your needs and goals

It is well-documented that athletes spend a considerable amount of time conditioning their bodies for the demands of competition through cross-training outside their own sport discipline. For example, in addition to their on-field practice, football players also utilize mental practice by reviewing videos of games and learning different plays. They also spend a considerable amount of time in the gym improving their physical condition. Athletes will tell you that much of their time is spent off the field, or out of the pool, preparing for their events, unlike dancers who spend the majority of their training time in the studio. All these athletes have specific physical needs and goals with regard to their training. For example, runners who require the explosive power for a quick start off the blocks would benefit from plyometric training, rather than spending hours in a hot yoga class that would not be specific to their needs in this instance. This book is designed to guide you through suggestions not only for general dance conditioning, but also for creating a tailored program to meet any specific demands that you are facing.

When determining your needs it is helpful to assess your short-term and long-term goals. Short-term goals typically focus on specific aspects of technique. That may be *fouettés* in ballet, tilts in jazz, or inversions in a modern class. These short-term goals usually require specific additional training, outside of the dance studio, that focuses on strength, flexibility, balance, and muscular coordination. Long-term goals may be directed toward your future aspirations as a dancer, such as specific auditions, the repertoire of a particular dance company, or the style of work in the concert/commercial industry. If, for example, you have your eyes set on a job with a very physical dance company, then now is the time to address the cardiovascular and possibly upper-body strength training necessary to be successful in performing that company's repertoire safely. It is important to keep in mind that your needs and goals will change over time as your training progresses and your work opportunities develop. Regardless of their goals, dancers who undertake supplemental conditioning will come to class with an instrument that is better prepared for their technical training. These dancers will be less vulnerable to injury and better prepared to meet the challenges of both technique and performance.

Past ideas vs. current knowledge

As previously mentioned, supplemental conditioning programs were not commonplace in the dance world of the past. So we may wonder why we should place such an emphasis on this idea today. Over the decades, dance technique has continually increased in difficulty and has in many ways become more athletic. Many steps that were considered technically demanding fifty years ago are now common dance vocabulary, thus it would have been easier for dancers of past generations to acquire the necessary technique by class participation alone. Just as the level of difficulty in dance technique has increased with time, so have the physical demands of a performing career. Today's dancers often perform more frequently and in a wider range of movement styles and venues than past dancers did. Because dancers in earlier times did not have to meet these demands, their regular technique class was often sufficient preparation for a successful performing career.

Furthermore, we will never know how many potentially wonderful dancers did not have the chance to perform. Perhaps their technique classes were not sufficient to fully develop the height of their jump or leg extensions, for example. Consequently, they may have been passed over in favor of another dancer with a better *ballon* or *développé*. Perhaps potential careers were cut short or completely prevented due to injury. All of these situations may have been avoided by adopting an appropriate dance conditioning program. Since the 1990s, an increasing body of research has been developed in the field of dance medicine and science that validates the need for supplemental conditioning. While dancers today may be aware of the need for supplemental conditioning, choosing the appropriate training program can be a difficult process.

Dancers today may be aware of the need for supplemental conditioning, but choosing the appropriate training program can be a difficult process. The Internet is awash with apps and programs stating that they have all the answers. Even in the published research, while there is agreement that dancers need to develop a balance between stability and mobility, along with aerobic training, the advice on how to achieve these goals may vary greatly. Dancers are faced with many options, such as free weights, resistance machines at gyms, multiple forms of yoga, Pilates, Gyrotonics, and cardio boot camps, to name a few. This book will help you to navigate the pros and cons of some of the current training options and help you tailor your program toward your individual needs and goals.

3

BASIC ANATOMICAL INFORMATION

THIS SECTION WILL INTRODUCE YOU to the basic anatomical terminology that will be used throughout this book. To facilitate your understanding of their respective roles in strength and flexibility training, it will also describe the properties and functions of the various body tissues, such as bones, muscles, tendons, and ligaments. These structures will then be placed into the context of neutral body alignment, as this forms the basis of many of the exercises throughout this book. This material is, therefore, key to understanding how to evaluate your dance technique and how to create and perform an appropriate conditioning program.

Body orientation

The following anatomical terms will be used to describe the various aspects of the body:

> *Anterior:* the front of the body or part of the body.
>
> *Posterior:* the back of the body or part of the body.
>
> *Midline:* the imaginary line that divides the body into a right and a left side.
>
> *Medial:* the part of the body closest to the midline of the body.
>
> *Lateral:* the part of the body farthest from the midline of the body.

Body movements

> *Flexion:* This movement involves a decrease in the angle between two body parts. For example, elbow flexion involves bringing the hand

toward the shoulder, decreasing the angle between the forearm and upper arm. A front kick is an example of hip flexion, as the angle between the thigh bone and the pelvis is decreasing (i.e., they are coming closer together).

Extension: This movement involves an increase in the angle between two body parts. For example, elbow extension involves moving the hand away from the shoulder, thus increasing the angle between the forearm and upper arm. An *arabesque* movement of the leg is an example of hip extension, as the angle between the thigh bone and the pelvis is increasing (i.e., they are moving farther apart).

Abduction: This involves a movement away from the midline. Raising the arm sideways to second position is an example of shoulder abduction.

Adduction: This involves a movement toward the midline. Bringing the arm down sideways from second position is an example of shoulder adduction.

External (outward) rotation: This involves a rotational movement away from the midline. Dancers' turn-out is an example of external rotation of the hip.

Internal (inward) rotation: This involves a rotational movement toward the midline. Turning the legs inward (where dancers don't like to go!) is an example of internal rotation of the hip.

Body tissues

Bones: These form the skeleton and come in many different shapes and sizes. There are approximately 206 bones in the body and they articulate with one another at joints. They provide the levers for body movement. (Figure 3.1)

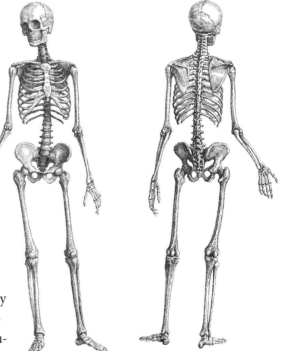

Figure 3.1 The skeleton

Ligaments: These are tough but flexible soft-tissue structures that strap two or more bones together at joints, providing passive stability and facilitating movement. As ligaments do not share the same level of elasticity as muscles, they can only be stretched by a slow, sustained force over time. Once stretched, however, they will remain lax, potentially creating instability of the underlying joint.

Muscles: These are bundles of elastic fibers that are able to contract and change shape or size, then return to their original state. They cross one or more joints and act as the pulleys that move the levers (bones), allowing us to ambulate through, and to interact with, our surroundings. They provide the active stability at our joints and are often paired with other muscles to facilitate controlled movement.

Tendons: These are tough bands or cords of inelastic tissue that serve to attach muscles to bones. They provide a means to transmit the contraction force of the elastic muscles to the bones for movement. At rest, the tendon fibers are wavy, then, under the contraction force of the muscle above, the waves are pulled flat (like a concertina or accordion), thus producing an increase in length. However, the fibers themselves do not stretch.

Cartilage: Where bones meet at joints, their surfaces are covered with a highly glossy surface layer of cartilage that facilitates movement, reduces friction on the bone surfaces, and transmits the loads produced by movement. Some joints, such as the knee, also contain pads of cartilage that help with shock absorption. In a growing child, the ends of many bones are still made of cartilage and do not fully become bone until approximately the age of 18 in females and 22 in males.

Fascia: This is a thin, membrane-like sheath that surrounds many of the body structures including the muscles, tendons, bones, and internal organs. It runs in various tracks throughout the body, encompassing and connecting many structures along its path. It is an important component of the body's structural integrity and facilitates the integration of movements across distant areas of the body.

Types of muscle action

In order to produce the complexities of human movement, muscles can act in three different ways:

> *Concentric muscle action:* This occurs when the attachment points of the muscle move toward each other and the muscle shortens as it exerts force. The hip flexor muscles perform this action when a dancer kicks his or her leg to the front, thus pulling the thigh bone toward the hip and spine.

> *Eccentric muscle action:* This occurs when the attachment points of the muscle move away from each other and the muscle lengthens as it exerts force. The hip flexor muscles perform this action when lowering the leg from a kick—they must exert enough force to counter gravity to control the descent, but the fibers also lengthen as the thigh bone moves away from the hip and spine.

> *Isometric muscle action:* This occurs when a muscle contracts and exerts a force without any change in its length. The muscles that move our arms perform this action when we hold the arms in second position—they contract to balance the weight of the arm against the force of gravity.

Neutral alignment

All the structures in the body are designed to work optimally from a neutral alignment. However, when we are dancing we are taking our bodies through all kinds of dynamic and static positions that may well be far from the neutral ideal. The body is perfectly capable of achieving this, but what we must consider is that any movement away from neutral alignment may have an increased biomechanical cost. This could manifest as increased energy requirements, increased forces or loads on body structures, and compromises in balance and stability, all of which may also increase the risk of injury. We must therefore have strategies in place to ensure that our bodies are well prepared to compensate for these risk factors, and the content of this book is aimed at doing just that.

If we liken the body to a stack of "Jenga" bricks, the stack will be at its most stable when the weight is transferred through the center of each brick. The moment we pull a brick out of line, the stability of the stack is compromised. In our bodies, this means that the weight needs to be transferred through the center of each joint. For example, the weight of the head needs to be transferred centrally through each vertebra down the gently curving spine to the pelvis, then on through the center of both hip joints to the knees and feet below.

A common way to measure neutral alignment is to use a plumb line. Viewed from the side, the plumb line should begin just under the ear lobe and run through the center of the shoulder, the center of the hip, just slightly in front of the center of the knee joint, and slightly in front of the outside ankle bone. The arms should hang easily at the side. This can be seen in Figure 3.2.

When we are out of neutral, the weight is not being transferred through the center of the joints and this can result in increased stress on the bones, ligaments, and cartilage. This can begin to cause unnecessary wear and tear on these structures that could result in pain and injury.

When we are in a neutral alignment, there is a minimal amount of muscular effort required to keep us upright. If we balanced a tennis ball on our heads in this position, it would stay there without any effort to hold it in place. However, if we shift away from neutral, then the tennis ball is going to hit the ground under the influence of gravity, and the same is true of our bodies. In order to counter this force, we will have to contract some muscles in order to retain our stability. For example, if we pitch our weight toward the balls of the feet, then the muscles at the back of the legs and torso will have to contract to prevent us from falling forward. If this is a habitual issue, then those muscles may become shortened, and thus weakened, reducing flexibility and power and leaving them more vulnerable to injury.

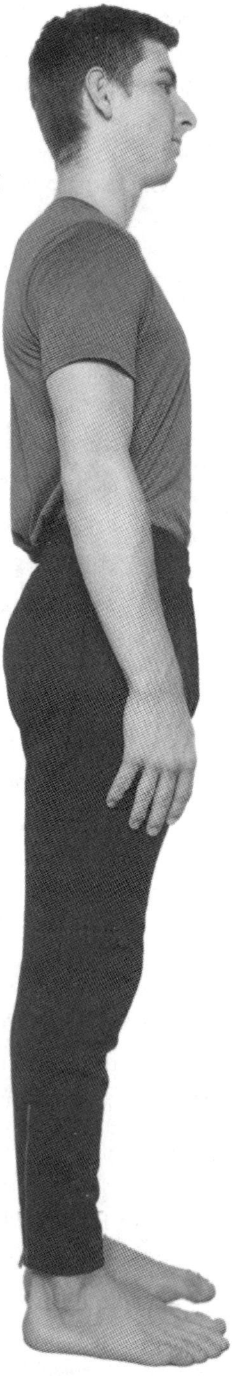

Figure 3.2
Optimal alignment

Many of the exercises you will find in this book begin with you lying on your back. It is important that we also know how to find a neutral spine in this supine position. While you are lying on the back with knees bent, the sacrum will be in contact with the floor, the lower spine (lumbar region) will rise just off the floor, and the upper back (thoracic region) will be on the floor. In this position the deepest abdominal muscle (*transverse abdominis*) will play a role in maintaining the support for the lumbar spine and attention should be paid to this when carrying out the exercises.

When we are dancing, there is always a part of the body in contact with the ground, except when we are in the air in jumps. Most often, it is our feet that are in contact with the ground, thus all the structures above are dependent upon them for their alignment. This is known as a *closed system*. For example, if a dancer is turning out the feet excessively in order to enhance the look of their fifth position, then this will have a reciprocal effect through the knees, hips, pelvis, and spine. This inefficient alignment provides a temporary solution that may have long-term costs in terms of increased injury risk.

Thus, the starting point for any conditioning program is to find that ideal neutral alignment. Once this has been established, strategies can be created to build the dynamic strength and balance mechanisms we need to support the body structures when they are away from this ideal. When the dancer finds this neutral placement, and the body systems learn how to find and return to it, then every time they pass through neutral between more extreme movements, the body is afforded a moment of respite where it can literally and metaphorically catch its breath. Movements will seem less effortful, the flexibility potential in the joints will be maximized, and we will have the appropriate muscle control to protect the body in its journey through the more biomechanically challenging positions.

4
CONDITIONING for STRENGTH

THREE PRINCIPLES SERVE AS THE FOUNDATION for strength training programs. They are: *overload*, *specificity*, and *reversibility*. *Overload* refers to increased exercise demands. *Specificity* indicates the similarity of a conditioning exercise to the dance idiom that an individual is performing. *Reversibility* describes the loss of strength when you stop training. The strength conditioning exercises in this book are based on these principles.

The overload principle

The overload principle states that strength cannot be increased unless the muscles are stressed beyond their normal workload. They need to be worked to the point of fatigue. To achieve this overload, you can increase the frequency, duration, or intensity of your exercise program. Here, *frequency* means how often an exercise is performed; *duration*, how long an exercise lasts; and *intensity*, the difficulty of an exercise.

There are many factors that help to determine the intensity or difficulty of an exercise. In this book, intensity will be primarily determined by the amount of weight a muscle must lift or move. The overload principle also suggests that the frequency, duration, or intensity must be progressively increased for consistent gains in strength.

Overload and flexibility

Some dancers are concerned that flexibility will decrease if they begin a program that uses weights to increase strength. This will not happen if flexibility exercises are also performed. All of the strength conditioning exercises in this book have flexibility exercises included as part of the conditioning program.

Overload and muscle size

Many dancers and teachers are worried that working with weights will build big muscles. In fact, one of the most common misconceptions about strength training is that it will *always* result in large bulky muscles, even in women. This is not true. *Hypertrophy*, an increase in muscle mass, is influenced by several factors. One is the presence or absence of certain hormones; another is the type of exercise program that is followed.

Before puberty, growth hormone increases the size of the muscles, in both men and women, as the body grows. After puberty, the male hormone testosterone continues to increase muscle size. If men perform certain types of strength training exercises, the presence of testosterone makes it possible for them to increase the size of their muscles even further. Because the female body produces very little testosterone, women who engage in strength training do not develop the same muscle mass as men.

Muscular hypertrophy is also affected by the type of strength training program that is followed. Exercise programs that use maximal resistance result in greater hypertrophy. *Maximal resistance* is afforded by a weight so heavy that it can be lifted only a few times before fatigue occurs.

When the weight to be lifted is light enough that the exercise can be performed a moderate number of times, very little hypertrophy will result. The small degree of hypertrophy that does occur is considered *muscle tone*. A strength training program that involves moderate resistance and moderate repetitions will not cause muscular hypertrophy, but it will result in modest, functional increases in strength. It can also help to delay muscular fatigue. The exercises provided in this book are moderate resistance, moderate repetition exercises, so they will not produce excessive muscular hypertrophy.

Muscular size and strength

Two main factors determine strength. The first is the size of the muscle and the second is the ability of the nervous system to control the muscle. Inside each muscle are numerous muscle fibers. When these fibers receive a signal from the nervous system, they shorten or contract. If a task requires very little strength, then relatively few muscle fibers will be directed to contract. As more strength is required, more muscle fibers are called into action. When you consider that a skeletal muscle may contain as many as 300,000 fibers, you can understand the complexity of the controlling process. Through strength training, the nervous system learns to better coordinate the contraction of muscle fibers. This increases the strength of muscles without increasing their size.

The specificity principle

The *principle of specificity* states that the exercises you choose for your strength conditioning program should be as similar as possible to the dance movements you perform in class and onstage. It has been suggested that dancers could adhere to both the specificity and overload principles by wearing ankle weights to class. In this way they would be able to add resistance while performing specific dance movements. This resistance could be increased by wearing heavier weights. However, there is some question as to whether wearing ankle weights is wise. For some warm-up exercises, light ankle weights may be acceptable. There is always the possibility, however, that extra weight at the ankle could hurt a knee or ankle that is not yet strong enough to support the additional load. Another problem is that ankle weights distort the timing of your movement. To produce movement, the fibers inside each muscle act in a complex coordination of contractions and relaxations. The timing of these contractions and relaxations is altered by ankle weights. This potentially means that any training performed with ankle weights is not transferable to regular dance movement. Ankle weights will also distort the centrifugal force your muscles have to control when performing turns. For these reasons, using ankle weights can actually reduce the specificity of this training choice.

We therefore believe that a dance conditioning program is a better way to build muscle strength than wearing ankle weights during dance class. A dance conditioning program will allow you to condition your body with exercises that incorporate the principles of overload and specificity without the problems associated with ankle weights.

The reversibility principle

Reversibility refers to the fact that a loss of strength occurs rapidly when a person stops exercising. In fact, two weeks after training ends, a marked decrease in strength can occur. After one month, as much as a 35 percent loss in strength can occur. To maintain gains in strength, one must continue a strength conditioning program. Generally speaking, a muscle needs to be conditioned at least two times a week in order to maintain its level of strength.

Periodization

The concept of periodization in training is well established in the sports world. This concept is based upon the principle that training should be focused toward developing the physiological, psychological, and biomechanical aspects of an athlete's performance, as well as addressing specific skills. The aim is to support the individual as a whole person and to use a methodological approach to achieve a given goal. Thus training programs are constructed with specific aims that can be measured using physiological outcomes, such as aerobic fitness capacity. Such programs are designed to maximize the potential for the body to adapt to new increases in load, while minimizing the risk of muscle fatigue that can lead to injury. This is achieved by cycling through various aspects of training to allow different body structures to adapt and recover. An important component of periodization is the use of a "tapering" period in the run-up to an event. This is where physical activity is systematically reduced to allow for physical and mental recovery, and the mind can then be refocused from practice to the mastery of performance. Research has shown that such a training approach can improve strength and skill acquisition while minimizing the risk of injury.

The concept of periodization has not commonly been adopted by the dance world, although some dance companies are beginning to introduce some elements of this practice into their scheduling. It is even less commonly adopted in dance training establishments. Part of the difficulty lies in the timing of the professional dance season that many companies adhere to, and also the need for schools to follow standard 12- to 15-week semesters. Neither of these situations lends itself well to the introduction of periodization. However, with the physical demands of dance becoming ever more strenuous, and the injury rates in the profession still being unacceptably high, perhaps this concept should be explored and adapted to work for dancers.

Here we have explored the "big picture" of periodization and the obstacles it poses in dance training, but introducing elements of this concept into your supplemental training program can be much more readily achieved. While the structuring of your dance classes or rehearsals may be beyond your capacity to control, you can certainly make some decisions about how best to focus the timing of your own supplemental training program to both meet your goals and to manage your fatigue.

Here is an example of how you can implement the concepts of periodization by making adjustments to your supplemental training routine in the context of a collegiate dance program. A college semester is typically 12–16 weeks long and usually has a dance concert placed toward the end of the semester (due to the time it takes to choreograph and prepare a piece for performance). As a college dancer, the first thing you should do is map out the level of your physical activity each week. Bear in mind that rehearsals that take place toward the start of the semester tend to be lighter and have more downtime as the creative process tends to dominate at this stage. As you get closer to the performance date, rehearsals will become more physically demanding as you are now running the entire piece full-out. Regular classes also tend to begin at a more modest level of activity and then build toward the end of the semester. Now that you have the physical demands of the semester mapped out, you can plan the level of supplemental training each week. You are likely to have more free time and a lower physical work load in the early part of the semester, so at this point a complete supplemental training program is attainable. Once you draw closer to areas of high physical demand, such as midterms, dress rehearsals, and performances, you will want to pull back on your full-body workouts and focus more directly on the specific areas of need, such as muscle weakness or imbalance and injury. The closer you get to performance, the more important it is to find the time to rest. This follows the sports concept of "tapering," which allows for muscle recovery and repair, mental preparation, and the conservation of energy for the show (Wyon 2010).

5

CONDITIONING for FLEXIBILITY

FLEXIBILITY IS INCREASED by stretching the muscles, especially the connective tissue within the muscles. Muscles are held within a connective tissue sheath known as *fascia*. Within each muscle lie bundles of individual muscle fibers. Each muscle fiber is itself surrounded by a layer of this fascial connective tissue, and the grouped bundles of fibers are contained within another fascial sheath. The fascial connective tissue that runs through and surrounds each muscle maintains its structural integrity and is one of the determinants of the muscle's elasticity. When the muscle is stretched, the connective tissue stretches and the flexibility of the muscle is increased. Temperature is an important factor in increasing the length of connective tissue. When the body is warm, the connective tissue is more amenable to elongation.

When stretching, we are usually trying to increase the flexibility of our joints. However, the architecture of the joint itself is ultimately the restricting factor that governs the potential range of motion. For instance, the hip joint has a ball and socket design. The shape of the socket (known as the *acetabulum*) varies among individuals. Some have a relatively shallow socket that will allow for a greater range of motion, but is less stable. Others may have a deeper socket resulting in increased stability, but less flexibility. Where bones meet at joints, they are strapped together by ligaments. These ligaments can also determine the degree of joint flexibility, depending on their length, degree of laxity, and whether they have been previously damaged.

Hypermobility

No discussion about flexibility in dancers is complete without mentioning the issue of joint hypermobility. While most dancers are likely to have increased flexibility when compared to the average non-dancer, some display extreme levels of flexibility. These dancers may have Joint Hypermobility Syndrome (JHS), a genetic condition characterized by a collagen deficiency. Collagen, one of the main constituents of connective tissue, contributes to its strength. A lack of collagen results in connective tissue laxity and this includes the ligaments that surround our joints. This can result in a high degree of flexibility but a lack of stability in the joints, rendering these dancers more prone to injury (Weber et al. 2015). Other characteristics of this condition include slower healing rates from injury and slower response times to strength training. Hypermobility is a spectrum disorder, with many dancers falling somewhere along its scale, however those at the extreme end are less likely to be able to sustain a long dance career due to increased injury risk (McCormack et al. 2004). Good muscle strength is key to controlling joint laxity and can be protective of injury, therefore strength training is essential for hypermobile dancers.

Hypermobility is assessed using a test called the Beighton Scoring System. This is a 9-point measurement that looks at several joints in the body, including the knees, elbows, wrists, and fingers, and assesses their flexibility against normal joint ranges of motion. A score of 0–3 is considered normal, and scores of 4–9 indicate an increasing degree of joint laxity. You can find the criteria for the Beighton Score via an Internet search, but if you suspect that you fall into this category it is advisable to have this diagnosed by a medical professional.

The relationship between strength and flexibility

Movement occurs when muscles pull on the bony structures of the body. Muscles always *pull*, they never *push*. Muscles also work in pairs. When one member of the pair contracts and pulls, the other member of the pair will relax and stretch. The more the one muscle contracts, the more the other is stretched. In any pair of muscles, the contracting muscle is called the *agonist* and the relaxing muscle is called the *antagonist*.

The same muscle can be the agonist in one movement and the antagonist in the opposite movement. For example, when you point your foot and extend your ankle, the *gastrocnemius* muscle (located in the back of the calf) contracts. The *gastrocnemius* is the agonist. The *tibialis anterior* muscle (located in the front of the lower leg), acts as the antagonist and relaxes. When you flex the ankle, the muscles switch roles. The *tibialis anterior* becomes the agonist and contracts to flex the ankle. The *gastrocnemius* becomes the antagonist and relaxes.

Because the same muscles act in both agonist and antagonist roles, they must be both strong and flexible. They must be strong enough to act as agonists to produce movement, and they must be flexible enough to stretch when they are in the antagonist position. If the muscle pairs are not balanced in strength and flexibility, technique can suffer and injury can result. For example, a muscle that is not flexible can be torn when it acts as the antagonist. Furthermore, its lack of flexibility can prevent the agonist from fully contracting. This limits both motion and strength.

A flexible body without strength is a useless dance instrument. A strong body without flexibility is a very limited dance instrument. That is why a well-rounded dance conditioning program develops both strength and flexibility. Such a program prepares the muscles to act as either agonists or antagonists.

When to stretch

The timing of stretches is very important in order that they are both safe and effective. While dancers have traditionally always liked to perform deep stretches before and during class or rehearsal, we now know that this is not advisable. When muscles are stretched statically (where the position is held for upward of 30 seconds), they will actually lose power temporarily, making them weaker and more prone to injury (Deighan 2005). So any sustained, static stretching should be limited to the end of the day's final activity when you no longer require power from the muscles. Immediately after exercise is ideal, but if this is not possible, then at the end of the day have a warm bath or shower and perform your stretches before you retire to bed. This will help to unravel any tensions that have built up during that day and give you a clean slate for starting the next day. Always ensure that muscles are warm before stretching—if the muscles are cold, then they will not receive the stretch well and will be prone to damage.

6

ADDITIONAL TRAINING PROTOCOLS

Cardiovascular fitness

Research has shown that dancers often lack the appropriate level of cardiovascular fitness to sustain them in performance. Standard technique classes do not typically provide endurance training due to their stop/start nature. It is therefore necessary to address cardiovascular fitness in your supplemental training program (Rodrigues-Krause, Krause, and Reischak-Oliveira 2015). Dancers can do this in several ways and should choose an option that complements their current training and avoids loading any vulnerable joints.

The basic rule for improving cardiovascular fitness is that you should engage in sustained exercise at your maximum heart rate for 20 minutes and that this should be done three times a week. Options include running, elliptical machine, swimming, rowing, static bicycle, and so forth. Dancers should choose an option that avoids muscle groups that they are currently working elsewhere to prevent overload and should avoid loading injury sites or otherwise vulnerable areas. Specific exercises for this will be covered in Chapter 22.

Balance and proprioception

Dancers need to have a highly refined sense of balance, both in terms of achieving a balanced pose and through being able to swiftly "autocorrect" any movements that may have strayed from optimal alignment. Balance is not a static state. It is a function of the body's ability to make many subtle, fine-tuning adjustments to maintain dynamic alignment and poise. If we think in terms of structural design, a rigid building would have no tolerance to high winds or earth tremors.

Skyscrapers have a built-in mobility that allows them to flex and accommodate all that nature may throw at them. It is the same with the body: we must make subtle adjustments to hone our balance as we react to our own placement and the environment around us. To achieve this requires a sophisticated integration of many body systems.

The vestibular system

The complex workings of the inner ear are one of the central components of our balance system. This area is lined with hairlike strands called *cilia* and also contains a fluid called *endolymph*. As the body moves and rotates, the movement of the fluid is detected by the hair cells that send signals, to the brain, that tell it where we are in space. There are other structures in the ear that give additional information about our relationship to gravity and our vertical orientation.

The eyes

Sensory information from the eyes gives the brain vital information about our relationship and orientation to other objects in the environment. Some of the nerve fibers from our eyes interact with the vestibular system. Information from this sources can then be compared by the brain to account for our position in space.

The proprioceptive system

The body has a large sensory network of receptors that can be found in our skin, muscles, tendons, ligaments, and the capsules that surround our joints. These receptors can detect changes in the orientation of our body parts by assessing the length and tension of muscles and tendons and the movement of our joints. As our bodies bend and move, signals are sent from these receptors to the brain where they are then coordinated with the information from the eyes and ears. The brain can then create an accurate picture of where we are in space and activate appropriate muscle contractions to keep us balanced and oriented.

Being "on balance" involves much more than just hitting a static pose. All these systems need to be well-conditioned and therefore also need some attention in training. Chapter 22 will include some exercises for this vital and often overlooked aspect of dancer health.

7

The STRENGTH CONDITIONING
EXERCISES

Introduction to the exercises

Before you begin the exercises, there is some basic information that can help you to formulate your program. You will need to know how many repetitions to do, how fast or slow to do them, what rhythm to use, how to stretch appropriately, and how to increase the training intensity for continued improvement. The information in the following chapters can be applied to all the exercises throughout the book.

The exercises we have selected are a combination of injury-rehabilitation protocols, Pilates-based work, and dance-specific exercises. In many instances, it was necessary to choose between several effective exercise options. The following criteria were used in making those choices: (1) exercises had to be simple enough to be taught by written description; (2) exercises needed to be performed without the assistance of a partner; and (3) any equipment required had to be easily obtained. Some exercises provided in the book will have variations to increase the intensity or difficulty, and, to suit personal preferences, some have additional options for the same muscle group. Part VI contains some suggested programs for various situations. These include a suggested warm-up routine and a full-body workout for both beginner and intermediate/advanced levels. In addition, exercise combinations that address some of the common, specific needs for dancers are also offered.

While some of the exercises are described in terms of a specific muscle group or action—for example, the lower trapezius muscle—in reality the body works as an integrated unit. It is extremely difficult to isolate a single muscle or muscle group as all movements involve a combination of muscles that work in an integrated fashion. Where exercises are described in the context of an isolated muscle, this is simply to help you to focus on the appropriate body area. The exercises provided in this book provide a strong foundation to create efficient movement activation that can then build to more complex, integrated muscle activity. Imagery can be extremely useful to enhance the benefits of the flexibility and strength exercises. Some basic imagery is provided in this book, but we have kept this relatively simple. The work of both Eric Franklin and Irene Dowd are great resources for more detailed information on the use of imagery in dance.

The number of repetitions of an exercise that you perform is an important consideration in strength conditioning programs. The following material describes how to determine the number of repetitions to perform and contains information on resistance, tempo, adding variety to the program, and some words of caution.

Determining the number of repetitions

When you first begin a strength conditioning program, you will probably find that different muscle groups vary in strength. As a result, the number of repetitions you can perform will vary from one exercise to another. To determine how many repetitions you should perform of any given exercise, repeat the exercise until you feel that the muscle reaches a point of fatigue, but not exhaustion. If the feeling of fatigue goes away within an hour after exercise, you have performed the correct number of repetitions. Use this number as the starting point for that particular exercise.

If you experience extreme soreness the next day, you may have done too many repetitions and pushed the muscle too hard. The resulting muscle soreness may then cause your performance to suffer. However, if you do not work the muscle hard enough to become tired, you will not build strength. A quick check for deciding where the line is between too much and too little lies in the answer to this question: Do my muscles feel like they have been worked but the soreness is not impacting my regular activities, or is the soreness causing me to alter my usual movement patterns? If the soreness causes you to groan every time you move from sitting to standing, then you did too much!

Increasing the repetitions

You can add a few more repetitions as soon as the muscle no longer feels tired at the end of the exercise. Increases should be in small, gradual steps. Your body will tell you if you are asking too much, too soon. Listen to it! Several of the exercises outlined in this book involve using the right and left sides of the body or limbs. It is important to notice if there is a side-to-side difference in either strength or flexibility. If a there is a noticeable difference between the two sides, this indicates an imbalance. The side that is noticeably weaker in strength would benefit from performing an extra set of exercises. Also spending a few more minutes stretching the less flexible side will help with increasing range of motion. Imbalances between right and left sides can be a predisposing factor for injury, so these need to be addressed.

Generally speaking, more repetitions and less resistance helps gain strength without developing excessive bulk. Most of the exercises in this book recommend eight to ten repetitions. If after completing your repetitions you are not feeling muscular fatigue you can either increase your repetitions or increase the resistance.

Repetitions and sets

In strength training, a total program of eight to ten exercises for targeted muscle groups is a recommended goal, and these should be performed two to three times a week. It is generally recommended that you perform approximately ten repetitions of each exercise (Esco 2013). Many people like to divide the number of repetitions into groups, or sets, and rest for a few seconds between sets. For new exercises, you may want to start with fewer repetitions and work your way up. For example, if your goal is ten repetitions, you could begin with two sets of three repetitions. When you are no longer fatigued by these repetitions, you can progress to two sets of four repetitions, and finally work up to two sets of five. Some dancers prefer to divide their repetitions into three sets, particularly if working with greater resistance, as this provides an additional pause.

Repetitions and resistance

As a general guideline, you should try working up to ten repetitions of a specific exercise without any added resistance. When you can do this without muscular fatigue, you can begin to add resistance. The appropriate method of increasing resistance is unique to each exercise. Each section will discuss options to increase the workload as your strength increases. Typically you can add additional weight or shorten the length of an elastic band to increase the resistance. Any increase in resistance needs to begin with small increments to avoid muscular injury. You should be able to complete at least half as many repetitions as you performed without the added resistance; if not, cut back on the resistance.

It is important to evaluate your dance technique periodically as you build strength. There is no universal, preset level of resistance to be used in these conditioning exercises. Each individual will need to evaluate their technique and decide when they have reached their strength goals. Dancers who are uncertain about their level of strength should check with their teacher.

Timing patterns and tempos

Working slowly will help you to achieve your goal of improving strength. When you work slowly, you can be certain that you are working correctly and thoroughly. Dancers' bodies will tend to compensate for weaker muscles by recruiting other groups to join in the action. If you work too fast without control you are more likely to make compensatory movements and this defeats the purpose of following a training program. Focusing the mind and body is essential for all conditioning work to maximize your efforts and benefits. For these reasons, the strength conditioning exercises in this book are designed to be performed at a slow tempo. If at first an exercise seems too easy, try slowing down the tempo before you increase the difficulty in any other way. As you perform the strength building exercises you must move evenly and smoothly. Do not use abrupt upward movements or let go and collapse on downward movements. When returning to the starting position, it is very important that you do this with control, utilizing a fluid motion. Muscles will gain strength in both concentric (shortening) and eccentric (lengthening) contractions. Concentric contractions occur when the muscle belly shortens, moving the bones closer together at the joint. Eccentric contractions occur when the bones move away from each other under the control of the muscle. This means the muscle has to contract to provide a decelerating force while it is lengthening. This movement can be strengthening but it is also places a greater force on the muscle, making it more susceptible to damage. It is therefore essential to ensure good alignment when performing eccentric contractions and be cautious with regard to the associated load. Generally speaking, slow, steady, focused movement is the key to successfully developing muscular strength.

Variety in your exercise program

There is a certain amount of necessary repetition to conditioning work. In order to increase your strength, the repetitions and the resistance must be increased. If you are committed to improving your dance technique, you will have to accept repetition as part of the process. However, muscle groups need recovery time from conditioning, so building a varied program that allows respite for the worked areas is key. For instance, if you have worked on your legs one day, then perhaps do some upper-body conditioning the next day allowing the legs time to recover.

Exercising with a friend can make the repetitions more enjoyable, but be careful that you don't slip into a competitive mindset and try to outdo each other! You could also listen to music while exercising, but choose pieces that suit the optimal tempo of the exercise, as dancers' bodies will always follow the beat! There is research evidence that has shown that exercising to music produces better physiological outcomes, if you enjoy that particular music! These things can help to make exercising more interesting, but remember that it is important to maintain a level of awareness of the body while conditioning to maximize your efforts.

Once you have become familiar with the exercises and material presented in this book, you will have a good foundation from which to evaluate other strength and flexibility programs. The exercises recommended in this book are by no means the only set of appropriate exercises. As you become aware of other programs, you can analyze their effectiveness and judge how they might contribute to your conditioning work. As discussed earlier, every dancer has a unique musculoskeletal structure and it is important to take your own specific needs into consideration when developing your exercise plan. Having variety in your conditioning programs helps you to avoid becoming bored with the exercises and keeps you engaged in the work.

Finding the time

The dance world is laced with multiple obstacles to finding the time for supplemental training. Scheduling is often more related to the logistics of studio, rehearsal space, or theater availability rather than what is physically best for the dancer. Excuses for not finding the time for supplemental training include long rehearsal periods in the run-up to a performance, jumping from gig to gig to keep yourself in work, back-to-back classes in studio training, and schedules that fluctuate from week to week or month to month with little regularity. The reality is that supplemental training will take additional time. However, if you are committed to improving your dance technique and want to reduce your injury risk, you will have to find the time for a conditioning program. It is important to develop a flexible program that allows you to adjust to both the changes in your own physical demands (related to your current workload and choreographic needs) and the issues of time availability. You can divide the exercises up and do a few throughout the day, as long as you remember that the body should always be warmed up first. By taking a few minutes before and after dance class or rehearsal, or a few minutes after a hot bath or shower, you can make the time.

There are three points you should consider when beginning any strength conditioning program:

Top Priorities

1. the use of the breath during the exercises;

2. the correct organization of a conditioning session;

3. maintaining a balance.

Optimal breathing

Many strength training experts recommend that you exhale as you perform the action and inhale as you return to the starting position. However, you should not hold your breath during the movement. If you hold your breath during a muscle contraction, an increase in pressure on the heart can occur: this is called the *Valsalva maneuver*. One way to prevent this is to exhale as you perform the motion. Another way is to talk or count out loud as you perform the muscular contractions—this ensures that you are breathing out. The resistance recommended for the exercises in this book is relatively light, compared to competitive weight training, therefore it is unlikely that you would enter into the territory where a *Valsalva maneuver* might occur. However, as a precaution, we recommend that you remain aware of your breathing patterns as you exercise.

Breathing is a natural function for the human body. Using the out-breath while exercising engages the *transversus abdominis* muscle. This is the deepest layer of the abdominal muscles that helps to stabilize the lower back during movement. Exhaling as you initiate movement ensures that the spine is stabilized and ready for the action. Developing an awareness of your breathing can create a stronger mind-body connection while facilitating dynamic movement.

Correct organization of a conditioning session

Some dancers prefer to do all of their conditioning work in one session while others prefer to divide up the exercises into smaller chunks. This can often be dictated by their schedule and takes some careful consideration. For instance, you shouldn't be selecting exercises that require maximal resistance or pushing the muscles to fatigue right before a class or rehearsal.

It is also important to plan the sequence in which you perform your exercises to ensure that you get the most from your training while minimizing injury risk. The following guidelines will help you to organize your conditioning session for optimal performance:

1. Strength conditioning in which the muscles are worked to the point of fatigue should not be done when the body is cold. You should always perform a warm-up before starting a strength building session. This should include light intensity activities that begin to increase the heart rate and blood flow.

2. Strength conditioning exercises for one muscle group should be followed by flexibility exercises for that same muscle group. For example, strength conditioning work for the knee extensors should be followed by flexibility exercises for the knee extensors. In the chapters that follow, various "exercise prescriptions" will be given to help improve technique and prevent injury. Whenever a recommendation is made to strengthen a particular muscle group, the flexibility exercise for that muscle group will also be

listed. This is to serve as a reminder to include flexibility work in your strength conditioning program. Stretch what you strengthen and strengthen what you stretch.

3. Large muscle groups should be exercised before smaller muscle groups. For example, the muscles of the hip and knee should be conditioned before the muscles of the ankle and foot.

4. As you perform a series of exercises, it is important to listen to your body. It will provide important information as to which particular sequence of exercises "feels right" and works best for you.

5. A proper cooldown is an important part of any exercise session. In the cooldown process, you need to gradually decrease the intensity of the exercise, and stretch the muscle groups that have been conditioned for strength. If you follow the previous guidelines, you will have met the requirements for a proper cooldown. Leaving the smaller muscle group exercises to last naturally decreases the intensity, and performing the appropriate flexibility exercises will ensure that muscle tension is reduced and the waste products of exercise have been dissipated.

It is recommended that a muscle group be conditioned for strength three times a week to produce gains in strength without chronic fatigue (Esco 2013). Not all muscle groups need to be exercised on the same day. You should be aware that it may take up to six weeks of strength training before you see a significant improvement.

Maintaining a balance

Various "exercise prescriptions" will be suggested throughout the book. These will recommend strengthening or stretching specific muscle groups. As you work with these exercises, it is important to periodically evaluate your technique and placement. Additionally, remember the importance of keeping an overall balance of strength and stretch in the muscle pairs throughout the body. If you do not keep this goal in mind, you could find yourself overcorrecting a muscular imbalance and creating a new problem. The best way to maintain a balance of strength and stretch is to follow a regular conditioning program for the entire body. Chapter 23 presents examples of programs that may be designed from the exercises in this book.

8

The FLEXIBILITY EXERCISES

PERFORMING FLEXIBILITY EXERCISES should be approached mindfully and without judgment. Often, the positions you will be using (such as for a hamstring stretch) will not be representative of the position you usually use in class. This is because you will be targeting specific muscles for stretching rather than incorporating several muscle groups, as happens in many dance movements. Through being accurate with your alignment in flexibility training, you will then be able to contextualize this facility safely into dance technique.

Stretches should only be performed when the muscles are warm, either after activity or after a hot bath or shower. Stretches should be slow and controlled, with no bouncing. Bouncing causes muscles to contract in response to the sudden movement and this could lead to injury. More information on stretching, including the timing and intensity of the stretches, is presented below.

Timing the stretch

The question of the optimal length of time for sustaining a stretch is a complicated one. The degree of elasticity of muscles has many determinants. These include things like muscle fatigue, scar tissue from previous injury, levels of hydration, and muscle temperature. While considering that there may be individual differences among dancers, research has shown that a generalized recommendation of a 30-second stretch duration is optimal for most people (Critchfield 2011). Anything less than this has been shown not to have any lasting effects. Similarly, no significant increases were noted for stretches of 60 seconds. Therefore the "30 second rule" has become best practice. However, be sure to time your stretch using a clock or timer—if you are counting to 30, you may speed up and not reach the actual target.

Intensity of the stretch

The intensity of the stretch should be determined by the way your muscle "feels" during the stretch. You should feel the muscle stretching, but it should be a "friendly" stretch, not an "angry" one. Furthermore, the stretch should be felt in the middle of the muscle rather than at the ends of the muscle where the tendons attach to the bones.

Flexibility is increased by working *with* your muscles, not *against* them. Easy does it. There is a difference between feeling the muscle stretch and feeling pain while the muscle is stretching. Listen to your body. Let it guide the intensity of your stretch.

Use of breath

The breath can either help or hinder effective stretching so we should pay attention to its use. Holding the breath encourages muscle tension and does not predispose you to the ease required for "friendly" stretching. Using an out-breath to ease yourself into the stretch is a great way to ensure that there is no muscle tension and allows the body weight to sink into the stretch. Then you can breathe normally during the stretch, perhaps taking a deeper inhalation part way through and exhaling further into the stretch for the final remaining seconds.

Exercise sessions per week

The major muscle groups should be stretched three times per week outside of your dance classes. As for strength training, you do not need to stretch all of your muscles on the same day. You might want to stretch the lower body muscles on Monday, Wednesday, and Friday and the upper body on Tuesday, Thursday, and Saturday. You should be aware that it may take five to six weeks before you see significant improvements in flexibility.

There is one exception to the suggestion that you stretch a muscle group three times per week. If you use one particular muscle group a great deal in class or rehearsal, you should take time afterward to stretch that muscle group. For example, if class includes a lot of *relevés*, *pointe* work, or jumps, you should stretch the ankle plantar flexors as well as the knee and hip extensors. A wise dancer makes a mental check at the end of each day to be certain that the muscle groups used the most often for strength have also been stretched.

Other flexibility exercises

There are other forms of flexibility training that are used by healthcare professionals, such as Proprioceptive Neuromuscular Facilitation (PNF), Muscle Energy Technique (MET), or Contract-Relax. These methods are an effective way of stretching to increase flexibility that involves neuromuscular pathways. We do not include these stretching techniques in this book for the following reasons: (1) many of these stretches require a partner; (2) the partner must be carefully trained or injury could result; and (3) training the partner requires on-site, personal guidance that cannot be adequately obtained by reading a book.

9

EQUIPMENT and SETUP

Required equipment

Although the exercises do not require elaborate equipment, a few small items are necessary. All of these items can easily be purchased online or in any store that carries exercise equipment. These items are the following:

1. **Exercise mat.** All the floor exercises can be done without a mat, but in the interest of comfort, a yoga or Pilates mat is recommended, if available.

2. **Elastic resistance band.** TheraBand® (brand name) is the most commonly available option. This product, which is a six-inch-wide piece of rubber fabric, comes in eight color-coded resistances. We recommend most dancers purchase an 18-foot roll of the blue, or heavy-resistance, TheraBand®. Other brands are available but color-coding may differ.

3. **Small hand or ankle weights** ranging from two to five pounds. These are used in a few exercises and can also be used in place of an elastic band in some exercises.

4. **Foam roller.** This is a tool commonly used by dancers for rolling out muscles.

5. **Balls.** Racquetballs or tennis balls are helpful for self massage. Six-inch playground balls are useful for inner thigh work and for the under surface of the foot.

Selecting your exercise space

Supplemental training can be as much mental as it is physical. Whether you are on tour, backstage, in class, or in rehearsal, once you have developed your program, it is important to keep consistency for the strength and flexibility benefits to occur. The more consistent you are in your routine, the less of a chore working out will feel. Try to find a quiet space in your dance environment where you can exercise without getting sidetracked or distracted by everything going on around you. Losing focus on the accuracy of your training may negate the benefits of exercising. If a quiet space at work isn't available, then exercising at home may be a better option.

If you are going to invest the time on supplemental training to improve your skills, then find yourself the best possible environment in which to make that happen. The space you choose needs to be clean and safe for you to exercise. If you are traveling, finding some space in the hotel room may be your best option; you could use a bath towel on the floor if you don't have a mat. The exercises presented in this book take up minimal space, so even in a limited environment you can usually make something work. Much of the recommended equipment, such as elastic bands and balls, will fit in your dance bag, so you will have your own portable gym with you wherever you go.

Part II
FOOT, ANKLE, and LOWER LEG

Dancers must be able to flex and extend (point) the ankle fully, balance on demi-pointe *or full* pointe, *and to jump and move quickly. To perform these basic dance movements, the muscles of the foot and ankle must be both strong and flexible. In this part of the book, we discuss these muscles and describe ways in which dancers can improve their technique and prevent injury to the foot, ankle, and lower leg.*

10

STRUCTURAL ANATOMY

THE FOOT HAS 26 BONES that allow for motion in many planes and help us to fine-tune our balance. They are divided into three groups known as the *tarsals*, *metatarsals*, and *phalanges* (Figure 10.1). The bones of the foot are connected by a complex network of 117 ligaments.

There are two additional bones called *sesamoid* (floating) bones located under the ball of the foot at the base of the big toe.

The alignment of the bones in the foot creates three arches: the transverse arch, the medial arch, and the lateral longitudinal arch (Figure 10.2). Much like a bridge, these arches create a dynamic structure for stability and movement. The *medial longitudinal arch* extends along the inner border of the foot from the heel to big toe and is known as the "dancer's arch." The *transverse arch* extends crosswise from the medial to the lateral side of the foot, from the middle of the medial arch toward the fifth metatarsal. The height of these arches can vary in different people, but they function to help with changing directions, locomotion, coping with uneven surfaces, and absorbing the impact of jumps. The *lateral longitudinal arch* extends along the lateral border of the foot from the heel to the baby toe. When making

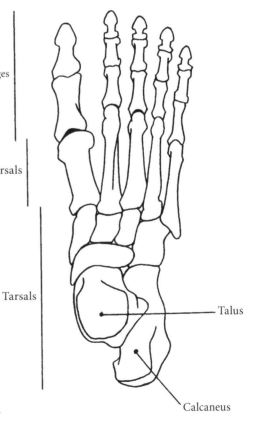

Phalanges

Metatarsals

Tarsals

Talus

Calcaneus

Figure 10.1 Dorsal view of the right foot

41

a footprint, this is the arch of the foot best seen in the impression. As the lateral arch spends most of its time in contact with the ground it is particularly important for stability and weight-bearing. If the bones of the feet stay in alignment, the three arches work efficiently to assist you in turning, jumping, balancing, and traveling through space. Unfortunately, if the structures break down due to weak muscles, poor flexibility, or misalignment, this can lead to pain and injury.

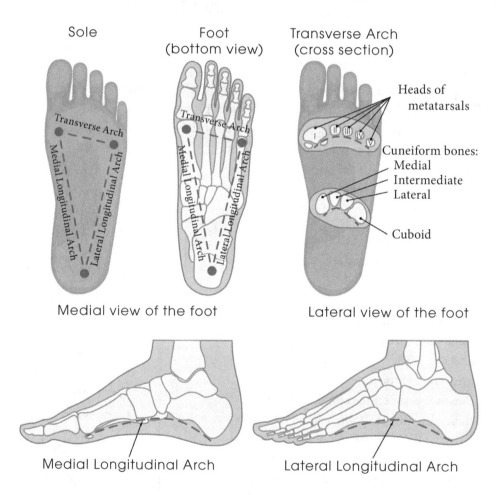

Figure 10.2 Arches of the feet

The bones of the lower leg are the *tibia* and *fibula*. The ends of the *tibia* and *fibula* are what most dancers call their ankle bones—the *tibia* on the inside and the *fibula* on the outside. The far ends of the *tibia* and *fibula* form the shape of a house (two side walls and a roof) around the *talus*. The *talus* sits on top of the *calcaneus*, or heel bone. Efficient movement of the *talus* in the space created by the *tibia* and *fibula* is crucial for all flexing and pointing actions of the foot.

As discussed in Part I, bones need muscles to create movement. The majority of muscles that flex and extend the foot or ankle have their origin on the *fibula* or *tibia* and run over the ankle onto specific bones of the foot. This chapter does not include a description or discussion of all bones, ligaments, and muscles of the foot and ankle. We will concentrate instead on those muscles primarily involved in producing the basic dance movements.

Movements of the foot and ankle

There are many types of motion at the foot and ankle, giving us a variety of movement possibilities. Here we have listed just the basic ones used in dance.

Dorsiflexion—the flexing of the ankle in dance.

Plantar flexion—the dancer's *pointe*.

Pronation—rolling in toward the medial arch.

Supination—rolling out toward the lateral arch.

Eversion— the "winging" or "beveling" of the foot.

Inversion— the "sickling" of the foot.

Through a dynamic combination of any of these possibilities, we can create a variety of movements. For instance, "winging" or "beveling" is produced by a combination of plantar flexion and eversion. "Sickling" involves a combination of supination and inversion.

Muscles of the foot and ankle

The names of muscles reflect the parts of the body they act upon. For instance, in toe movement, the word *hallucis* refers to the movements of the big toe only. The term *digitorum* refers to the movements of the four other toes. Have you ever wondered why you can move your big toe independently from your four other toes, but you struggle to differentiate the four toes from each other? This is because the big toe works on its own muscular system that is separate from the other four toes. Take a moment to try and move the toes independently and notice what you can and can't control.

The primary muscles used in the movements of the ankle and foot begin at different points on the lower leg (*tibia* and *fibula*). Based on their connections to the bones of the foot, they can create various movement options. In the chart below, the muscles have been listed based on their actions.

Table 10.1 Muscle actions of the ankle

Movement of the Ankle	Dancer Terminology	Muscles (abbreviation)
Dorsiflexion	Flexing	Tibialis Anterior (TA) Extensor Digitorum Longus (EDL) Extensor Hallucis Longus (EHL)
Plantar Flexion	Pointing	Gastrocnemius Soleus Tibialis Posterior (TP) Peroneus Longus (PL) Peroneus Brevis (PB)
Eversion	Wing/Bevel	Peroneus Longus (PL) Peroneus Brevis (PB) Extensor Digitorum Longus (EDL)
Inversion	Sickling	Tibialis Anterior (TA) Tibialis Posterior (TP)

Dorsiflexion of the ankle

The primary muscles that dorsiflex the ankle are the *tibialis anterior*, the *extensor digitorum longus*, and the *extensor hallucis longus*. These three muscles are located on the anterior aspect of the lower leg (Figures 10.3a and 10.3b). As you flex the ankle, notice the tendons that appear at the bend of the joint. When a dancer moves into a *demi-plié* position, the tendon of the *tibialis anterior* is often visible as it engages and becomes prominent on the top of the ankle. This can result in a restriction of the *plié*, limiting its depth. Techniques to address this restriction are discussed in Chapters 11 and 12.

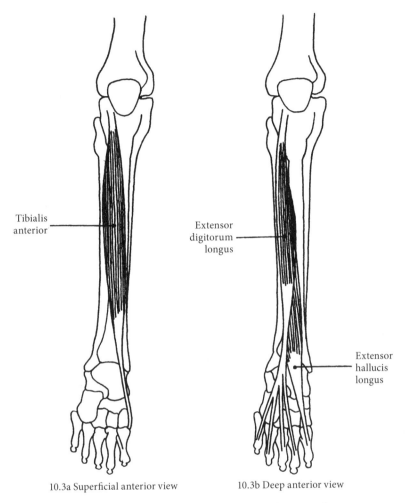

Tibialis anterior

Extensor digitorum longus

Extensor hallucis longus

10.3a Superficial anterior view

10.3b Deep anterior view

Figure 10.3 Anterior view of lower leg muscles

Find It
Place fingers on front of lower leg.

Feel It
Flex the foot toward your shin.

Notice the muscle popping up under your fingers. This is the *tibialis anterior.*

Dance It
Tendu to the front and then flex at the ankle.

Plantar flexion of the ankle

There are a significantly greater number of muscles on the posterior (back) surface of the lower leg than on the anterior surface. Due to the greater number of muscles that can engage to produce plantar flexion, it is important that they share the workload. Two muscles located on the posterior aspect of the lower leg that feed directly into the *Achilles tendon* are the *gastrocnemius* and *soleus* muscles.

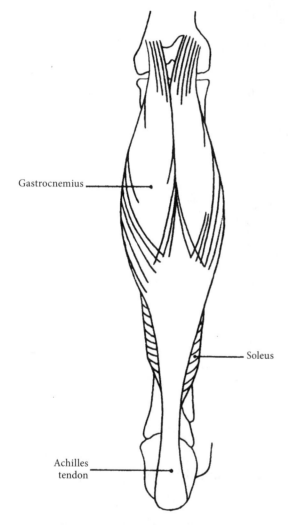

The *gastrocnemius* is attached to *the femur* (the upper leg bone) at one end and to the *calcaneus* (the heel bone) at the other (Figure 10.4). The tendon connecting the *gastrocnemius* to the *calcaneus* is known as the *Achilles tendon*. Because the *gastrocnemius* originates on the upper leg bone, therefore crossing the knee joint, it can also bend the knee when the foot is not bearing weight. The *gastrocnemius*, generally referred to as the "calf muscle," can be visualized or palpated when plantar flexing the ankle.

The *soleus* is attached to both the *tibia* and the *fibula* at one end. As is the case for the *gastrocnemius*, it is attached to the *calcaneus* by way of the *Achilles tendon* at the other end (Figure 10.4). However, because it does not cross the back of the knee joint, its movements are limited to the ankle. As it is located deep to the *gastrocnemius* muscle, it cannot be easily palpated.

While the *gastrocnemius* and *soleus* are powerful plantar flexors, we should be cautious about overusing them for generating the dancer's *pointe*. As these muscles attach to the *calcaneus*, forceful contractions can result in this bone rising up and compressing some of the other structures at the back of the ankle. This congestion can result in soreness and joint restriction,

Figure 10.4 Superficial posterior view of lower leg muscles

Gastrocnemius

Soleus

Achilles tendon

Find It

Stand with the right foot behind in the calf stretch position.

Feel It

Shift your weight forward with right knee straight. You are now stretching your *gastrocnemius*.

Bend your right knee and notice that the stretch drops toward the ankle. You have now found the *soleus*.

Dance It

Stand with the feet in parallel and rise up to three-quarter *pointe* without bending the knees. The *gastrocnemius* muscle will be dominating here, as the knees are straight.

Now perform a *sauté* (jump) in first position. The propulsion for this jump will mainly be generated by the *soleus*, as the jump begins from the *demi-plié* (knees bent) position.

---

and can increase the risk of developing a condition known as *posterior ankle impingement*. There are other important muscles that assist the *gastrocnemius* and the *soleus* in plantar flexion, namely the *peroneus longus, peroneus brevis*, and the *tibialis posterior* muscles (Figure 10.5). These can efficiently contribute to plantar flexion of the ankle but, as they do not act on the *calcaneus*, they will not add to the congestion at the back of the ankle (see exercise 12.F). Due to their added functions of inversion (*tibialis posterior*) and eversion (*peroneals*), the balance of these muscles will also guide optimal alignment of the ankle while moving into plantar flexion.

Eversion of the foot

The muscles that cause the foot to evert are the *peroneus longus*, the *peroneus brevis*, and the *extensor digitorum longus* (Figures 10.5a and 10.3b). The *peroneus longus* and *brevis* can be found by placing your hand on the lateral side of the lower leg and everting the foot. The tendons of the *extensor digitorum longus* can be seen running over the top of the foot when flaring the second to fifth toes upward into a "beveled" or "winged" position.

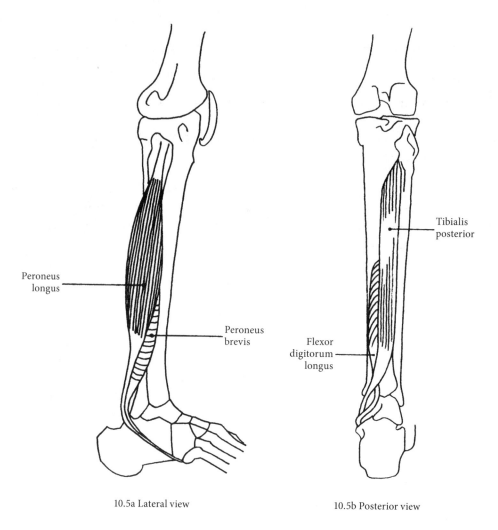

10.5a Lateral view   10.5b Posterior view

Figure 10.5 Lateral view and posterior view of lower leg muscles

Inversion of the foot

The muscles that cause the foot to invert are the *tibialis anterior* and the *tibialis posterior* (Figures 10.3a and 10.5b). Other muscles can be recruited, however this encourages inefficient movement patterns and can lead to injury and pain. Dancers are not usually encouraged to invert or "sickle" their foot as this creates an unpleasant aesthetic. Where these muscles do play an important role is in the maintenance of the medial longitudinal arch of the foot.

Table 10.2   Muscle actions of the toes

Movement of the Toes	Dancer Terminology	Muscles (abbreviation)
Extension	Flaring or lifting the toes	Extensor Hallucis Longus (EHL)—big toe Extensor Digitorum Longus (EDL)—four toes Extensor Digitorum Brevis—four toes
Flexion	Curling under	Flexor Hallucis Longus (FHL)—big toe Flexor Digitorum Longus (FDL)—four toes Flexor Digitorum Brevis—four toes

Extension of the toes

The muscles that extend the toes are the *extensor hallucis longus*, the *extensor digitorum longus*, and the *extensor digitorum brevis* (Figure 10.6a). The *extensor hallucis longus* lifts up the big toe. The *extensor digitorum longus* and *brevis* muscles lift up the four other toes. These muscles are located on the anterior aspect of the lower leg or on the top of the foot (Figure 10.3b)

The *extensor digitorum longus* is attached to both the *tibia* and the *fibula* at one end and to the tops of the four outer toes at the other end (Figures 10.3b and 10.6a). Extend the four toes several times and the tendons of this muscle on the top of the foot will become apparent.

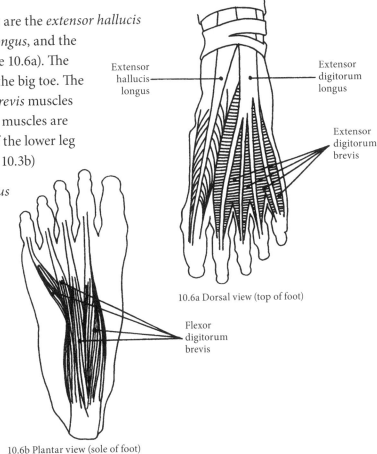

Extensor hallucis longus

Extensor digitorum longus

Extensor digitorum brevis

10.6a Dorsal view (top of foot)

Flexor digitorum brevis

Figure 10.6 Dorsal and plantar views of the foot

10.6b Plantar view (sole of foot)

Find It

Place fingers on the top of the joint at the big toe.

Feel It

Extend the toe toward the shin.

Notice the tendon popping up under your fingers. This is the *extensor hallucis longus*.

Dance It

In most forms of dance, we rarely actively lift the big toe in an isolated way as we spend most of the time working toward plantar flexion or just full ankle dorsiflexion. However, in some forms of Indian dance active extension of the toes is used.

Flexion of the toes

The three muscles that flex the toes are the *flexor hallucis longus* (FHL) (Figure 10.7), the *flexor digitorum longus* (FDL) (Figure 10.5b), and the *flexor digitorum brevis* (Figure 10.6b). The *flexor hallucis longus* flexes the big toe, while the four outer toes are flexed by the *flexor digitorum longus* and *brevis*. These muscles are located on the posterior aspect of the lower leg and on the bottom of the foot.

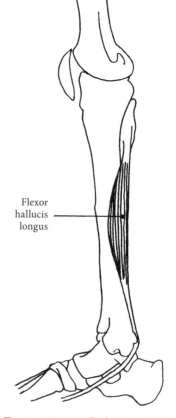

Flexor
hallucis
longus

The *flexor hallucis longus* is attached to the posterior aspect of the *fibula* at one end and to the bottom of the big toe at the other end (Figure 10.7). Take a moment to flex and extend your big toes. Do they crack or pop? Does the big toe seem to get stuck? Do you have issues standing on a full *demi-pointe* position on either foot? Do you have issues at the back of your heel near your *Achilles tendon*? These may all be issues associated with dysfunction in the FHL. The FHL and FDL can both be used to

Figure 10.7 Medial view of the lower leg muscle

assist plantar flexion of the ankle and dancers tend to overuse these two muscles by crunching their toes in an effort to increase their *pointe*. Crunching the toes under limits the function of these muscles and actually detracts from a beautiful foot line. It can also lead to the painful condition known as *Dancer's Tendonitis*. Specific exercises will be discussed in Chapter 12 to assist in developing a healthy FHL and FDL.

Intrinsic muscles of the foot

On the bottom surface of the foot are four layers of intrinsic muscles. These muscles are attached at both ends to the bones within the foot. All the intrinsic muscles of the foot function to move the toes and are important for rising up to *relevé* and for propulsion. According to some experts they also prevent the toes from "clawing" or curling under when the foot is pointed (Howse and Hancock 2014).

Plantar fascia

This is a thickened band of fibrous fascial tissue found on the sole of the foot. It runs from the edge of the *calcaneus* to the heads of all the metatarsal bones (Figure 10.8) it supports the arch and acts as a shock absorber during movement. One of its main functions is to aid propulsion for our gait. At rest, the foot is just a loose bag of bones that is not very efficient for movement. However, when the toes are extended (as during the toe-off phase in gait), the *plantar fascia* is stretched, thus creating a compressive force through the bones of the foot. They are now transformed into a rigid lever for efficient propulsion.

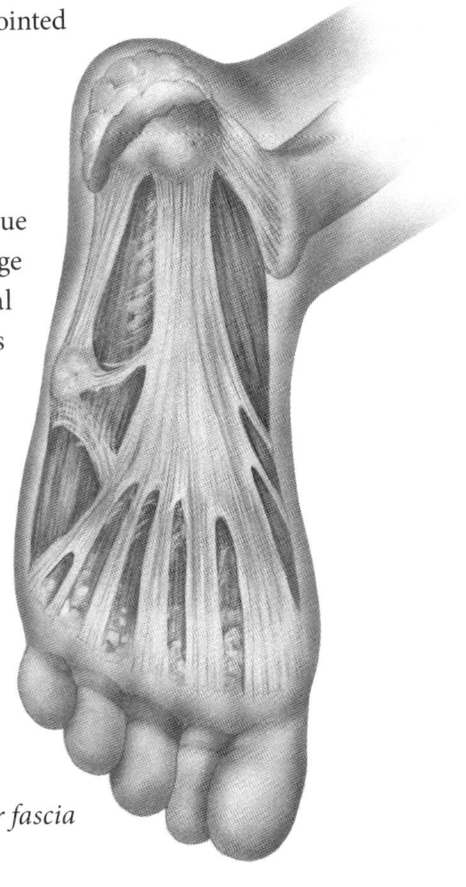

Figure 10.8 Plantar fascia

Find It

In a seated position take hold of your foot with both hands and waggle it around getting a sense of all the 26 bones. Now pull your toes back (extend) with one hand and palpate underneath your medial arch.

Feel It

You should feel the hard edge of the *plantar fascia*; it is often quite sensitive. Trace it from the *calcaneus* down to the big toe. It runs to all the toes, but the medial edge is the easiest place to locate it.

Dance It

The *plantar fascia* is not a muscle so it doesn't have a specific action. However, it will be busy stabilizing your foot in the *demi-pointe* position as well as providing shock absorption when you land from jumps.

Neutral alignment

When the foot and ankle are neutrally aligned with the lower leg, the weight of the body is transmitted through the *tibia* to the *talus* and *calcaneus* and then distributed across the ball of the foot. The body's weight is equally supported by the heel and ball of the foot, allowing the toes to relax. The toes should be in contact with the floor for balance, but they should not "claw" the floor. The medial longitudinal arch should be in a neutral position. It should not be depressed by excessive rolling in, nor unnaturally elevated by excessive rolling out. Looking upward, the foot should be aligned centrally under the knee in both parallel and in turn-out. A good way to find neutral alignment of the foot is to envisage a diagonal line pointing from the center of the heel down into the ground.

11

QUESTIONS and ANSWERS: The FOOT, ANKLE, and LOWER LEG

The following questions relate to common dance training issues, such as alignment and movement execution, that could result in injury. A few common injuries are also addressed.

1. Why is the alignment of the foot and ankle important?

The feet are the foundation for the entire body so a small misalignment or compensation here can create a ripple effect throughout the body. As the body's weight is distributed across the surface of the foot, optimal alignment is essential for efficient movement. The basic neutral alignment of the foot and ankle is described on page 52. A common tendency in dancers is to "roll in" (over-pronate) the foot in an attempt to control or improve the look of their turn-out. This will begin a chain of events that has repercus-

sions throughout the body. One way to evaluate alignment in this area is to look at the
relationship between the medial longitudinal
arch and the *Achilles tendon* as it runs down
the back of the heel. If the tendon bows medially (inward), the dancer is rolling in (Figure
11.1). If the tendon bows laterally (outward),
the dancer is rolling out. This can cause an
increase in injury risk for the *Achilles* itself,
as well as affecting the efficiency of the calf

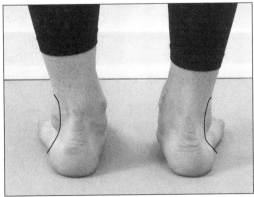

Figure 11.1 Tendon bowing

53

muscles. For instance, those with a tibial torsion may not be able to view the big toe in *demi-plié*.

Optimal placement allows the muscles of the foot and ankle to work efficiently, while sub-optimal placement jeopardizes the structural components of both the foot and the ankle. Because the entire weight of the body is transmitted to the ankle and foot, even a small deviation in placement can place a great deal of stress on the structures in this anatomical area.

The ligaments are primarily responsible for holding the bones of the ankle and foot together, and these can become permanently stretched if they are subjected to the continual pressure of misalignment. It is important to understand that ligaments do not have the same elastic property that muscles have. Once a ligament is overstretched, it remains elongated and is no longer able to hold the bones in their appropriate place. As a result, the optimal architecture of the foot and ankle can no longer be maintained. This leaves the foot and ankle vulnerable to further injury.

Jumps are performed frequently both in dance classes and choreography. Every time you land from a jump, the force of gravity increases the weight of your body. This extra weight is transmitted to the ankle and foot. If they are not aligned optimally, the ligaments, tendons, and sometimes even the muscles can be badly injured.

The relationship of the foot to the knee is another important consideration. The middle of the foot should be centered under the middle of the knee. This is true in parallel as well as in turned-out positions. One way to check this alignment is to stand in parallel first position *demi-plié*. If you look down at your feet, you should be able to see your big toe. If you can see only your knees, your foot and knee are not aligned. You need to move your knees wider apart until they are centered over the midline of your feet.

Next, you should try the same test in a turned-out first position *demi-plié*. If you cannot see your big toe, you can address this in one of two ways. Either you can increase the external rotation of your legs at the hip, which will cause the knees to move laterally, or you can decrease the turn-out of the foot and ankle, which will cause the feet to move medially.

It is important to recognize that some alignment issues may be due to an individual's inherent anatomical design. They are therefore structural, rather than functional, issues. These cannot be changed by improving technique or performing conditioning exercises. If you suspect your problem is structural and not due to technique, you may want to consult a dance medicine professional for an evaluation.

2.   What is the optimal alignment of the foot when a dancer is *en pointe*?

When a dancer is *en pointe*, the line of gravity should pass through the *tibia*, ankle, foot, and toes. Inside the *pointe* shoe, the toes should be extended and straight (Figure 11.2a). If one of the lesser toes is longer than the others, it would have to curl under to even out the line. However, this is not healthy for the toe in question. Inserts can be used in the *pointe* shoe box to even out such discrepancies. The toes should also not hyperflex or curve back toward the sole of the shoe. Knuckling under or hyperflexing the toes can stress the joints and make them vulnerable to injury (Figure 11.2b).

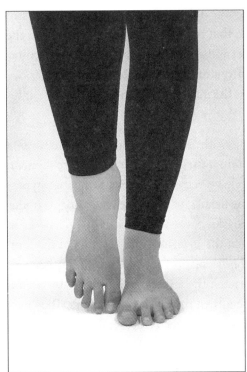 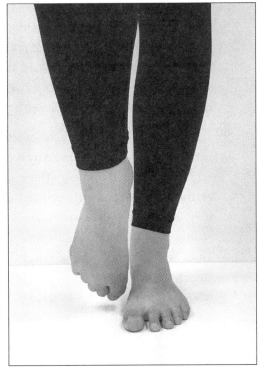

11.2a Extended toe pointe   *11.2b Scrunched toes*

Figure 11.2 Extended toe pointe.

The weight of the body should be distributed across the entire *pointe* box surface of the shoe. Pronating (rolling in) will send the weight toward the big toe and medial edge of the *pointe* surface. Pronation can aggravate the big-toe joint and lead to injuries such as *tendonitis* and *shin splints.*

Equally, the dancer should not roll out. This sends the weight of the body toward the little toe and the lateral edge of the *pointe* surface. Rolling out stresses the lateral structure of the foot and ankle, as well as the muscles on the lateral side of the leg.

It is also very important that a dancer be "all the way up" on the toe box when *en pointe*, as this is the position of greatest mechanical stability. If the dancer does not reach the full *pointe* position, the weight will be primarily supported along the rear edge of the *pointe* surface. This causes compensatory changes in body alignment. It also puts excessive strain on the ankle plantar flexors, which must contract with considerable force to maintain the position. This can lead to tendonitis and muscular tightness.

Just as it is important to get all the way up *en pointe*, it is equally important not to exaggerate the *pointe* position so that the weight shifts to the front of the *pointe* surface. Dancers with flexible feet and ankles need to control their plantar flexion so they do not roll toward the front of the *pointe* shoe. Rolling over can stress the ligaments of the foot as well as the muscles and tendons along the anterior surface of the foot and lower leg.

Dancers who have been working with compromised placement over a period of time may need to address certain muscular imbalances before they can achieve optimal alignment. Those who have been working with the toes hyperextended may need to strengthen the toe flexors, while those who knuckle under may need to strengthen the intrinsic muscles of the foot. Dancers who have been rolling in or out may need to strengthen the invertors and evertors of the foot. Those who have not achieved the full *pointe* position may need to strengthen and stretch the ankle plantar flexors and stretch the ankle dorsiflexors. Others who have been rolling over may need to strengthen the ankle dorsiflexors. They may also find it helpful to use a *pointe* shoe with a longer vamp.

This last group of muscles (the evertors) are difficult to stretch. Exercise 12.D.2 (pp. 86–88) offers an option for rolling these muscles. Massage can help to relax the muscles that lift and support the arch (exercise 12.A.2); massage and gentle hand manipulation in the direction of toe extension can help relax the toe flexors; massage and gentle hand manipulation in the directions of inversion and eversion, as well as performing ankle circles, can help relax the foot invertors and evertors.

3.   I have been told that I am forcing my turn-out from the foot and ankle. What can I do about this?

Turn-out should be directed by the availability of external rotation at the hip socket. When you try to increase your turn-out by forcing your feet into greater rotation than the hip allows, you run the risk of injuring not only your feet and ankles, but many other structures in the body as well. In addition, you will reduce the efficiency of your muscular system, creating compensations in your technique.

When turn-out is forced at the foot and ankle, the body's weight can no longer be properly transmitted through the center of the *talus* and *calcaneus* to the ball of the foot. In forced rotation, the weight falls to the medial side of the ankle and foot. This stress will increase the injury risk at the ankle, longitudinal arch, and big-toe joint. If the stress on the arch continues over a period of time, the ligaments can become overstretched and the bones can actually shift position. This can cause the arch to fall and can be very painful. Forcing rotation also affects the muscles, tendons, and bones. Not only does it decrease muscular efficiency, it can also contribute to *tendonitis*, *shin splints*, and *stress fractures* of the lower leg bones. Forcing can also cause a dancer to excessively grip, or "claw," the toes as the weight is not naturally supported over the center of gravity.

When turn-out is forced at the foot and ankle, the effects are registered throughout the body. Excessive rotation, for example, can strain the medial side of the knee, cause the pelvis to tilt forward, and cause the back

Figure 11.3 Forced turnout

to hyperextend (Figure 11.3). This posture can weaken the abdominal muscles and lead to lower-back injury. Forcing can also cause a dancer to "sit" in the standing hip. This limits optimal technique and can compromise the aesthetic line.

4.   Why is it important to keep my heels down in the *demi-plié* that precedes and follows a jump?

There are several reasons why it is important to ensure that your heels contact the ground in jump sequences. In terms of injury prevention, allowing the heels to pop up when you land from a jump may lead to *tendonitis* or *shin splints*. Double heel strikes can also cause *shin splints*. These occur when a dancer lands from a jump with the heels down, momentarily releases the heels, then presses them down again before the next movement occurs.

Another reason for keeping your heels down is to improve the height of your jump. A muscle can exert greater force when it contracts from a slightly stretched position. When you allow your heels to contact the ground in *demi plié*, you stretch the ankle plantar flexors. This stretched position allows them to generate greater force as they contract and plantar flex the ankle for the next jump.

If you have trouble keeping your heels down, it could be that your ankle plantar flexors are tight and need to be stretched. It could also be that you are contracting the *tibialis anterior* muscle as you *plié*. This will show as the large tendon that becomes visible on the top surface of the ankle crease. If this muscle is activating on landing, the tendon will restrict the depth of the *plié*. Activating this muscle may be habitual, but may also be indicative of the weight not being centered over the foot.

5.   I am a commercial dancer and need to take class and perform in heels. What should I be looking for when choosing shoes?

Ideally, dancers should only work in shoes that are specifically designed for dance. There are many heeled shoes that have been especially created to provide the necessary support and stability for all the potential moves they may be subjected to in various forms of dance. They are designed to provide flexibility in the appropriate places for pointing the foot while also providing support for vulnerable areas. They will also usually have a means of securing the shoe to the foot via either a buckled or elastic strap. Attention will also have been paid to the surface of the shoe, ensuring it strikes the balance between grip and glide that is essential for moves such as turns. Such shoes are commercially available from most dancewear stores. There are even some companies that will custom-make shoes for individual dancers, but these are inevitably rather expensive.

However, dancers often find that dance-specific shoes do not have the appropriate "look" for the aesthetic of commercial work. They are then faced with buying regular street shoes that are not necessarily fit for the purposes of dance. If you find yourself in this position, there are some things you can look for and adjustments that you can make to customize shoes for dance. If you are required to wear very high heels, then it is best to find a shoe that has a platform underneath the toe area (Figure 11.4). This has the effect of retaining the look of the higher heel, but by raising the toes, the angle of ankle plantar flexion is reduced. This is particularly useful for dancers with smaller feet. It is also a wise move to choose a shoe that does not narrow excessively toward the toes. A narrow shoe will lead to bunching of the toes and can exaggerate any tendency for developing bunions. Allowing the toes to spread evenly in the shoe is essential when all the body weight is being forced into the *metatarsophalangeal* joints in the forced plantar flexion position induced by wearing heels. Weight-bearing

with the toes in a compromised position increases injury risk.

If the shoe is not securely fitted to the foot and feels like it might come off, then it is key to make some adaptations. If the shoe does not feel secure, there will be a tendency to "grip" with the feet in an effort to

Figure 11.4 Heels

stop the shoe from slipping. This will create tension in the foot and lower leg muscles, and narrows the base of support for the whole body. To address this issue, you can sew a wide flesh-colored elastic strap into the shoe so that it runs across the arch. If it is not possible to stitch the elastic in, you can create an external elastic strap. Wrap a piece of inch-wide elastic around the entire arch/instep with your foot in the shoe. Measure it so that it feels snug but not too tight. Cut it to size and stitch the ends together. This now becomes an elastic "sleeve" or "cuff" that you can slide over the arch area to secure the shoe to the foot.

If the sole of the shoe is slippery and doesn't provide enough grip, you can use a pocket knife or the blades of a pair of scissors to score the sole of the shoe in a cross-hatch pattern. This can provide the necessary friction to stop you from slipping while still facilitating glide for turns. If the floor surface is particularly slippery, you can have a rubber sole fitted by a cobbler.

Even if you have modified your shoes as much as possible to accommodate the choreographic requirements, dancing in heels is always a risky proposition. This can be exacerbated if you are working on a raked (sloped) or uneven stage surface. You will also need to modify your body alignment to counter the ripple effect of being in forced plantar flexion. See Question 6 below for further information on this. You will also need to pay attention to good stretching techniques for the muscles of plantar flexion. These can be found below in section 12.C.2.

6. After dancing in heels, I often experience discomfort in my toe joints, ankles, and lower back. What can I do to reduce these symptoms and be able to perform in heels without pain?

Dancing in heels will alter whole-body alignment. As soon as we change the relationship of the foot to the floor, the whole kinetic chain will have to compensate. This means taking some joints away from the optimal neutral alignment, and this can cause discomfort. Essentially, when wearing heels the foot is forced into a plantar-flexed position with the toes extended. This forces much of the body weight into the balls of the feet, which can lead to discomfort in the toe joints and bruising to the under surface of the metatarsal heads. This is known as *metatarsalgia* and can be slow to resolve if we continue to dance. Under the big-toe joint there are two small *sesamoid* (accessory) bones and these can also become inflamed: this is known as *sesamoiditis*. This is a particular risk for dancers who tend to "wing" or "bevel" their feet in heeled shoes, thus placing more weight on the big-toe joint.

While dancers are quite used to working with the foot in plantar flexion, they are usually passing in and out of this position, allowing for some respite in dorsiflexion. In heels, the feet are permanently plantar-flexed, which can lead to an accumulation of pressure in certain structures. One area that can suffer is the posterior compartment of the ankle—the space between the *Achilles tendon* and the back of the *calcaneus* and *talus*. In plantar flexion, the *calcaneus* will push the *talus* that sits above it upward toward the back of the *tibia*. This can compress some of the soft-tissue structures in the area and can irritate the joint surfaces. Additionally, some individuals have an extra bone in this area, known as an *Os Trigonum* (Figure 11.5), and this can also become irritated and inflamed if compressed.

In heeled shoes, the foot is essentially placed in the *demi-pointe* or three-quarter *pointe* position. The full *pointe* and flat positions of the feet both have the advantage of added stability from the relative joint positions. Between these two positions the ankle is at its most unstable. The risk of lateral ankle sprains and fractures is heightened here. This could be particularly dramatic if the shoe also has a platform, as the ankle will have farther to fall.

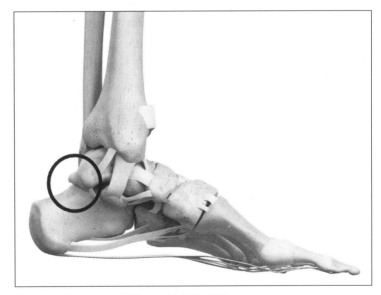

Figure 11.5 Os Trigonum

The midfoot is also vulnerable to injury when dancing in heels. The joint where the *second metatarsal* meets the *medial cuneiform* bone is stabilized by the *Lisfranc ligament*. This joint can be vulnerable during turns and jump takeoffs. If the dancer starts to rotate or push off, but the shoe sticks to the floor surface and is unable to glide, this ligament can become sprained or torn—and may even pull a piece of bone away. This leads to pain in the midfoot and marked instability. This can be a significant injury that may require surgery.

Farther up the kinetic chain, the plantar flexion caused by wearing heels will often result in the dancer pushing the knees back into hyperextension, particularly if they are hypermobile. This sets up a compensatory pattern that will also often result in an anterior tilt of the pelvis, causing an increase in the lumbar curve. This can lead to pain in both the knees and the lower back. The disruption of the neutral alignment at the pelvis and lower back also reduces the efficiency of the core stabilizing muscles, rendering the dancer less stable and more vulnerable to injury.

Wearing heels is required for several forms of dance and performance genres, so it cannot be avoided in many cases. While it will always pose increased risks for injury, there are some things that dancers can do to modify the effects of wearing heels. First, you must try to select the most appropriate shoe (see Question 5 on page 58). Then you need to modify your alignment by ensuring that your body weight is not being driven too far over the balls of the feet. Moving the weight back toward the midfoot or heel, and making sure you are not pushing the knees into hyperextension, will bring the weight more toward neutral. Additionally, check the pelvic and lower-back alignment for any tendency to tilt. This should be easier to do if you have already modified the body-weight placement from the feet. You should also take regular breaks out of the shoes, and be sure to stretch both the calf and hamstring muscles well at the end of your working day.

7.   When I point my feet I tend to "sickle." Does this put me at risk for injury?

"Sickling," or inverting, the foot can be problematic and does not represent the true aesthetic line for dance (Figure 11.6). Some individuals have a natural tendency toward the inverted position, so they may find this hard to adjust. When the foot is plantar-flexed (pointed) and inverted (the movements that make up the "sickle") it is most at risk of a *lateral inversion sprain*. This is the typical "twisted" ankle that many dancers experience. Having the foot habitually in this position can contribute to weakness in the stabilizing ligaments on the outside of the ankle, thus making it more prone to this type of sprain.

Another issue is that "sickling" may create an imbalance in the muscles that control the ankle position. For a foot to be well controlled in the neutral position, there needs to be a balance between the invertors and evertors. If the foot is habitually being "sickled," the invertors will become tight and the evertors will become lengthened and weak. This will further reinforce the tendency to "sickle," and a vicious circle ensues. As alignment at the feet and ankles is fundamental to optimal placement of all the joints above, it is crucial to address this habit as soon as possible.

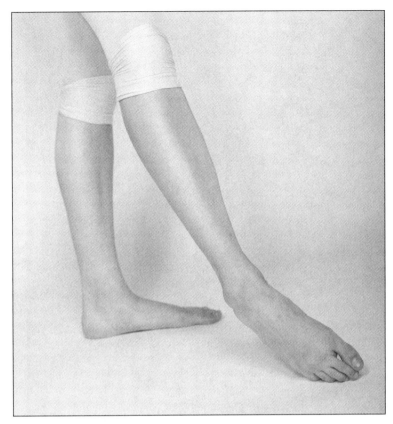

Figure 11.6 Sickled foot

8. I have been taught to "wing" my ankle when dancing. Is this a problem?

As for the question on "sickling" above, "winging," or everting, also represents a move away from the neutral position. However, everting the foot tends to be more accepted, and sometimes even favored, in the dance aesthetic (Figure 11.7). While this position does not pose the same risks for a lateral inversion sprain, it will have a weakening effect on the ligaments on the inside of the ankle. If the tendency to "wing" is also accompanied by a tendency to "roll" or over-pronate, then this adds to the injury-risk picture. If you are "winging" in the *demi-pointe* or full *pointe* position, then this will place the majority of the load into the

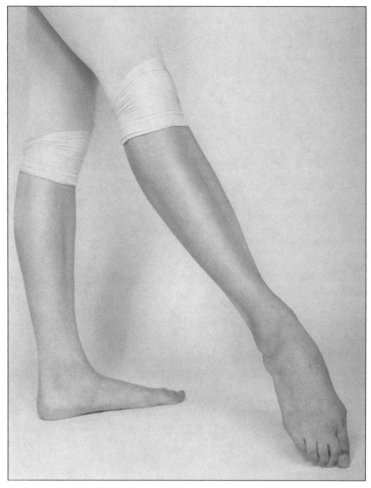

Figure 11.7 Winged foot

big-toe joint. This can lead to pain and inflammation of this joint and, if a dancer has the genetic predisposition, it may exacerbate the risk of developing bunions. This joint can also subsequently become restricted, thus limiting the *demi-pointe* position. This will then set up further compensations in the kinetic chain. "Winging" the foot will create tension in the evertor muscles and weakness in the invertors. This muscle imbalance will further reinforce the issue. Again, the knees, hips, and lower back will all be affected by this deviation from the neutral position.

"Winging" or "fishing" may be a choice for some non-weight-bearing positions, such as to augment the *arabesque* line, but should be avoided in weight-bearing positions because of the abnormal loads it will place on certain structures. Attention should be paid to the *peroneal* muscles to ensure they are not becoming overly tight, and exercises to address the balance of the invertors and evertors should be performed.

9.   Is it correct to stand with your weight shifted onto the balls of the feet?

Many styles of dance require the weight to be shifted slightly toward the ball of the foot so that it is easier to move. It means that minimal adjustments need to be made to transition to the *relevé* position. However, it is important that you do not shift the weight so far forward that the heels lose contact with the floor. When this happens, all of your weight is pressed onto the *metatarsal* heads instead of being partially distributed to the heels. This could put undue stress on the ball of the foot and overwork the ankle plantar flexors. This forward shift should also be minimized to reduce the compensatory effect on the joints above, such as hyperextending the knees, tilting the pelvis, and hyperextending the lower back. Having the weight too far forward can lead to "gripping" with the feet in order to maintain stability. This will increase the tension in the lower leg muscles, particularly the *tibialis anterior*, and in some cases this may lead to *shin splints*. Attention must be paid to stretching the *gastrocnemius* and *soleus* muscles, as they will also be affected by this forward weight shift.

10. What is restricting the depth of my *demi-plié*?

In some individuals, the bones of the lower leg and ankle are shaped and positioned in such a way as to limit the depth of the *demi-plié*. However, restriction can also result from tension in the plantar flexor muscles. The *gastrocnemius* and *soleus* muscles attach to the *calcaneus* by way of the *Achilles tendon*. In the *demi-plié* position, these structures need to stretch and glide to facilitate the movement.

Tension in this complex will result in a tendency for the heels to "pop" up instead of remain in contact with the floor. Another structure that can affect the depth of the *demi-plié* is the *tibialis anterior* muscle. If the dancer is tensing this muscle during *plié*, the tendon at the front of the ankle will be engaged and will restrict the movement (Figure 11.8).

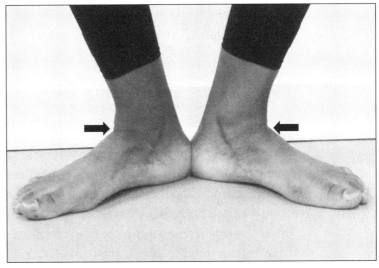

Figure 11.8 Tibialis anterior popped

11.   When should a dancer go *en pointe*?

There are many factors to consider before a dancer is allowed to go *en pointe*. One important consideration is the physical development of the bones in the ankle and foot. The bones must be sufficiently mature to accommodate the additional demands of *pointe* work. This physical development typically takes place around the age of twelve, but this can vary between individuals. Another factor is the dancer's muscular strength. If the dancer is unstable on *demi-pointe* due to muscular weakness, then she will have increased difficulty on full *pointe* and be at risk of injury. Muscular strength for *pointe* work is not just a consideration for the feet. Strength in the muscles at the top of the leg and hip is equally important. When these muscles are well controlled, they guide top-down alignment into the lower leg and serve to hold body weight out of the foot and ankle.

In addition to muscular strength, alignment must be evaluated. If the dancer cannot perform the basic ballet vocabulary while maintaining optimal alignment, she will not be able to do well *en pointe*. Any alignment and technique issues will be exaggerated *en pointe* and, once again, the risk of injury is increased.

Because each dancer develops at an individual rate, the decision to go *en pointe* should be based on the dancer's level of physical and technical development. It should not be arbitrarily determined by chronological age or years of dance training.

12.   I notice that many ballet dancers have bunions. What causes them and are there conditioning exercises that can help with this problem?

The tendency to form bunions is inherited (Figure 11.9). Technique issues such as forcing turn-out and rolling in can exacerbate the situation in a dancer with this genetic tendency. Shoes that are too narrow at the toes, particularly high heels where the weight is being forced forward into the toe joints, can also be an issue. This includes *pointe* shoes, which should be fitted carefully. Adaptations can be made to accommodate an existing bunion, such as a wider *pointe* shoe box, slitting the part of the box that presses on the bunion, or placing a pad around the bunion. A careful evaluation of technique is also important, including turn-out control, weight placement, and foot alignment. Someone with painful bunions should see a physician for assessment. Generally, it is not recommended that bunions be surgically treated until after a dance career is over. This is because surgery may result in a restriction of the range of motion in the big-toe joint. Exercises should be focused on upper leg muscular control, foot alignment, and intrinsic foot muscle strength.

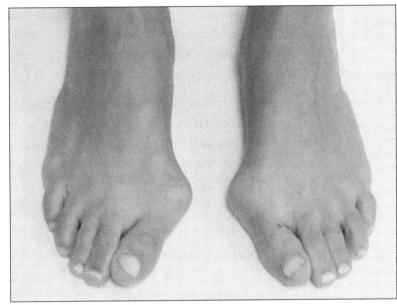

Figure 11.9 Bunions

13.   How should a dancer manage ankle tendonitis?

Tendonitis, an inflammation of a tendon or tendon sheath, is a problem dancers frequently encounter. At the ankle, it usually occurs in the tendon sheath of the *flexor hallucis longus*, or in the *Achilles tendon*. In either case, the dancer experiences pain at the back of the ankle during *demi-plié* or *relevé*.

Tendonitis may be caused by technique issues, such as forcing turn-out at the ankle, rolling in, rolling out, "sickling," and "popping" the heels on jump landings. The condition may also be a result of extrinsic factors such as jumping on hard floors; a sudden increase in class or rehearsal schedule; prolonged, unaccustomed *pointe* work; or choreography that makes unaccustomed demands on the ankle and foot muscles. Finally, this condition can also be caused by excessive tension in the attached muscle group placing an increased load on the tendon. Additional risk factors include "gripping" or "clenching" muscles in the foot and ankle and failing to stretch appropriately after exercise.

Dancers with mild *tendonitis* can try rest, massage to the calf muscles (not the tendon), and careful stretching of the associated muscle group. If pain continues, a physician should be consulted. Once the immediate symptoms have been controlled and any muscle imbalances have been addressed, you can work to change any other factors that may have led to the problem. Developing the habit of regularly stretching the ankle plantar flexors can help to avoid one cause of *tendonitis.*

It is worth noting that *tendonitis* is an acute condition that lasts from 24 to 72 hours. For those who are having ongoing tendon symptoms lasting days or weeks, the appropriate term is *tendonosis.* This condition arises from chronic wear and tear of the tendon and needs to be addressed as early as possible to avoid slipping into the cycle of chronic pain.

14. Sometimes the front of my shins hurt when I perform a series of jumps, and I develop shin splints. Is there something I can do to prevent this from happening?

The term *shin splints* is a generic term that is used to describe any pain in the lower leg that can arise from a variety of causes. Typical presentations involve pain along the anterior-lateral or posterior-medial lower leg. The muscles most commonly involved are the *tibialis anterior* and *peroneals* on the anterior-lateral aspect, and *tibialis posterior, soleus,* and *flexor digitorum longus* on the posterior-medial aspect.

Shin splints can be brought on by a variety of factors. Some dancers develop this condition when they return to dance after time out. This can be due to a loss of muscle strength and alignment control. Similarly, a sudden or excessive increase in jumps or leaps can also lead to this condition. In other cases, lack of optimal turn-out control in the hip external rotators can lead to "rolling," or foot pronation, and this places asymmetrical forces on the plantar flexor muscles. The result is an excessive load on the medial attachment of the *soleus* muscle, causing pain along the medial border of the *tibia.* Additionally, tension in the *soleus* muscle can lead to restriction of the *demi-plié* that, in turn, leads to "popping" the heels when landing from jumps. This places increased stresses into the lower legs and further tightens the plantar flexors.

If the cause is muscular weakness or muscular imbalance, you can perform conditioning exercises to help address this issue. These involve strengthening and stretching of all the muscle groups around the ankle. Where pronation is involved, strengthening exercises for the intrinsic muscles of the foot and for the muscles that control turn-out are key. Dancers who develop *shin splints* each time they return from vacation are advised to do conditioning exercises during their time out.

If the causes are extrinsic, such as from dancing on hard floors, then attempts should be made to modify the environmental issues as much as is feasible. For instance, if you know you will be performing on a hard stage you should build your exposure to it gradually and be mindful of how much jumping you are doing in rehearsals. Ensuring that you have a good stretch routine for the lower legs is key to undo any tension that builds up.

Dancers with severe and/or chronic *shin splints* should consult a dance medicine professional. Many times the necessary conditioning work is more complex than the strengthening and stretching exercises recommended here. In these cases it is important to have an expert prescribe a conditioning program that is specifically tailored for the individual.

It is important to know that pain in the lower leg may be caused by conditions other than *shin splints*. You should consult a physician regarding pain in your lower leg if the pain persists during activity as well as at rest, or if it lasts for more than one week.

12

STRENGTH and FLEXIBILITY EXERCISES: The FOOT, ANKLE, and LOWER LEG

THIS SECTION PROVIDES STRENGTH, FLEXIBILITY, and integration exercises for the ankle and foot. Where appropriate, injuries are also discussed. Each section will provide the exercise name, any equipment needed, and starting positions. Step-by-step descriptions of the action of the exercise, and suggestions for self checks and comments on what you might feel are offered.

Table 12.1   Roadmap

Action	Strength Exercises	Flexibility Exercises
Combination Movements		
Foot Articulation	12.A.1	12.A.2
Individual Movements		
Ankle dorsiflexion	12.B.1	12.B.2
Ankle plantar flexion	12.C.1	12.C.2
Eversion	12.D.1	12.D.2
Inversion	12.E.1	12.E.2
Functional Movements		
Pointing without the calf	12.F	12.C.2

Note: Be sure to read Part I before performing the following exercises.

12.A Foot articulation

12.A.1 Strength exercises

The following exercises for strength and flexibility are designed to strengthen the intrinsic muscles of the foot and to maximize your pointe.

Doming (Figure 12.1)

Starting position

Sit on a chair or on the floor with the feet flat on the floor. The working foot should be flat on the floor but not bearing weight.

Action

a) Keep your toes relaxed and lift the arches of your feet so they make a dome shape (Figure 12.1). The height of the dome does not matter as much as the activation of the intrinsic muscles of the arch. The goal is to keep all five toes relaxed, lengthened, and in contact with the floor.

b) Once you reach the full dome position, relax the foot back to the neutral starting position.

Repetitions

5–10 times on each foot.

Quick self checks

When learning to dome, be sure not to fall into these common traps: pushing the toes into the floor, initiating the movement by curling the toes under, or inverting or everting the ankle. This simple exercise

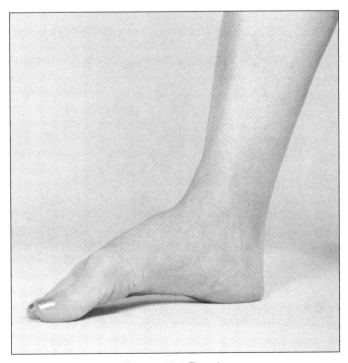

Figure 12.1 Doming

takes concentration so take your time to avoid these errors. As you work the arch of the foot you may begin to feel the muscles in your arch come to life. Some dancers may experience a small cramp under the arch when they are new to this exercise. If this happens take a break and stretch out the foot (see exercise 12.A.2).

TOE SWAPPING (FIGURE 12.2)

Starting position

Sit barefoot with the feet flat on the floor. The working foot should be flat on the floor but not bearing weight.

Action

a)   Keeping your ankle in a neutral position (and avoiding rolling out), attempt to lift just the big toe off the floor while keeping the four smaller toes on the floor. (Figure 12.2a)

b)   Place the big toe back on the floor and lift the four smaller toes off the floor, avoiding rolling in. (Figure 12.2b)

c)   Alternate between the big toe and the four toes.

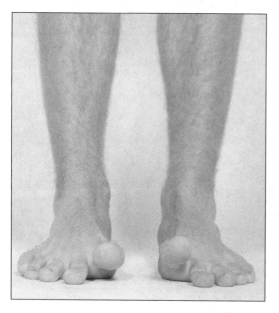 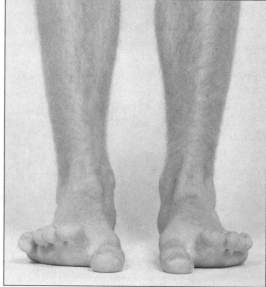

Figure 12.2a & 12.2b Toe Swapping

Repetitions

5–10 repetitions on each foot.

RIPPLE

Starting position

Sit barefoot with the feet flat on the floor. The working foot should be flat on the floor but not bearing weight.

Action

a) Keeping the ankle in a neutral position, attempt to lift each toe, one by one, in sequence, until they are all up. Then place them back down on the floor one at a time.

b) Start with the big toe then move to the second toe and so on until you reach the baby toe. Then reverse the process.

c) You can vary the exercise by starting with either the big toe or the baby toe.

Repetitions

5–10 repetitions on each foot.

SPREADING

Starting position

Sit on the floor with legs extended and toes directed toward the ceiling.

Action

a) Similar to the ripple exercise, but now you are articulating the toes side to side instead of up and down.

b) With feet extended in front of you abduct your baby toe by moving it away from the toe next to it. Continue until you have spread all five toes apart.

c) Return to the starting position. This can be done with a pointed or flexed foot.

Repetitions

5–10 repetitions on each foot.

Quick self checks

In the beginning start with a smaller number of repetitions. As you improve, you can increase the number of repetitions. If you are finding it hard to move the toes at all, or only a few toes seem to respond, don't worry. As the fingers are more able to articulate than the toes, mimic the movement in your hands. This will give you a visual and kinesthetic experience of your goal that may help you to find the same movement in the toes. You can also use your fingers to assist wayward toes that don't want to participate. You will be surprised that, after a few minutes, your toes will start to respond. After finishing the doming and toe play exercises, stand up and be aware of how your feet feel on the floor. Do they feel alive and active—ready to participate? Play with rising up on the ball of the feet in parallel and turned-out first position and notice if you feel more stable.

Toe flexors with towel

Equipment

Chair or bench, hand towel.

Starting position

Sit on a chair with your legs parallel, toes pointed straight ahead. Place the hand towel on the floor in front of your feet.

Action

a) Grasp the edge of the hand towel with your toes and pull the towel toward you.

b) Once the toes have completely flexed allow the midfoot to lift off the floor, straighten your toes releasing the towel back to the floor.

c) Relax your toes and return to the starting position.

d) Grasp the towel again and pull it toward you, then relax your toes.

e) Continue this action until the far end of the towel is under your toes.

f) Straighten the towel and begin again.

g) If you would like to increase the challenge, start with placing a two-pound weight at the end of the towel. You can increase the weight over time up to ten pounds.

Repetitions

Repetitions for this exercise are counted by the number of times your toes grasp the towel and pull it toward you. 5–10 repetitions.

Quick self checks

Keep an eye on your ankle alignment. It is important to keep your ankle in neutral alignment in order not to encourage a "sickled" or "beveled" foot. Fully flex all the toes that pull the towel with each contraction. Think of elongating the toes each time you place the foot back down to grab the towel again. The toes will begin to fatigue as you work toward the end of the towel. If you start to cramp up, take a few minutes to stretch out the bottom of your foot and then resume with a less intense contraction of the toe flexors. Once you have finished, stand up and walk around, noticing the toes on the floor. Practice a *tendu* and feel the articulation of the toes.

12.A.2 Flexibility exercise

The muscles under the foot are difficult to stretch, so this massaging technique is a useful way to relieve tension here.

MASSAGING THE SOLE OF THE FOOT INCLUDING THE HEEL, ARCH, AND BALL.

Equipment

Small ball. The size and firmness of the ball will change the intensity of the massage. You can use racquet, golf, tennis, or high-bounce Pinky balls.

Starting position

Either standing or in a sitting position, place the ball on the floor and the foot on top of the ball.

Action

Start with a gentle massage rolling the foot from toe to heel. If you find a tender point you can spend a little more time and pressure on that spot.

Repetitions

Spend a few minutes on each foot.

Quick self checks

Relax the bottom of the foot, in particular the medial arch. Before you begin, notice how your feet feel on the floor. Do you feel pain? Are they tight? Where is your weight? After you roll out one foot, come back to a standing position and notice if there is a change in how your foot feels. Take a small walk around the room and notice how the foot and ankle feels. After you repeat the rolling on the other foot, repeat the quick check. Be aware of not overdoing the foot rolling. The goal is not to create pain, but to use as much pressure as feels comfortable. When you assess the feet after rolling them out, you may notice that each foot seems wider and in greater contact with the floor. You can also rise up to the balls of your feet and see if it is easier to keep the toes long without clawing under.

12.B Dorsiflexion

12.B.1 Strength exercise

This exercise is for the muscles responsible for flexing the foot toward the shin.

RESISTED DORSIFLEXION (FIGURE 12.3)

Equipment

Elastic band attached to the leg of a heavy piece of furniture. It is important that the furniture will not move while you pull on the elastic band.

Starting position

a) Sit on the floor facing the furniture. Place the elastic band around the ball of your right foot at the base of your toes. Move far enough away that the elastic is pulled taut and can offer resistance to the action.

b) Plantar flex (point) your right ankle and foot as much as possible without allowing the elastic band to slip off. Keep the toes long and extended.

Action

a) Dorsiflex (flex) your right ankle and foot as much as possible (Figure 12.3). The elastic should provide resistance. If there is not enough resistance, sit farther away from the furniture or shorten the loop around the furniture.

b) Return to the starting position.

c) Complete all repetitions on the first side before changing sides.

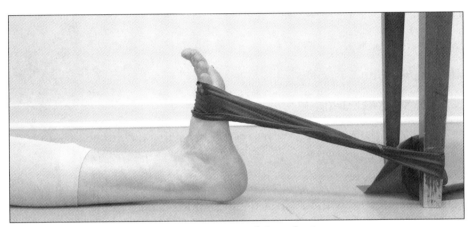

Figure 12.3 Resisted dorsiflexion

Repetitions

8–12 repetitions. To increase the resistance, either sit farther away or shorten the band.

Quick self checks

From the sitting position, it is easy to watch the alignment of the foot and ankle as you move from a pointed to a flexed position. Be aware of any tendency to "sickle" or "bevel" as you move. Imagine that the ankle is in a narrow hallway and that you don't want to touch the walls on either side. Make sure that your knee is extended to a straight, but not hyperextended, position. As with the other ankle work, take your time and move with awareness and flow. As you are working the muscles located primarily on the anterior surface of the lower leg, you may begin to feel these muscles fatigue as they reach the end of a set. Place a hand on the top of your shin to feel which muscles engage.

12.B.2 Flexibility exercise

The tibialis anterior *muscle is difficult to stretch, particularly for dancers who have flexible ankles. This exercise is an active release technique that can help to relieve tension in this muscle of dorsiflexion.*

ACTIVE RELEASE FOR *TIBIALIS ANTERIOR* (FIGURE 12.4A)

Equipment

Chair or bench.

Starting position

a)   Sit on a chair.

b)   Bend the right knee toward the chest, holding the shin with both hands and flex the foot.

c)   Locate the *tibialis anterior* muscle just to the outer side of the *tibia* (shin bone) with the fingertips of your left hand. With the foot flexed, this muscle should be activated (Figure 12.4a).

d)   To be sure you are on the muscle, alternatively point and flex the foot, feeling the muscle engage in flexion.

Action

a)   Relax the foot and press the fingertips of the left hand into the belly of the muscle about midway up the shin (Figure 12.4b). You may reinforce the pressure by placing the palm of the right hand over the top of the left .

b)   Apply gentle pressure straight down into the muscle and slightly up toward the knee.

c)   Holding the finger position steady, point the foot into full plantar flexion, then invert ("sickle") the ankle (Figure 12.4c).

d)   Release the finger pressure and relax the foot. Move the fingers a little farther up toward the knee and repeat.

Repetitions

Moving the finger position upward with each repetition, repeat 2–3 times until you have covered the length of the entire muscle. Repeat on the other leg.

Quick self checks

Be sure you are not applying excessive pressure with the fingers into the muscle. The muscle belly is quite shallow and may bruise with too much force. You need just enough pressure to stop the muscle from gliding as the foot moves into a *pointe*. You should experience only a mild discomfort. If the muscle is painful, even with minimal pressure, then do not

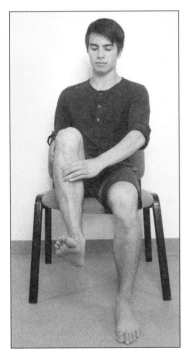

Figure 12.4a Finding the tibialis anterior

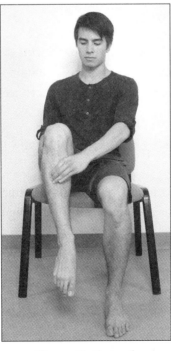

Figure 12.4b Apply gentle pressure

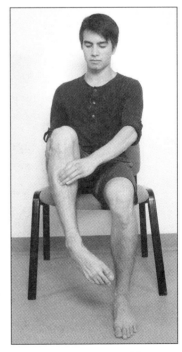

Figure 12.4c Sickle the ankle

continue the exercise. Gentle massage with the heel of the hand may be used instead. If the symptoms last more than two days, seek help from a dance medicine professional.

12.C Plantar flexion

12.C.1 Strength exercise

This exercise is for the muscles that point the foot.

RESISTED PLANTAR FLEXION (FIGURE 12.5)

Equipment

Elastic band.

Starting position

Sit on the floor and extend the working leg straight in front of you. Place the band securely under the ball of the foot and include the toes. Hold the ends of the elastic band in your hands.

Action

a)   While holding on to the band with your hands, start with a fully dorsiflexed ankle and then, in a fluid motion, lengthen the foot into plantar flexion. Beware of crunching or curling the toes under.

b)   Lengthen the toes by pushing on the band until you are in a full *pointe*.

c)   In a fluid motion, reverse the movement by pulling the toes up toward the shin and then continuing into a fully dorsiflexed position of the ankle.

Repetitions

8–12 repetitions.

Quick self checks

As discussed previously, it is important to create efficient movement patterns. Fewer repetitions with greater control and strong alignment are preferred over a higher number of repetitions and before increasing the resistance. Whether you are sitting or standing, notice the pathway of your feet and ankles as you point. Are you easily moving into plantar flexion and pushing evenly on the elastic band? When not aware, dancers often recruit the larger muscle groups around any joint. When it comes to pointing the feet, dancers commonly over-recruit the *gastrocnemius* and *soleus*, and ignore the smaller muscles. However, it is the smaller muscles that are more efficient at pointing the foot without jamming the tissues at the back of the ankle. Practice with the elastic band first in a seated position then see if you can translate this action into standing work, such as *tendus* and *dégagés*.

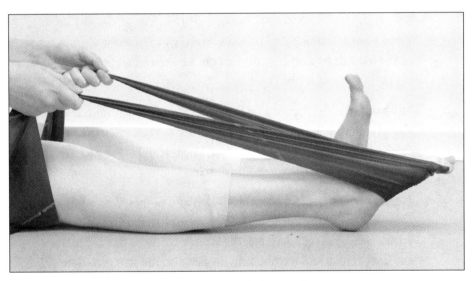

Figure 12.5 Resisted plantar flexion

12.C.2 Flexibility exercise

This exercise will stretch the muscles of plantar flexion (pointing).

CALF STRETCH (FIGURES 12.6A AND 12.6B)

Equipment

Wall or *barre*.

Starting position

a) Stand approximately two feet from the wall or *barre* with your feet in parallel first position. Do not turn out.

b) Step forward with your right leg and *demi-plié* on your right leg. Lean your hands against the wall or *barre.* Your left knee must be straight and your left heel must be touching the floor. In order to get the best stretch, the left foot must be absolutely parallel, toes pointing straight ahead. If you are accustomed to dancing in a turned-out position, this parallel position may feel turned in. Be sure to maintain the medial longitudinal arch, preventing pronation of the left foot.

Action

a) From your starting position, allow yourself to increase the stretch of the left calf by keeping the heel on the ground while you deepen the bend in the right leg.

b) Hold the stretch (Figure 12.6a) for 30 seconds to 1 minute. Feel the stretch in your left calf muscle, closer to your knee than to your ankle. While keeping the back knee straight, the focus of the stretch is on the *gastrocnemius* muscle.

c) Gently come slightly out of the stretch and without changing anything else bend the left knee. When you are stretching your calf with a bent knee you will feel the stretch closer to the ankle than the knee. This is now stretching deeper into the *soleus* muscle (Figure 12.6b). Hold this position for 30 seconds to 1 minute.

d) Straighten out the left knee again and repeat the straight leg stretch.

Repetitions

Repeat the stretch cycle 2–3 times on one side and then switch to the other calf.

Quick self checks

Double check the alignment of the feet and knees. Play with how the stretch feels in both a turned out and parallel position. You will find that in a true parallel position the stretch will feel stronger. Take a moment to check your lower back, abdominal muscles, and the alignment of your pelvis. To help maximize the stretch, have your pelvis in a neutral position with the abdominal muscles lifted to avoid an overly arched lower back. Again, you might experiment with the stretch by tilting your pelvis and then finding a neutral position.

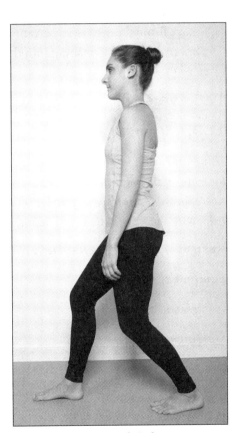

Figure 12.6a Gastrocnemius   *Figure 12.6b Soleus*

It is possible that these muscles will be very tight if you have been doing a lot of *relevés*, jumps, or *pointe* work without stretching this muscle group. If so, you may become frustrated with the limited range of movement and force the area into an "angry" stretch. Tight muscles can be stretched if you attend to them regularly and listen to your body. Remember you want to feel a "friendly" stretch, not a painful one. Pay close attention to where you are feeling the stretch. With a straight leg, the stretch will be felt high in the calf closer to the knee, and with a bent back knee the stretch will drop down toward the ankle. If you are not feeling a stretch in the back of the lower leg and only feeling a pinch in the front of the ankle or if the depth of the stretch feels restricted, then you may have a limited range of ankle dorsiflexion. This may be caused by structural limitations rather than tightness in the ankle plantar flexors. If you suspect that this is the case, consult a dance medicine professional. Understanding why you may have limited range is important to make sure that you are not creating more damage by pushing into the stretch.

12.D Eversion

12.D.1 Strength exercise

Using an elastic band, this is a resistance exercise for the muscles on the lateral (outside) of the lower leg that create eversion or a "beveled" foot. If you have weak, unstable ankles or have suffered from one or more ankle sprains, this exercise will help to develop dynamic strength and support for dance.

RESISTED ANKLE EVERSION (FIGURES 12.7A AND 12.7B)

Equipment

   Elastic band.

Starting position

   a)   Sit on the floor with the elastic band wrapped once around the middle of your left foot.

   b)   Take the ends of the elastic band to the right and use the right foot to hold the band at about a 90-degree angle to the working foot.

   c)   Hold the ends of the band together in one hand (Figure 12.7a).

d) Plantar flex your right ankle as much as possible, then invert your foot. Do not let the toes "claw" or curl under excessively.

e) Optional starting position—tie the elastic band off to a piece of furniture that will not move when you pull on it. Sit with your right side to the furniture so the band loops around the outside of your left foot.

Action

a) While holding the elastic band on the medial side of the working foot, allow the left foot to come into a full inverted or "sickled" position. From there engage the lateral side of the lower leg and move the foot into a full everted or "beveled" position (Figure 12.7b).

b) Slowly allow the foot to return to the starting position.

 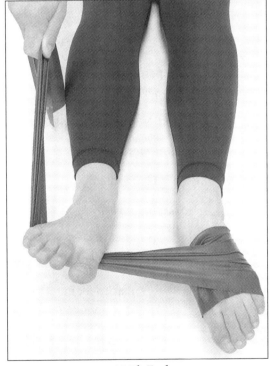

12.7a Start   *12.7b End*

Figure 12.7 Resisted ankle eversion

Repetitions

5–10 repetitions.

Quick self checks

As you are moving the foot from inversion to eversion, be sure that the movement is isolated to the foot. Try to avoid rocking your heel from side to side with the movement of the foot, or allowing the whole leg to become involved in the action. These are small muscles, so the more precise you can be, the better the results. Pay attention to whether the movement is fluid or jumpy. The goal is to have fluid control as you take the foot from inversion to eversion and then also to have a slow fluid return. If you find the foot jumps back quickly, then slow down until you can refine your control over these muscles. The lateral aspect of your ankle should begin to feel slightly fatigued. If you place your hand on the outside of your calf, you will feel the *peroneus longus, peroneus brevis,* and *extensor digitorum* muscles contract under your fingers.

12.D.2 Flexibility exercise

The peroneal *muscles are difficult muscles to stretch. This rolling exercise will help to relieve tension in this often overlooked and over-tight muscle group.*

PERONEAL MUSCLE ROLLING (FIGURE 12.8)

Equipment

Foam roller.

Starting position

a) Sit on the floor or mat in the seated fourth position with the front knee bent at 90 degrees.

b) Place a foam roller vertically under the outer aspect of the front shin about a third of the way up from the ankle.

c) Lean the upper body forward resting the arms on the front leg.

Action

a)   Roll the outer aspect of the shin in a downward motion, allowing
     the roller to travel up toward the knee.

b)   You may vary the pressure of the body weight via the arms to
     increase or decrease the force.

c)   Release the pressure before the roller reaches the knee, then reset
     down to the starting point.

d)   If a particular area of tension is noted, you can use smaller, local-
     ized rolling motions over this spot.

Repetitions

5 upward sweeps of the roller, or until a release is felt. Repeat on the
other leg.

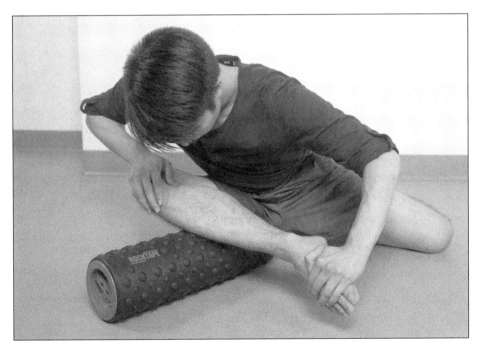

Figure 12.8 Peroneal muscle rolling

Quick self checks

> Be sure not to use excessive pressure via the body weight. This is a shallow muscle that can bruise easily. You should feel only mild discomfort. If the muscle is painful, you can simply use a massage motion with the heel of your hand while you are in a seated position with the knee bent and foot on the floor.

12.E Inversion

12.E.1 Strength exercise

Using an elastic band, this is a resistance exercise for the muscles of the lower leg that create inversion or a "sickled" foot. If you have weak, unstable ankles or have suffered one or more ankle sprains, this exercise will help to develop the strength on the inside of your ankle, creating dynamic support for dance.

RESISTED ANKLE INVERSION (FIGURE 12.9)

Equipment

> Elastic band.

Starting position

> a) Sit on the floor with the elastic band wrapped once around the middle of your left foot.
>
> b) Take the ends of the extra elastic band to the left. Cross the right leg over and use the right foot to hold the elastic band at about a 90-degree angle to the working foot.
>
> c) Hold the ends of the elastic band together in one hand (Figure 12.9a).
>
> d) Plantar flex your left ankle as much as possible, then evert your foot. Do not let the toes "claw" or curl under excessively.
>
> e) Optional starting position—tie the elastic band off to a piece of furniture that will not move when you pull on it. Sit with your right side to the furniture so the elastic band loops around the inside of your right foot.

Action

a) While holding the elastic band on the lateral aspect of the working foot, allow the left foot to come into a full inverted or "sickled" position. This engages the medial aspect of the lower leg as the foot is brought into inversion (Figure 12.9b).

b) Slowly allow the foot to return to the starting position.

Repetitions

5–10 repetitions. As you improve in strength, increase the resistance on the elastic band.

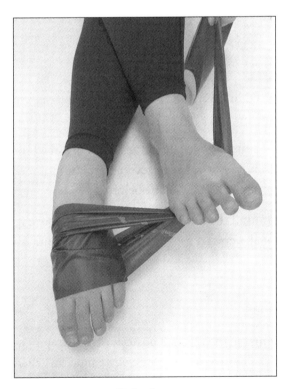 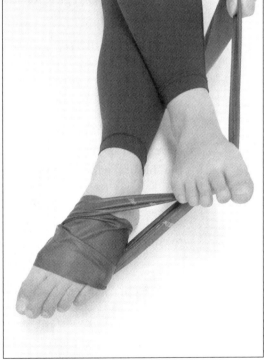

12.9a Start   *12.9b End*

Figure 12.9 Resisted ankle inversion

Quick self checks

As you are moving the foot from eversion to inversion, be sure that the movement is isolated to the foot. Try to avoid rocking your heel from side to side with the movement of the foot or allowing the whole leg to become involved in the action. These are small muscles, so the more precise you can be, the better your results. Pay attention to whether the movement is fluid or jumpy. The goal is to have fluid control as you take the foot from eversion to inversion and then also to have a slow fluid return. If you find the foot jumps back quickly, then slow down until you can refine your control over these muscles.

The medial aspect of your ankle should begin to feel slightly fatigued. After you have completed the eversion and inversion exercises, stand up and do some *pliés* and *relevés* feeling the inside and the outside areas of the ankle engaging for stability.

12.E.2 Flexibility exercise

The *tibialis anterior* muscle is involved in inversion. To stretch this muscle, use exercise 12.B.2 on page 78.

The *tibialis posterior* muscle is difficult to locate for any kind of stretch or active release. As the tendon of this muscle attaches to several structures under the sole of the foot, the rolling exercises in 12.A.2 will be helpful.

If you are experiencing pain around the inside ankle bone or just above it, consult a dance medicine professional who can use manual therapy techniques to address this muscle.

12.F Pointing without the calf

This exercise is important for minimizing the risk of a posterior ankle impingement injury. Over-recruitment of the *gastrocnemius* and *soleus* muscles when pointing the foot will result in a traction force that draws the *calcaneus* (via the *Achilles tendon*) up into the back of the ankle. This can compress the soft tissues and bony surfaces in the area resulting in pain, inflammation, and possibly ankle restriction. By focusing on using the muscles of plantar flexion that do not connect to the *calcaneus*, a strong pointing action can be achieved without causing posterior ankle compression.

Starting position

Sitting on the floor with the legs extended.

Action

a) With the leg extended, point your foot and observe the engagement of the calf muscles. You should clearly see the outline of the *gastrocnemius* muscle as it contracts. Also, observe the skin creases around the back of the *Achilles tendon* and feel the sensation of the *calcaneus* being pulled up into the space at the back of the ankle.

b) Now dorsiflex (flex) the ankle and feel the space that is created at the back of the ankle by the downward movement of the *calcaneus*. Holding this sensation, then begin to point the foot and attempt to maintain this space. You can do this by focusing on pointing from the middle of the foot and extending the toes away. Do not allow the calf muscles to engage and pull the *calcaneus* upward, keeping the creasing around the *Achilles* to a minimum.

Repetitions

Repeat 5–10 times, building the repetitions slowly. Do not repeat if you begin to recruit the calf muscles.

Quick self checks

If you are in the habit of over-recruiting the calf muscles, you will find this exercise difficult to master as these muscles will want to dominate. A good trick is to use your hand to gently shake the calf muscles to keep them soft as you begin to point. As soon as they begin to engage, stop and shake them again. As you practice this exercise, you should be able to point a bit further each time until the calf muscles engage again. Envision the deep, midfoot, plantar flexor muscles engaging instead of the calf muscles, and "think" your way to a new muscle-firing pattern. Using "mind over matter" and your hand to monitor calf activity, you will gradually get the hang of it. You should feel the pointing action located under the midfoot area and the toes extending away to continue the line. You should also be aware of maintaining the space at the back of the ankle. You should *not* feel the calf muscles over-firing, the *Achilles* creasing, or the *calcaneus* crunching up into the posterior ankle compartment.

Part III
The KNEE and HIP

The knee joint and the hip joint are discussed together in this part of the book as they are influenced by many of the same muscle groups. These muscles originate at the pelvis and end below the knee on the bones of the lower leg. They are often called "two-joint muscles" because they cause movements at two joints, the hip and the knee.

13

STRUCTURAL ANATOMY

THE KNEE JOINT IS ONE OF THE MOST COMPLEX JOINTS in the body. It is the meeting point of the *femur* (thigh bone) and *tibia* (shin bone). The *femur* has two enlarged processes called *condyles* at the lower end of the bone (Figure 13.1). These condyles articulate (fit together) with the enlarged surfaces of the *tibia*, known as the *tibial condyles*.

The other bone associated with the knee is the *patella*, commonly known as the knee cap. It is classified as a sesamoid (floating) bone because it is held within a tendon, in this case the tendon of the quadriceps muscle group (Figure 13.1). This tendon transmits the forces of the four knee extensor muscles above to the *tibia* below, encasing the *patella* on the way. This system allows the knee extensor muscles to produce greater force during knee extension than would be possible without the *patella*.

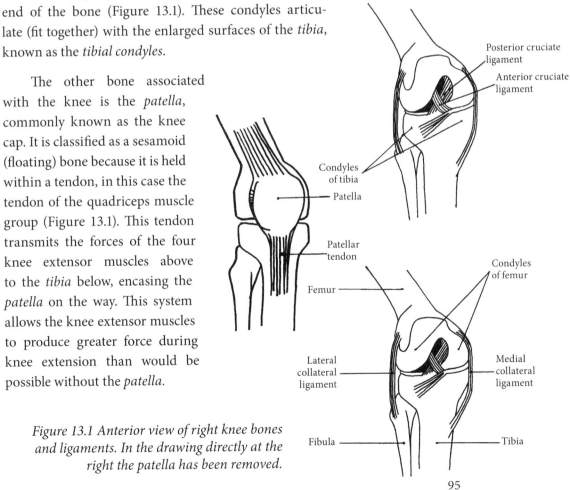

Figure 13.1 Anterior view of right knee bones and ligaments. In the drawing directly at the right the patella has been removed.

95

The surfaces of the bones of the knee joint are lined with cartilage to provide cushioning and ease of movement. Ligaments and tendons provide strength and support. Some of the knee ligaments include the *cruciate* and the *collateral ligaments* (Figure 13.1). The *cruciate ligaments* "cross" within the knee joint between the *tibia* and the *femur*. These ligaments provide internal stability for the knee joint. The *collateral ligaments* are found on the medial and lateral aspects of the knee and provide an external support for the knee joint.

Movements of the knee joint

Movements at the knee include *flexion* (bending the knee) and *extension* (straightening the knee). A slight degree of *inward* and *outward rotation* accompanies the

Table 13.1 Muscle actions of the knee

Movement of the Knee	Dancer Terminology	Muscles

Flexion	Bending—*plié* or *passé* movement	Hamstring Group
		    Biceps Femoris
		    Semitendinosus
		    Semimembranosus
		Popliteus
		Sartorius
		Gracilis
		Gastrocnemius

Extension	Straightening the leg	Quadriceps Group
		    Rectus Femoris
		    Vastus Lateralis
		    Vastus Intermedius
		    Vastus Medialis

Inward rotation	Turning the legs in	Semitendinosus Semimembranosus
Outward rotation	Turn-out	Biceps Femoris

movements of *flexion* and *extension*. *Inward* and *outward* rotation can only occur when the knee is bent. Rotation is not possible once the knee is fully extended and straight. There are also some other very subtle movements possible, such as a rocking motion (side to side) and shearing motion (forward to back) of the *femur* on the *tibia*. These are known as intrinsic movements and help with the subtleties of balance.

Flexion of the knee

The muscles responsible for knee flexion include the hamstrings, the *popliteus*, the *sartorius*, and the *gracilis*. The hamstrings and *popliteus* are found on the posterior aspect of the thigh; the greater part of the *sartorius*, on the anterior aspect; and the *gracilis*, on the medial aspect. The *gastrocnemius* (described in Chapter 10) is attached to the *femur* and can also assist with knee flexion when the lower leg is not bearing weight.

The hamstrings consist of the *biceps femoris*, the *semitendinosus*, and the *semimembranosus*. The *biceps femoris* has two heads (Figures 13.2 and 13.3). The long head is attached to the pelvis and the short head to the *femur*. Both muscles are attached at the other end to the lateral aspect of the *fibula* as well as to the lateral condyle of the *tibia*. You can feel the tendon of the *biceps femoris* on the lateral aspect of the posterior thigh, near the knee.

The *semimembranosus* and the *semitendinosus* are attached at one end to the pelvis and at the other end, to the medial aspect of the *tibia* (Figure 13.2). You can feel these muscles on the medial aspect of the posterior thigh, near the knee.

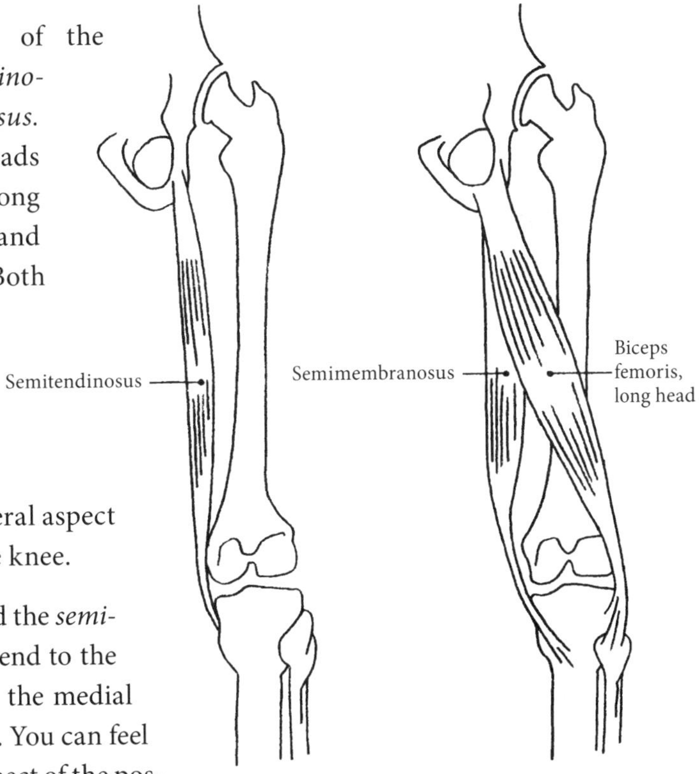

Figure 13.2 Posterior view of knee and hip muscles

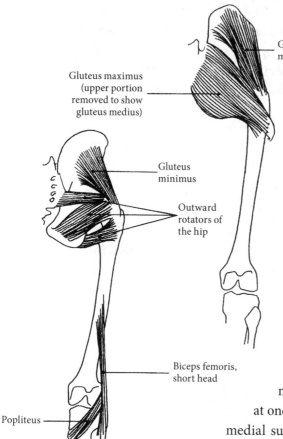

Gluteus medius

Gluteus maximus (upper portion removed to show gluteus medius)

Gluteus minimus

Outward rotators of the hip

Biceps femoris, short head

Popliteus

Figure 13.3 Posterior view of additional hip and knee muscles

The *popliteus* is a small muscle that is attached to the lateral condyle of the *femur* at one end and to the *tibia* at the other (Figure 13.3). It is a deep muscle and is difficult to palpate. The *popliteus* serves to flex the knee and is the only one-joint muscle that performs this function. It also acts with the *cruciate ligaments* to stabilize the knee.

The *sartorius* is a slender muscle that is attached at one end to the anterior aspect of the pelvis (Figure 13.4a). At the other end it is attached to the anterior and medial surface of the *tibia*. It may be visually identified as the slender muscle running diagonally across the front of the thigh.

The *gracilis* is another long slender muscle located on the inner thigh. It is attached at one end to the pelvis and at the other end, to the medial surface of the *tibia* (Figure 13.4a). To feel this muscle in action, place your hand on the medial side of the thigh, two to three inches below the *pubic* bone as you flex the knee.

Find It

Sit on the floor with the legs extended to the front. Lift one leg and place your fingers behind and just above the knee.

Feel It

Bend your knee. Notice the tendons on the inside and outside of the back of the knee engaging. These are the hamstring tendons.

Dance It

Place your leg in a low *arabesque* then bend into *attitude*.

Extension of the knee

The quadriceps muscle group, located at the front of the thigh, is responsible for knee extension. It is comprised of four muscles: the *rectus femoris*, the *vastus lateralis*, the *vastus intermedius*, and the *vastus medialis*, all of which are shown in Figure 13.4a and 13.4b. Of these, only the *rectus femoris* is a two-joint muscle, crossing both the hip and knee joints. The lower tendons of all four muscles encase the *patella* and then blend to form the *patellar tendon*, which inserts on the anterior surface of the *tibia* just below the knee joint.

The *rectus femoris* is attached at one end to the pelvis and at the other end, to the *tibia* by way of the *patellar tendon* (Figure 13.4b). Of the four quadriceps muscles, it is closest to the surface and can be easily palpated on the front of the thigh. If you have been told by your instructor that you are "gripping your thigh muscle" when performing a *développé*, that muscle is usually the *rectus femoris*.

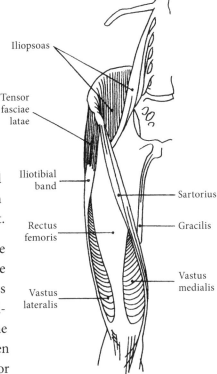

Figure 13.4a Anterior view of knee and hip muscles

The *vastus lateralis, vastus intermedius,* and *vastus medialis* muscles are attached on one end to the *femur* and on the other end to the *tibia* by way of the *patellar tendon* (Figure 13.4b). The *vastus lateralis* is the largest and can be palpated on the lateral mid-thigh. The *vastus intermedius* is located beneath the *rectus femoris* and cannot be palpated. The *vastus medialis* may be palpated on the medial aspect of the anterior thigh near the knee.

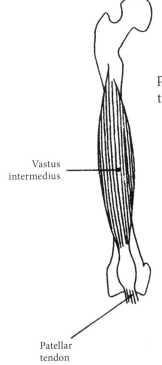

Figure 13.4b Deep anterior view of knee muscles

Find It

> Stand on one leg with the knee of the raised leg bent. Place a hand on the front of the lifted thigh.

Feel It

> Straighten the knee and feel the quadriceps muscles engaging.

Dance It

> Place the leg in *attitude devant* and then fully extend the knee.

Inward and outward rotation of the knee

A small degree of *inward* and *outward rotation* can occur when the knee is bent. *Inward rotation* is performed mainly by the *semimembranosus* and the *semitendinosus.*

Outward rotation is performed mainly by the *biceps femoris.* All of these muscles have been described above.

Find It

> Sit in a chair with your legs bent to 90 degrees, feet on the floor. Flex one foot keeping the heel in contact but raise the toes off the floor. Place your fingers on the hamstring tendons—behind and just above the knee.

Feel It

> Keeping the thigh in neutral, pivot on your heel to rotate the lower leg inward and outward.
>
> Notice the tendon on the outside of the knee engages when you rotate outward, and the tendons on the inside engage when you rotate inward

Dance It

> In tap dancing, the movement of the front lower leg in a *Suzi Q* displays this knee motion.

The structure of the hip joint

The bones of the hip joint include the *femur* and the *pelvis* (Figure 13.5a). The *femur* is comprised of the head, a short neck, a prominent bony projection

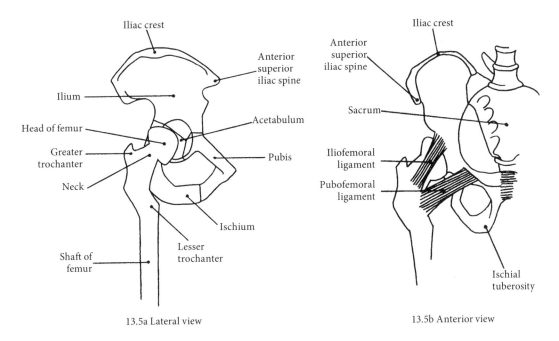

13.5a Lateral view

13.5b Anterior view

Figure 13.5 Lateral and anterior view of right hip joint and ligaments

called the *greater trochanter,* a smaller bony projection called the *lesser trochan-ter,* and the shaft with its condyles at the knee joint. The head of the *femur* articu-lates with the pelvis at the *acetabulum,* or hip socket. The lower end articulates with the *tibia* to form the knee joint.

Three bones—the *ilium, ischium,* and *pubis*—are fused together to form the pelvis (Figure 13.5a). The right and left sides of the *ilium* form the upper portion of the pelvis. The right and left sides of the *ischium* form the posterior and lower portions, while the right and left sides of the *pubis* form the anterior and lower portions.

The *ilium* (plural *ilia*) is the largest bone. On the front of the *ilia* are the bony projections commonly referred to as the "hip bones." Anatomically they are referred to as the *anterior superior iliac spines.* The crest of the *ilium* is the top ridge of the hip bone just below the waist. If you carry books or packages in one arm and let them rest on your "hip," they are resting on the crest of the *ilium.* The *sacrum,* or lowest part of the spine, fits between the right and left portions of the posterior *ilia.*

The "sitting bones" are found on the *ischium* and they are referred to as the *ischial tuberosities*. They bear the weight of the body when sitting.

Several ligaments attach the *femur* to the hip socket. Two of these ligaments, the *iliofemoral* and *pubofemoral*, are of great interest to dancers (Figure 13.5b). They are located at the front of the hip socket, and their names indicate the bones that they connect. The *iliofemoral* ligament joins the *ilium* and the *femur*. The *pubofemoral* ligament joins the *pubis* and the *femur*. If these ligaments are relatively short, they can limit outward rotation of the leg at the hip. For a dancer this can mean a reduced ability to turn out.

Movements of the hip joint

Movements at the hip include *flexion* (bending at the hip) and *extension* (straightening of the hip). There is a difference of opinion among experts as to whether *hyperextension* (a continuation of extension beyond 180 degrees) is possible at the hip joint. Some experts believe a small degree of hyperextension is possible (Luttgens and Wells 1982). An example of this would be a *tendu* back. Other experts believe that all posterior movement, from *tendu* back to *arabesque*, is more correctly classified as hyperextension of the spine, rather than hyperextension of the hip (Fitt 2001). For the purpose of this book we will simply use the term *extension* when referring to movements such as *tendu* back, back *attitude*, and *arabesque*.

Other movements at the hip include *abduction* (sideward movement of the leg away from the midline of the body), *adduction* (sideward movement of the leg toward the midline of the body), and *inward* and *outward rotation*. An example of abduction is the lifted leg position in a modern dance class (Figure 13.6). *Adduction* would occur if the lifted leg moved to parallel first position. *Inward* and *outward rotation* refer to turning in and turning out.

Movement of the hip usually involves a combination of the actions just described. For example, a ballet dancer's *grand battement* front would involve hip flexion and outward rotation. If the same dancer were to lift the leg in a forward diagonal direction, as usually occurs in a *grand battement* to the side, movements at the hip would include flexion, abduction, and outward rotation.

Just as there can be a complex interaction of movement occurring at the hip, there can also be a complex interaction of the muscles that produce this

Figure 13.6 Hip abduction movement in modern dance

movement. Many of the muscles at the hip are involved in more than one action. Sometimes different parts of the same muscle are active in producing entirely different actions. In the material that follows we will only discuss those muscles that are primarily involved in producing a certain movement. Understanding this simplified discussion will give you the general background you need to proceed with the questions and exercises that follow.

Flexion of the hip

Some of the muscles responsible for hip flexion are the *iliopsoas*, the *pectineus*, the *sartorius* and the *rectus femoris* (both already described), and the *tensor fasciae latae*. These muscles are located on the anterior aspect of the thigh and pelvis, except for the *tensor fasciae latae*, which is located on both the anterior and lateral aspects of the thigh.

The *iliopsoas* is the most important hip flexor muscle. It is actually composed of two muscles, the *iliacus* and the *psoas* (Figure 13.7). The *psoas* is attached to the lower vertebrae and the *iliacus* is attached to the inner aspect of the *ilium*.

Table 13.2 Muscle actions of the hip

Movement of the Hip	Dancer Terminology	Muscles
Flexion	Bending at the hip	Iliopsoas Pectineus Sartorius Rectus Femoris (quadricep muscle) Tensor Fasciae Latae

Extension	Straightening or extending the hip	Hamstring Group
		    Biceps Femoris
		    Semitendinosus
		    Semimembranosus
		Gluteus Maximus

Iliopsoas
Psoas portion

Iliacus portion

Patella

The two muscles blend and attach to the *femur* at the lesser trochanter. The *iliopsoas* is a powerful muscle. If its strength is not balanced by the abdominal muscles, the *iliopsoas* can pull down on the front of the pelvis, flexing the hip and tilting the pelvis forward. When the pelvis tilts forward, the spine often hyperextends or over-arches. This tipping action and the balancing role of the abdominal muscles will be discussed in Part IV.

The *pectineus* is a small muscle attached at one end to the *pubic* bone and at the other, to the medial aspect of the *femur* (Figure 13.8). Like the *iliopsoas*, the *pectineus* tends to pull the pelvis downward in front, thereby flexing the hip and tilting the pelvis forward. The *tensor fasciae latae* is another small muscle (Figure 13.4a). It is attached at one end to the *ilium* and at the other end, to the *iliotibial band* (connective tissue) of the lateral

Figure 13.7 Anterior view of the iliopsoas

thigh. The *iliotibial band* runs the length of the lateral leg, crosses the lateral aspect of the knee joint, and inserts on the lateral condyle of the *tibia*. Not only does the *tensor fasciae latae* flex the hip, it also exerts a pull on the *iliotibial band*. In this way it stabilizes the knee joint in weight-bearing positions.

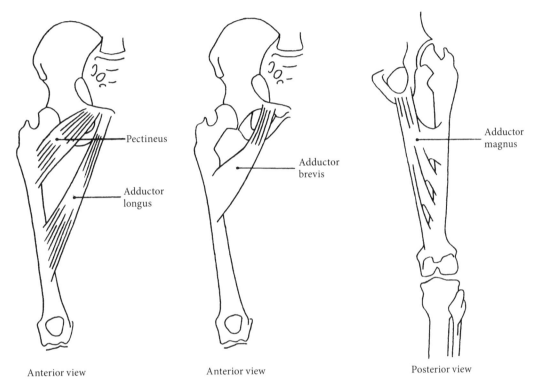

Figure 13.8 Anterior and posterior views of hip muscles

Find It

Find the prominent hip bone on the front of the pelvis. Place your fingers just below this point

Feel It

Bring your knee up toward your chest.

Notice the tendons engaging under your fingers. These are the *tensor fasciae latae*, *rectus femoris*, and *sartorius* tendons.

Dance It

Perform a *grand battement devant*.

Extension of the hip

Some of the muscles responsible for hip extension include the hamstring group (already described) and the *gluteus maximus*. These muscles are located on the posterior aspect of the body. They are responsible for lifting the leg in *arabesque*, back *attitude*, and other hyperextended positions.

The *gluteus maximus* is attached to both the *ilium* and *sacrum* at one end (Figure 13.3). At the other end it is attached to the *femur* and along the iliotibial band (connective tissue) of the lateral thigh. The *gluteus maximus* muscle is a powerful hip extensor against resistance. For example, it is very active in stair climbing or coming up from a deep lunge. It also assists with *outward rotation* when the hip is extended. This muscle can easily be palpated in the area of the buttocks.

Find It

Stand with your legs parallel, with your hand on the left buttock area.

Feel It

Lift the left leg to the back.

Notice the muscle popping up under your fingers. This is the *gluteus maximus*.

Dance It

Perform a *grand battement derrière*.

Table 13.3 Muscle actions of the hip

Movement of the Hip	Dancer Description	Muscles
Abduction	Kick to the side or the out phase of a tendu or jumping jack	Gluteus Medius Gluteus Minimus Tensor Fasciae Latae
Adduction	Closing the leg from a side movement like a tendu	Adductor Longus Adductor Brevis Adductor Magnus

Abduction of the hip

Some of the muscles responsible for hip abduction are the *gluteus medius*, the *gluteus minimus*, and the *tensor fasciae latae* (already described). The *gluteus medius* and *minimus* are located on the lateral aspect of the hip.

The *gluteus medius* is a small muscle that lies under the *gluteus maximus*. It is attached at one end to the lateral surface of the *ilium* and at the other end, to the top of the greater trochanter (Figure 13.3). It is the chief abductor of the thigh at the hip and is also important in stabilizing the standing leg.

The *gluteus minimus* is another small muscle that lies under the *gluteus medius*. It is attached to the lateral aspect of the *ilium* and to the top of the greater trochanter (Figure 13.3).

Find It
Standing in parallel, place your hand on the side of the pelvis with fingers pointing downward.

Feel It
Lift your leg to a parallel second position.
   Notice the muscle popping up under your fingers. This is the *gluteus medius*.

Dance It
Perform a side layout.

Adduction of the hip

The muscles generally classified as hip adductors are the *adductor longus*, the *adductor brevis*, and the *adductor magnus*, as well as the *gracilis* and the medial hamstrings (described previously). These muscles are located on the medial aspect of the thigh.

The *adductor longus*, *adductor brevis*, and *adductor magnus* are attached at one end to the *pubic* bone or *ischium* and at the other end, to the medial or posterior aspect of the *femur* (Figure 13.8). The *adductor magnus* is attached to the largest area of the *femur* and can be palpated midway down the thigh on the medial surface. The *adductor brevis* cannot be palpated. The *adductor longus* can be felt by placing your hand just below the *pubic* bone on the medial side of the thigh as you adduct the thigh against resistance.

Find It

Sit on floor with legs extended and parallel. Open one leg to the side and place your fingers on the inner thigh.

Feel It

Draw the open leg back toward the other one.

Notice the muscles popping up under your fingers. These are the adductors.

Dance It

Close the leg from a *dégagé* to the side.

Table 13.4 Muscle actions of the hip

Movement of the Hip	Dancer Description	Muscles
Inward rotation	Turning the legs in	Gluteus Medius Gluteus Minimus Semimembranosus Semitendinosus Gracilis Tensor Fasciae Latae Adductors

Outward rotation	Turn-out	Deep 6 outward rotators
		  Piriformis
		  Obturator Externus
		  Obturator Internus
		  Gemellus Superior
		  Gemellus Inferior
		  Quadratus Femoris
		Gluteus Maximus
		Sartorius
		Biceps Femoris

Inward rotation of the hip

The primary *inward rotators* are the *gluteus medius* and *minimus*, the *minimus* being the most effective. Other muscles that assist in inward rotation are the *semimembranosus, semitendinosus, gracilis, tensor fasciae latae*, and some of the adductors. All of these muscles have been described previously.

Find It

Place your fingers just below and to the outside of the prominent hip bone, pointing downward. Place the fingers of your other hand on to the innermost hamstrings and inner thigh.

Feel It

Rotate the leg inward.

Notice the muscles popping up under your fingers. These are the *tensor fasciae latae* and *gluteus medius* on the outside of the hip, and the *semimembranosus, semitendinosus,* and adductors on the inner aspect of the leg.

Dance It

The front leg in a "Fosse" walk.

Outward rotation of the hip

Some of the muscles responsible for *outward rotation* are the six outward rotators, the *gluteus maximus, sartorius, biceps femoris,* and the adductors. With the exception of the six outward rotators, these muscles have been described previously.

The six outward rotators are very short muscles that attach at one end to the posterior surface of the *sacrum, ilium,* and *ischium* (Figure 13.3). At the other end they attach to the greater trochanter. These muscles are very deep and are responsible for most of the turn-out control in dance.

Find It

Stand with legs in parallel. Place your fingers at the top of one leg just under the curve of the buttock.

Feel It

Rotate the leg outward from the hip.

Notice the muscles popping up under your fingers. These are known as the "deep six" rotators.

Dance It

Développé devant feeling the down-and-under rotation of the hip.

Neutral alignment for the knees and hip

Starting at the knees, it is key to note that neutral alignment here is ultimately dependent upon the placement of the feet below and the pelvis and spine above. Knees should always be viewed in this global context particularly, if a dancer is experiencing knee symptoms.

When viewed from the front or back, the knee caps should ideally face straight ahead and not point inward. Some people may have a slight bowing to the lower legs that can affect this alignment of the knee, but this can be minimized by using hip external rotation control (see Chapter 14, Question 1 and the exercises at 15.G below). When viewed from the side, a plumb line should pass through the center of the hip, continue behind the *patella* passing slightly forward of the center of the knee, and finish in front of the ankle bone. If the plumb line passes through the front of the knee, the knee is considered to be hyperextended. If the plumb line passes through the back of the knee, the knee is said to be hyperflexed.

Next we must consider the relationship of the knee to foot alignment. In all dance positions, the knee should be in line with, or centered over, the middle of the foot. If in turned-out positions this is being forced from the knee and ankle, rather than turning out the entire leg from the hip, then the knee will be aligned with the floor in front of the foot rather than being centered over the middle of the foot. This will be particularly notable in *pliés* (Figure 13.9).

The pelvis should be neither tilted forward (anterior tilt) nor backward (posterior tilt). This will be discussed further in Part IV.

Figure 13.9 Knee alignment (left image incorrect, right image correct)

14

QUESTIONS and ANSWERS: The KNEE and HIP

The following questions relate to common dance training issues, such as alignment and movement execution that could result in injury. A few common injuries are also addressed. As we have noted in Chapter 13, the knee and hip are interrelated. This section provides answers to questions that are related to individual areas and how these areas interact in movement.

1. When I have to stand in parallel I struggle to align my knees over my toes. When my knees are straight my feet want to be turned out but if I align my feet my knees face in. I also struggle with alignment control in turn-out. Why is this?

Many dancers experience this issue and it is usually related to the underlying anatomy. In some individuals, the *tibia* is slightly rotated (either inward or outward) in relation to the *femur* (Figure 14.1). This is known as *tibial torsion*. An inward rotation will make achieving turn-out particularly challenging. This rotation will cause the knee joint to be slightly misaligned resulting in an inability to have the knees placed over the center of the foot. This can lead to discomfort and injury. There are some exercises that may help to minimize this rotation but the results may ultimately be limited by the underlying anatomical structures. In such cases it may be prudent to focus on knee and foot alignment rather than the knee itself (Grossman et al. 2008).

Forcing the turn-out from the feet can also be a contributing factor to this issue. When the knees are straight, the joint surfaces do not allow for any *inward* or *outward rotation*. However, when the knees are bent, the joint surfaces are no longer in play, and the *collateral ligaments* that stabilize the joint will be lax. This allows for a slight degree of *inward* and *outward rotation* to take place, which is controlled and limited by the *cruciate ligaments*. When in *plié*, dancers may be tempted to exploit this extra degree of rotation by exaggerating the knee position or by popping the heels forward. This will increase the forces over the medial aspect of the knee and risk damage to the medial ligaments and cartilage. If they then attempt to maintain this increased rotation as they straighten the knees, that movement will stress both the *cruciate* and *collateral ligaments*, further increasing the risk of injury.

Ligaments do not have the elastic capability of the muscles. This makes them susceptible to being torn or permanently stretched. If knee ligaments are overstretched, their ability to stabilize the joint is impaired. Furthermore, when a *medial collateral ligament* is torn, the knee cartilage may be torn as well, as they are interconnected.

While dancers with tibial torsion are at risk of falling into the trap of exploiting their turn-out capacity from below the knee, it may

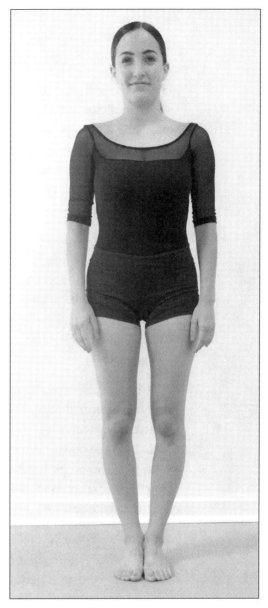

Figure 14.1 Tibial torsion

also be that young dancers who fall into this trap are actually at risk of developing a tibial torsion. To minimize the risk of injury to the knees, close attention must be paid to the technical control of turn-out at all levels of training.

2.   I am confused about the rules regarding *grand pliés*. Are they bad for my knees? Is there a good time in class to do *grand pliés*?

Many orthopedists and physical therapists who work with dancers, as well as dance kinesiologists, find the *grand plié* to be extremely taxing on the knee. Some believe it is an appropriate movement if it is executed correctly, but express concern that the majority of dancers may not have the requisite strength in the optimal alignment to achieve this. Dancers with knee issues should avoid performing *grand pliés*, particularly in the fourth and fifth positions, until their symptoms have resolved.

Most of these experts agree that the *grand plié* should be regarded as an advanced skill and taught only when dancers have sufficient strength to control the alignment of the torso, hip, and leg throughout the entire movement. Even then, they should be practiced with moderation and their placement in the class structure should be considered. It is often recommended that *grand pliés* should be placed later in the warm-up, so that the body is prepared before this exacting work begins.

Considerable stress is placed on the knee during a *grand plié*. On the downward movement, the quadriceps muscles function eccentrically and on the upward movement, they function concentrically. The pull of these knee extensors in both the downward and upward movements creates a compressive force, via the *patellar tendon*, in which the *patella* is pressed against the condyles of the *femur*. If there is any deviation in the pull of the extensors, the compressive force can damage the *patella*, leading to anterior knee pain.

Another issue is that during a *grand plié*, gravity requires the knee joint to control more than three times the body's weight. When this stress is accumulated over a period of time, it can lead to knee injury—especially if the body is not strong enough to maintain the proper alignment of the knee during this movement. The previously mentioned issues of forcing the turn-out in the straightening phase of the *plié* also apply to this question. See Question 1 on page 112.

3. The hurdle position has been recommended as a
    good way to stretch the outer thigh, but it causes
    me discomfort in the bent knee (Figure 14.2).
    The same thing happens to the back knee in the
    seated fourth position (Figure 14.3). Should I be
    doing these?

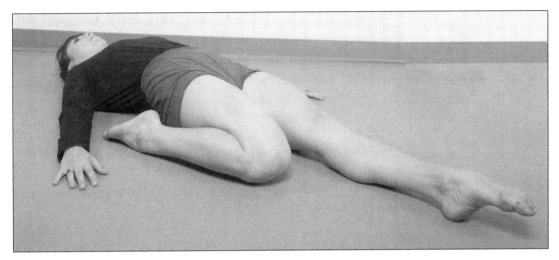

Figure 14.2 Hurdle

The hurdle position's bent knee and
the seated fourth position's back knee
are in essentially the same position.
Some dancers with laxity or looseness in the ligaments of the knee may
not experience knee pain in these
positions. However, many dancers do
encounter knee pain and should not
try to endure or work through it.

In Figure 14.3, you will see that
the *femur* is rotated in one direction

Figure 14.3 Seated fourth position

while the lower leg is rotated in another. If you are experiencing knee pain in the hurdle or seated fourth position, it is probably because you do not have enough natural rotation in the knee to accommodate the position of the thigh and lower leg. If you continue to work through the pain, you are at risk of injuring your knee ligaments. When the *medial collateral ligament* is seriously injured, it can often cause damage to the medial knee cartilage as well. This is why movement experts recommend these positions not be used by anyone experiencing pain.

In these two positions, it is necessary to have both buttocks in contact with the floor. Many dancers have enough natural rotation to be comfortable as long as the back hip is off the floor. However, when they try to lower it down, they experience pain. This is unlikely to improve with persistence, so again these dancers should avoid these positions.

4.   I am having trouble performing knee hinges and back hinge falls in my modern dance and jazz classes. How can I improve my performance of these movements?

If you look closely at the knee hinge and the back hinge fall, you will see that the knees flex about as much as they do in a *grand plié*. The stress that *grand pliés* can place on the knee is discussed in question 2 on page 114. Many of those concerns also apply to knee hinges and back hinge falls.

To prevent knee injury while performing knee hinge movements, keep the hips extended or "lifted up" and the torso in straight alignment. The descent in the knee hinge must be controlled. At no time should the weight be allowed to drop. Dancers who do not have the necessary control to perform a back hinge fall can bruise the shoulder structure and forcefully jam the knee into a fully flexed position.

Knee hinges and back hinge falls should be regarded as advanced techniques. These movements should be introduced only when the necessary strength to execute every phase of the movement properly has been acquired. It is also important to only attempt these taxing movements when the body is sufficiently warmed up and prepared. Both the knee hinge and back hinge fall require strong and flexible knee extensors. In addition, the hip extensors must be strong enough to prevent the hip from flexing, and the trunk muscles must be strong enough to maintain the alignment of the torso. The exercises listed below will help you condition the knee and hip muscles. Part IV discusses strength conditioning for the trunk.

5. My knees are often painful when performing kneeling work or knee falls. Is there something I can do to prevent this from happening?

Performing movements on the knees and falling or sliding to the knees can be traumatic to these vulnerable joints. There are several potential reasons for this pain that will depend upon the location of symptoms.

If the discomfort is being felt over the knee cap, this may relate to the *pre-patellar bursa*. A *bursa* is a small, fluid-filled "pillow" that is usually present at the site of a tendon attachment to bone. There are many of these in the knee joint, but the aforementioned *prepatellar bursa* lies between the kneecap and the skin. Constant kneeling can irritate this bursa and cause inflammation and swelling. The swelling generally occurs over the knee cap and causes consider-able pain during movement. Physicians recommend ice, rest, and elevation as an immediate treatment. If the swelling does not disappear, a specialist should be consulted.

In adolescent dancers, if the pain is occurring lower down on the *tibial tuberosity*, another condition should be considered. The *tibial tuberosity* is the bony prominence that can be felt just below the center of the knee at the top of the *tibia*. Before the age of 16 or 17, this area is yet to become fully formed bone and is still comprised of cartilage. This makes it prone to inflammation. This is the attachment point of the *patella tendon* that transmits the forces of the quad-riceps muscle group. During heavy knee work, this powerful muscle group can exert quite a traction force through the relatively soft tissue of the *tibial tuberos-ity* and cause it to become inflamed. This area is often the first point of contact with the ground during knee falls or slides. The added force of the body weight falling under gravity onto this potentially inflamed prominence, while it is also being influenced by the traction force of the quadriceps, causes a recipe for pain and swelling. This condition is known as *Osgood Schlatter's Disease*, and it often occurs after a growth spurt in adolescent dancers. During growth phases, bones often grow at a faster rate than muscles, with muscles sometimes taking as long as six months to catch up. If the *femur* has increased in length but the quadriceps have not, then they will now be stretched over a greater length, thus increasing the force exerted via the tendon to the *tibial tuberosity*. This condition is usually self-remitting once the muscles have caught up in length to the bones. However, you may wish to consult a medical professional to help you manage the condition and symptoms in the meantime.

Dropping into the kneeling position, rather than controlling the body's descent, may be another cause of this problem. Strong knee and hip extensors are needed to control the kneeling movement. Conditioning these muscles may help. If you are controlling the kneeling movement, then it may simply be the pressure of kneeling that irritates the surrounding structures. Knee pads can help to relieve this pressure, but it is important that these pads do not become a crutch. With the knee pads protecting the joints, dancers can sometimes overlook the need to develop the appropriate strength to control their descent into the kneeling position and simply drop to the floor at the end of the movement, using the pads as protection. However, many costumes do not accommodate for wearing knee pads, so in performance the knee can be vulnerable to injury when the requisite strength and control is lacking. Check with your teacher to be sure it is appropriate for you to wear knee pads in class.

6.   When dancing *en pointe,* I find it difficult to straighten my knees despite trying hard to do so. Why is this?

This is often related to an issue with the ankle rather than being isolated to the knee joint. In order to be stable *en pointe*, the body weight needs to be centered over the middle of the *pointe* shoe box. If a dancer is restricted in plantar flexion at the ankle, and is unable to achieve the necessary minimum of 90 degrees from the standing position, then she may bend the knees in order to exaggerate the ankle motion in an effort to center the foot over the box. This may also be an issue if the dancer is in the habit of curling the toes to achieve her *pointe*. This motion creates a tendency for knee flexion, which is then translated into the *en pointe* position. Solutions for these issues can be found in the previous chapter on the foot and ankle.

Another cause could be weakness in the knee extensor muscles that creates difficulty in straightening the knees. This is often true of beginner *pointe* dancers. For these dancers, a program to strengthen the knee extensors may be helpful in preventing the issue.

The importance of correcting bent knees while *en pointe* goes beyond aesthetic considerations. The bent knee is anatomically more unstable for placement and balance, and is therefore more prone to injury.

7. I have "swayback" knees. What causes this condition, and should I be concerned about it?

The anatomical term for *swayback* knees is *hyperextension*. The knee is said to be hyperextended when the joint extends more than 5 degrees beyond neutral

(Figure 14.4). This can be the result of laxity or looseness in the knee ligaments as well as muscular imbalances. It is often a feature of Joint Hypermobility Syndrome (see Chapter 5). Hyperextended knees can be recognized by their curved or bowed appearance when viewed from the side.

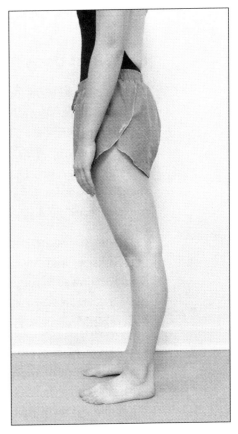

Some experts regard a slight degree of hyperextension as aesthetically advantageous for those who dance *en pointe*. Nevertheless, it would be unwise to assume that hyperextended knees present no problem. Many dancers have a hyperextension that goes beyond being "slight," and there are anatomical repercussions from this alignment that can lead to injury.

When a dancer "locks back" into the hyperextended position, the weight of the body is no longer transferred through the center of the knee joint. Instead, it is directed toward the back of the knee joint. This can further stretch the knee ligaments and affect the stability of the joint. When the dancer's weight falls toward the back of the hyperextended knee, it may then also be transferred to the

Figure 14.4 Swayback knees

heels rather than the center of the ankle and foot. This can make it more difficult to *relevé* or jump.

Because of the integrated nature of anatomical movement, it is not surprising that other problems may also occur in connection with hyperextended knees. These include weak forefeet, patellar instability, and hyperextended backs. All of these conditions can lead to further injury and limit technique.

If a dancer has a serious problem with hyperextended knees (i.e. is encountering pain or unable to find a stable neutral position for the knee), we recommend that he or she see a physician or physical therapist who specializes in dance. These experts can identify the extent of the specific problem and the related body compensations, and recommend the proper rehabilitation program. These programs may include exercises to improve proprioception as well as strength and flexibility work for muscles of the foot, ankle, lower leg, knee, hip, and spine.

8.   What does it mean to have bow legs?

The anatomical term for this alignment of the legs is *genu varum* (Figure 14.1). All babies have naturally bowed legs, but this usually resolves around the age of three. However, some people's legs do not fully resolve, leaving them with some degree of bowing. This manifests as a gap between the knees when the feet are together in parallel. Dancers in this category may find it challenging to reach the desired aesthetic for some positions, but careful attention to technique and muscle recruitment patterns can reduce the risk of injury.

Sometimes the effect of bow legs is created by a combination of hyperextended knees and inward femoral rotation. If the knees hyperextend and the *femur* is allowed to rotate inwardly, the dancer will appear to have bow legs. This can be corrected by external hip rotation control and addressing the issue of hyperextended knees discussed in Question 7 on page 119.

Bow legs can often precipitate problems in foot and ankle alignment. Early detection of these alignment problems is particularly important. Consulting a dance medicine specialist is recommended to create a program of supplemental training to address this issue. This may include work for the hip, knee, and ankle.

9.   Dancers often complain of pain in or around their knee cap. What causes this, and can I prevent it?

The *patella* is a sesamoid bone that is encased by the common tendon of the quadriceps muscle group. When neutrally aligned, the *patella* fits in a groove formed by the two condyles of the *femur*, known as the *intercondylar groove*. Sometimes the *patella* is drawn to one side and does not sit in the center of the intercondylar groove. When this happens, it can rub against the raised lip of the femoral condyle each time the knee moves. The underside of the *patella* is coated with articular cartilage that is designed to facilitate the smooth movement of this bone in its groove. If it is rubbing, this cartilage can become damaged, causing inflammation and soreness. The pain is usually felt directly behind the kneecap or along its inner border. This condition is referred to by several names: *patellofemoral syndrome, chondromalacia patellae,* and *anterior knee pain.*

The symptoms are experienced in dance movements that require flexion and extension of the knee as well as in daily activities such as stair climbing. Sitting with the knees bent for long periods also causes discomfort, particularly when then trying to extend the knees. Dancers with this condition must seek treatment and rehabilitation as prolonged symptoms can result in deterioration of the knee cap.

One cause of this condition is forcing turn-out from the knee. When the lower leg is forced into excessive lateral rotation, the *patellar tendon* will be pulled laterally, taking the *patella* with it. This situation can also lead to another cause—namely, an imbalance of the quadriceps muscle group. When these four muscles are balanced in terms of strength, they exert an even force on the *patella* allowing it to remain located in the center of the intercondylar groove. However, if one of these muscles is weak, the pull on the *patella* will not be balanced. It will be pulled off center, toward the side of the stronger muscle. Due to the propensity for dancers to work in turn-out, the strong muscle is usually the *vastus lateralis* on the outer aspect of the thigh. The weak muscle is generally the *vastus medialis* on the inner aspect, resulting in the *patella*'s being pulled to the lateral aspect of the intercondylar groove.

To help prevent this muscular imbalance, dancers can strengthen the entire quadriceps muscle group, paying particular attention to the *vastus medialis*. This muscle comes into action during the last 15 degrees of knee extension. In order to strengthen the *vastus medialis*, you should either keep the knee straight as the leg is raised and lowered, or work through the last 15 degrees of knee extension (without hyperextending the knee). The *vastus lateralis* may also need to be stretched.

It has also been recommended that dancers strengthen the adductor muscles in addition to strengthening the *vastus medialis*. When strong adductors assist in controlling the *plié*, there is less compressive force on the *patella*. Compression occurs when the knee extensors contract and pull the *patella* against the *femur*. Alleviating some of this force can lessen the possibility of harmful friction between the *patella* and the femoral condyles. Deep knee bends should therefore be avoided when recovering from this condition.

10. I want my *arabesque* as well as my parallel and turned-out back *attitudes* to be higher. What conditioning work will improve those positions?

The height of an *arabesque* or back *attitude* is determined by several factors. Some of these involve the spine and muscles of the torso, others involve muscles at the hip. Part IV will discuss spinal structure as it relates to *arabesque* and back *attitude* as well as the muscles of the torso that help achieve these positions.

At the hip socket, a high *arabesque* or back *attitude* position requires strength in the hip extensors and flexibility in the hip flexors. Turn-out in these positions can be improved by strengthening the outward rotators of the hip and stretching the inward rotators. Exercises for these muscle groups are listed below.

Sometimes dancers try to achieve a higher *arabesque* or turned-out back *attitude* by allowing the hip to raise and the pelvis to twist. This stresses the lower back and is not advisable.

11. I am always pulling my hamstring muscle. Is there a way to prevent this from happening?

A pulled hamstring muscle is generally referred to as a *hamstring strain*. Muscles that cross more than one joint, like the hamstrings, are particularly susceptible to muscle strains. These strains can result from a variety of causes. An explosive movement, such as a sudden high kick, can strain the muscle, especially if the dancer is not warmed up or has recently returned from time out. Hamstring strains can also be caused by incorrect stretching techniques, especially if performed when the body is cold.

Another technique issue that can contribute to hamstring strain occurs on the standing leg. Some dancers have a tendency to pull back on the supporting leg when performing a *grand battement* to the back or an *arabesque penchée.* This could injure the hamstrings on the supporting leg, particularly if the turn-out is also not well controlled. Muscle imbalance can also be a contributing factor. The hamstrings are paired with the quadriceps muscle group and imbalances can occur when the hamstrings are very tight or weak and the quadriceps are very strong.

Mild hamstring strains may be treated with rest and careful stretching. Dancers who sustain a more serious injury, or those with chronic problems, should consult a physician. Chronic problems can occur when areas of damaged muscle tissue are not addressed through treatment and rehabilitation. Over time, these damaged fibers can form into scar tissue that is inelastic. This will reduce the overall flexibility and power of the muscle and predispose it to further injury in the same area.

As is true with any injury, treatment and rehabilitation are only part of the process. Unless you identify the cause of your injury and correct any predisposing factors, you will continue to face chronic problems.

To help prevent strain related to muscle imbalance, you should be sure the hamstrings are both strong and flexible. If your quadriceps are tight they should be stretched.

12. My teacher is always telling me to stop "sinking" into the standing hip. I try to "get up on my leg," but I am not successful. What should I do to address this?

First you should check your foot position. Forcing turn-out at the foot and ankle can sometimes cause a dancer to "sink" or "sit" in the standing hip. If the muscles that control turn-out are weak, then when raising the gesture leg, the standing leg muscles will be unable to compensate and "sitting" can occur. It may also be an issue of strength in the hip abductor muscles. These play an important role in stabilizing the standing hip and again need to be strong to counter the weight and movement of the gesture leg. The lateral muscles of the torso also help with alignment when you stand on one leg, so these should also be considered for strength training.

13. I have a "snapping" or "popping" in my hip in certain leg movements, and sometimes this is painful. Why does this happen and what can I do?

"Snapping" or" popping" can be felt in different areas around the hip and is usually caused by a tendon passing over a bony prominence or other joint structure. The location of the snap indicates the probable cause. A snap at the side of the hip may be due to the *iliotibial band* sliding over the greater trochanter of the *femur*. The *iliotibial band* is the tendinous portion of the *gluteus maximus* muscle and it typically snaps over the greater trochanter during the landing phase of jumps, as the hip moves from flexion to extension. If the band is being pulled tight by the muscle above, it is more likely to "catch" instead of glide over the bony prominence. If there is concomitant weakness in the hip abductor muscles, this can also contribute to the problem. The hip extensors and abductors should be addressed in resolving this issue.

A snap at the front of the hip is often caused by the *iliopsoas* tendon sliding over the *iliopectineal eminence* (a mild ridge on the inner aspect of the *pubic bone*). If the *iliopsoas* is tight, then the tendon is more likely to "catch" in this area. A snap in this area can also be a result of the same tendon rubbing on the hip joint capsule or the hip *labrum*—a ring of cartilage that surrounds the rim of the hip socket (Figure 14.5). This can particularly be the case if the capsule or *labrum* are already damaged and inflamed.

The *rectus femoris* tendon can also be a cause of snapping at the front of the hip where it passes over the round head of the *femur*. This usually occurs during *hip flexion* and *extension* motions, or *inward* and *outward* motions of the femur. This will be felt slightly more laterally than snapping from the *iliopsoas*, which tends to be toward the middle or inner aspect of the groin area.

When the snapping hip is caused by muscular imbalance, stretching and strengthening specific muscle groups is recommended (these are shown below).

Hip Joint

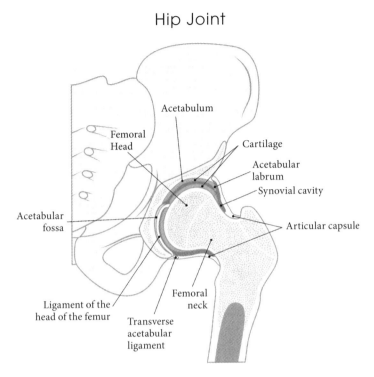

Figure 14.5 Hip labrum

Careful observation of the dancer's technique may reveal that subtle deviations in alignment are occurring simultaneously with the snap. For example, the anterior snap has sometimes been reported to be accompanied by a forward tilt of the pelvis (Clippenger-Robertson 1985). A program that combines strengthening the muscles that control pelvic tilt, along with correcting any other technique issues, may be the solution here. Appropriate exercises to help correct a forward tilt of the pelvis are discussed in Part IV.

Snapping may also occur in dancers with slightly uneven leg lengths. The snap is usually in the hip of the longer leg. While the leg lengths cannot be altered, and prescribing heel raises for the shoes is not possible for most dance shoes or for bare feet, the balance may be redressed by an appropriate stretch and strength program and technique adaptation.

If the hip snapping is causing pain, then you should consult a dance medicine specialist. Repeated snapping can cause inflammation that leads to *tendonitis*. Underlying many tendons are bursae (small, fluid-filled sacs) that can also become irritated, resulting in *bursitis*. When the symptoms are felt deep in the hip joint, this may be indicative of damage to the hip *labrum*, and this requires immediate evaluation.

Dancers should not fall into the habit of routinely "clicking" their hip joints, even if it is not painful to do so. The repeated wear and tear on the tendon may eventually lead to pain and injury. It is also a sign of a potential imbalance in the joint that needs addressing, so this should not be ignored.

14. I have heard that dancers often have hip issues and are prone to arthritis of the hip in later life. How can I prevent this?

The way we use the hip in dance takes it beyond the normal range for which it was designed, and this can make it vulnerable to injury. It is important to work with the inherent design of our anatomy when we are generating leg movements. One of the structures that can become damaged during extreme leg movements is the *labrum* (Figure 14.5). This is a ring of cartilage that lines the rim of the *acetabulum*, or hip socket, serving to deepen the socket for increased stability and to provide some shock absorption. The twisting and pivoting motions at the hip that are a feature of many dance movements can place the *labrum* under strain. The shape of both the hip socket and the head of the *femur* can vary between dancers, with some having extra bony prominences on these structures. This can increase the risk of the *labrum* becoming pinched and damaged. Hypermobile dancers who have laxity in the soft tissues that afford greater ranges of motion at the hip are also at risk. Muscle imbalances have also been implicated in the development of labral damage, particularly between the hip abductors and adductors (Weber et al. 2015).

Wear and tear of the *labrum* through repetitive motion in extreme positions can begin to cause degeneration and a *labral tear* can result. As the *labrum* functions to protect the hip socket, any damage to its structure can increase the risk of developing *osteoarthritis* later in life.

Osteoarthritis is a degenerative condition of the joint surfaces that usually manifests in later life and can result from joint overuse. Those dancers who have had previous hip injuries or surgery are at particular risk of developing this issue. Osteoarthritis of the hip occurs in older dancers more frequently than in the general population. Some experts suggest that forcing turn-out at the hip places dancers at increased risk (Laible et al. 2013). In extreme cases, osteoarthritis of the hip may require hip replacement surgery when the joint surfaces are no longer viable. It is therefore crucial for young dancers to be mindful of their placement and muscle recruitment patterns around the hip to reduce the risk of hip degeneration. See the exercises in Chapter 15 for strategies to address hip balance.

15

STRENGTH and FLEXIBILITY EXERCISES: The KNEE and HIP

THIS SECTION PROVIDES STRENGTH, flexibility, and integration exercises for the knee and hip. Where appropriate, injuries are also discussed. Each section will provide the exercise name, any equipment needed, and starting positions.

Table 15.1 Roadmap

Action	Strength Exercises	Flexibility Exercises
Individual Movements		
Knee flexion	15.A.1	15.A.2
Knee extension	15.B.1	15.B.2
Hip flexion	15.C.1	15.C.2
Hip extension	15.D.1	15.D.2
Hip abduction	15.E.1	15.E.2
Hip adduction	15.F.1	15.F.2
Hip external rotation	15.G.1	15.G.2
Hip internal rotation	15.H.1	15.H.2
Combination Movements		
Single-leg knee bend	15.I.1	15.E.2

Note: Be sure to read Part I before performing these exercises.

Step-by-step descriptions of the action of the exercise and suggestions for self checks and comments on what you might feel are offered. As there are several so-called "two-joint muscles" that act on both the knee and the hip, many of these exercises have dual roles across these highly interrelated structures.

(Pilates based exercises are denoted by an *.)

15.A. Knee flexion

15.A.1 Strength exercise

This exercise is designed to engage the hamstring muscle group. It also requires the cooperation of the quadriceps muscle group, promoting balance at the knee joint.

SINGLE-LEG KICKS* (FIGURE 15.1)

Equipment

    Exercise mat or cushioned surface to lay on.

Starting position

    a) Begin by lying on your stomach with your forearms on the mat and the spine in a slightly extended position.

    b) Legs are extended along the floor and as close together as is comfortable for the knees.

    c) Keep the abdominal muscles engaged to avoid an excessive curvature in the lower spine (Figure 15.1a).

Action

    a) Bring one foot toward the buttock at a time by bending the knee (Figure 15.1b).

    b) Pulse the heel twice as it reaches toward the buttock.

    c) Extend the back of the knee, lengthening the leg back to the floor.

    d) Repeat on the other leg.

Repetitions

    6–10 sets, 1 right and 1 left equals a set.

Quick self checks

Focus on the alignment of the lower leg, being sure it stays in line with the upper thigh. The tendency will be for the lower leg and foot to turn out. As the heel comes up, flex the foot and as the leg extends, point the foot. If you tend to have tight quadricep muscles your pelvis may lift up off the mat and your buttock may lift toward the ceiling as the knee flexes. Only flex as far as you can without these compensations. This is a balancing act between the flexibility of the quadriceps and the strength of the hamstrings. The work should be focused in the belly of the hamstring muscles on the back of the upper thigh. If your knee is "popping" or hurting, try to make adjustments, such as widening the thighs slightly or not flexing the knee as far. Dancers with extremely

15.1a Start

15.1b End

Figure 15.1 Single-leg kicks

tight quadriceps—especially on the outer side of the thigh—may feel the strain in the knee joint and should adjust to avoid this pain. By continuing to stretch the quadriceps and to build the strength in the hamstrings this pain should lessen.

15.A.2 Flexibility exercise

The benefits of a good hamstring stretch cannot be overestimated for dancers. However, many dancers fail to accurately target the hamstrings in their choice of stretches and this can lead to unnecessary injury. Be sure to follow these guidelines carefully to ensure accuracy.

HAMSTRING STRETCH (FIGURE 15.2)

Starting position

a)   Lie on your back maintaining a neutral pelvis and spine position.

b)   Bend the knee of your non-working leg and place that foot on the floor. This helps to stabilize the pelvis and maintain better alignment.

c)   Extend a straight working leg toward the ceiling. You can either use an elastic band or strap on the bottom of your foot to assist in the stretch, or hold the back of your leg with your hands.

Action

a)   Whether you are using a strap, elastic band, or your own hands, the most important component is to maintain pelvic alignment.

b)   From your comfortable starting position draw your leg toward your chest while keeping a straight knee.

c)   Once you have identified the stretch in the back of the hamstrings, hold the stretch and then slowly release before the next repetition.

Repetitions

Once the depth of the stretch is reached, hold the stretch for 30 seconds and repeat three to four times. Repeat on the other side.

Quick self checks

Remind yourself that the *gastrocnemius* muscle of the calf also crosses the back of the knee. Therefore, conducting hamstring stretches with a flexed foot will bring this muscle into play. When addressing flexibility for knee flexors, it is important to also include the calf stretches from Chapter 12. Triple-check your alignment and be aware of where you feel the stretch. Dancers tend to get carried away with their hamstring stretches and believe that the stretch only occurs when the foot is cranked past the head. Pulling your foot past your head is not a focused stretch on the hamstrings. A true hamstring stretch should be felt in the belly of the muscle and the focus is on creating distance between the back of the leg and your *ischial tuberosities* (sitting bones). As soon as you tuck your pelvis under or hike up your hip for the sake of the height of the leg, the focus on the hamstrings is lost. A true hamstring stretch can be a humbling experience even for the most flexible of dancers.

Figure 15.2 Hamstring stretch

15.B Knee extension

15.B.1 Strength exercise

This exercise focuses on the quadriceps muscle group. Strength here can provide support and protection for the knee joint. Working on the strength and flexibility of the knee extensors will help with knee tracking and control. These exercises will help with hinges, knee falls, control on landings, and plies.

KNEE EXTENSION

Equipment

Chair or bench.

Starting position

Sit on a chair and let your feet rest lightly on the floor. The knees should start at approximately 30 degrees of flexion. Both legs should be parallel and your torso should be held in neutral alignment.

Action

a) Completely straighten one knee, but do not lock or hyperextend the knee.

b) Return to the starting position.

c) Complete all repetitions on one leg and then repeat on the other side.

Variation

a) Sit on the floor with the non-working leg bent and the foot on the floor. Place a foam roller or rolled towel under the thigh of the working leg.

b) Completely straighten the working leg without locking or hyper-extending the knee.

c) An ankle weight can be added to this position once repetitions can be completed with minimal fatigue.

Repetitions

8–10 repetitions, 2 sets.

Quick self checks

Performing this exercise one leg at a time allows you to focus on the tracking of the knee and to stabilize your spinal alignment. As discussed earlier, the *vastus medialis* (the inner quadricep muscle) tends to be weaker than the outside of the thigh. Focus on engaging and seeing the muscle toward the inside of your *patella* engage. The quadricep muscles will begin to fatigue toward the end of your repetitions. If you can complete a full set with minimal fatigue, then, after working both legs, try adding a second set. Be aware to isolate the target muscle and do not allow your body to sway backward in an effort to help the leg extend. Once you have successfully completed two sets with minimal fatigue, you can add an ankle weight, starting with two pounds and not to exceed ten pounds. If you feel any strain on the knee joint, the weight is too much. Keep in mind that increasing repetitions but using less weight builds strength without bulk.

15.B.2 Flexibility exercise

Stretching the quadriceps muscle group is important for both knee and hip flexibility. It also facilitates efficiency in the hamstring muscle group.

Quadriceps stretch (Figure 15.3)

Starting position

a) Use a *barre*, wall, or the back of a chair for balance.

b) Standing with your legs parallel, flex your left knee and hold your left ankle behind your body with your left hand. Your left ankle must be in line with your left thigh, and your left knee should lightly touch or almost touch your right knee. Do not let your left hip flex.

c) Engage the abdominal muscles to prevent your back from over-arching. Bend slightly forward from the waist if you need to.

Action

    a)   Hold the stretch (Figure 15.3). Feel the stretch in the front of your thigh, between your knee and your hip.

    b)   Stretch the other side.

Repetitions

Once the depth of the stretch is reached, hold the stretch for 30 seconds and repeat three to four times. Repeat on the other side.

Quick self checks

Keep the stretch active in the belly of the muscle above the knee and toward the mid-thigh. Be careful when moving into this stretch to not stress the medial aspect of the knee joint. If you allow the knee to swing out to the side as you move into position you may feel knee strain. If you bring the foot closer to the buttock without changing your pelvic alignment you may feel an increase in the stretch. Be careful not to pull too hard on the foot as this can stress the knee joint and create pain.

Figure 15.3 Quad stretch

15.C. Hip flexion

15.C.1 Strength exercises

Strength in the hip flexors is key for achieving leg height and dynamic movement. However, finding a balance between the iliopsoas *and the other hip flexors can be challenging. The* iliopsoas *plays a vital role in stabilizing the lumbar spine during hip flexion and needs to be first in line in terms of muscle recruitment during leg extension movements. These exercises will help dancers to achieve this sequencing.*

Supine hip flexor exercise (Figure 15.4)

Equipment

Exercise mat or cushioned surface to lay on.

Starting position

a) Lie on your back on a mat with the right knee bent and right foot
    flat on the floor. This position helps to stabilize the pelvis and
    protects the lower back.

b) Extend the left leg straight along the floor keeping the leg in line
    with the hip.

Action

a) Raise the left leg to 90 degrees (Figure 15.4a).

b) Hold this position for a count of 10 and then lower back to the
    floor. A more challenging option to is lower the leg to just above
    the floor (Figure 15.4b).

Repetitions

Repeat 8–10 times on the same leg and then switch sides.

Quick self checks

Are you breathing? While you are working your *iliopsoas*, you also need to
use your out-breath to access your abdominal muscles. These will stabilize your lower spine and pelvis. When you begin to lift the leg, notice if
there is a shift in the pelvis or a hiking of the hip. This may indicate that
you have lost your torso control / core stability. One of the most common
complaints of a dancer while strengthening the *iliopsoas* is that they feel
tension in the hip. If you are feeling this exercise deep toward the inside
of the hip, then you have found the correct muscle. You may be surprised how quickly the muscle fatigues when you are maintaining your
alignment.

15.4a Start

15.4b End

Figure 15.4 Supine hip flexor exercise

ILIOPSOAS TRAINING

Starting position

a) Sit on the floor, leaning back slightly. You can either reach back and place your hands on the floor behind you or lower yourself down to rest on your elbows.

b) As with the first hip flexor exercises, extend your working leg and have your supporting leg in a bent position with the foot on the floor.

Action

a) Raise the straight leg as high as possible toward the chest without compromising the alignment of the pelvis or placement of the lower back.

b) Bend the knee at the top and draw the thigh in toward the chest a few more inches.

c) Extend the leg straight again and hold for a count of 4, then lower back to the floor.

Variation

a) When the leg is in the air and the knee is bent, pulse the thigh toward the torso 4 times, keeping the leg above 90 degrees. This can be repeated with legs parallel and turned-out.

b) The addition of an elastic band tied in a circle and placed around the thighs can add extra resistance. If you decide to use this version, both legs should remain in a bent position and the focus is solely on the activation of the *iliopsoas*, bringing the working thigh toward the chest while the other leg remains stationary.

c) As you improve in strength and coordination, maintain a neutral spine and transition to a vertical posture for the torso. Eventually work toward having the hands off the floor, holding them in a second or fifth position.

Repetitions

Repeat the hip flexion exercises 5–8 times per side.

Quick self checks

Try looking at a picture of the *iliopsoas* or find a video online to have a visual understanding of the movement of this muscle. Notice if the right and left side feels the same or different. Is the movement smooth or choppy? The more efficient the movement pattern, the smoother the action. Regardless of the variation above, you should be feeling the work deep in the hip and down toward the inside of the upper thigh. Be careful not to overdo these exercises, as when the muscle fatigues, you will quickly begin to compensate and lose your alignment. The goal is to find power in the *iliopsoas*, as this is the key to high legs and dynamic movement. Isolating the *iliopsoas* can be challenging for dancers who are used to powering through movements by recruiting everything and anything that is willing to help. Issues with snapping hip, lower-back pain, and other hip injuries are typically related to the dysfunction of the *iliopsoas*. The work of the *iliopsoas* is directly related to the abdominal muscles discussed in Part IV.

15.C.2 Flexibility exercises

Active and passive hip flexor stretch

Dancers need to strive to have strong and flexible hip flexors, but unfortunately many have tight (and therefore weak) hip flexors and this will impact the efficiency of their technique. Accurate stretching of the *iliopsoas* will not only help it to contract more efficiently but will also improve hip extension range. After completing the strengthening and stretching exercises suggested, stand up, try a *développé*, and notice whether the hips feel more open.

ACTIVE HIP FLEXOR STRETCH (FIGURE 15.5)

Starting position

a) Kneel on one knee and place the other foot in front of your body on the floor.

b) Start with the pelvis directly over the bottom knee and align the spine vertically in line with the bottom leg and pelvis.

c) Hands can go on your front knee, hold on to a wall, or be placed out to the side for balance.

Action

a) Slightly tuck the pelvis under and then shift your weight forward toward the front foot. If you have tight hip flexors you may immediately feel this deep in the hip and toward the inside of the inner thigh of the back leg. Once you feel the stretch, stop and hold. Remember to breathe and focus on creating space at the front of the hip.

b) Back out of the stretch and then repeat.

Variation

a) If you need more of a stretch, you can drop further into the back
    hip. However, make sure you are maintaining a slight tuck of
    the pelvis. As soon as your hips tip forward and your lower back
    arches you will lose the stretch of your *iliopsoas.*

b) You can add a long side stretch to deepen the stretch. Curve the
    torso toward the side of whichever leg is in front. Take the arm
    overhead and reach to the side, increasing the stretch at the hip
    and adding to the stretch to the waist.

Repetitions

Once the depth of the stretch is reached, hold the stretch for 30 seconds
and repeat three to four times. Repeat on the other side.

Quick self checks

Have you maintained the slight tuck of the pelvis? Did you make sure that
you were properly aligned at the beginning of the stretch and then moved
for greater range? Dancers will commonly drop into a lunge stretch with
very little awareness as to what they are actually stretching. The *iliopsoas*
stretch may feel different from those for other muscles in your body. You
may sense a tightening across
the front of your hip, which
is a different sensation than a
typical stretch. Dancers frequently report having "tight
hips" even though they stretch
in lunges and splits every day.
This is usually due to the body's
tendency to compensate in the
stretch and a lack of understanding of where the work truly
needs to originate.

*Figure 15.5 Active hip flexor
stretch*

PASSIVE HIP FLEXOR STRETCH (FIGURE 15.6)

Equipment

A table, bench, or a firm bed that is high enough to allow the leg being stretched to hang off the end without hitting the floor.

Starting position

a) Lie on your back with knees up to your chest on a table, bench, or firm bed. Your hips should be at the edge of the supporting surface.

b) Clasp your hands around one thigh and extend the other leg toward the floor. Keep the knee of the extended leg straight. If your lower back begins to arch and lose contact with the supporting surface, pull the thigh of your bent leg a little closer to your chest.

c) If you do not have enough space to extend your leg beyond the end of the supporting surface, you can position yourself in the middle of the table, bench, or bed and let your leg hang off the side. (Ensure the surface is stable before attempting this.)

Action

a) Breathe and hold the stretch (Figure 15.6). Feel the stretch across the front of your hip socket.

b) Stretch the other side.

Variation

Once in the stretch position, allow the knee of the extended leg to bend. If your foot touches the floor, you need to work on a higher surface. You will now feel the stretch across the hip and into the front of the thigh.

Repetitions

Hold for 30 seconds and then repeat on the other side.

Quick self checks

The straight leg version stretches the *iliopsoas* muscle whereas the bent knee version will stretch the *rectus femoris* muscle. As the knee bends, pay attention to the tendency for that bent leg to drift away from the midline and to lose its alignment to the hip. If you feel a strain on the outside of the knee, adjust the position or try placing a support under the foot to lessen the stretch and take the pressure off the knee joint.

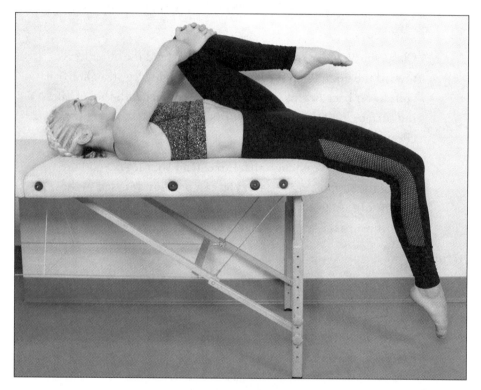

Figure 15.6 Passive hip flexor stretch

15.D. Hip extension

15.D.1 Strength exercises

Strengthening the hip extensors helps to stabilize the pelvic alignment. These muscles help with arabesques, *leaps, and jumps.*

Prone leg lifts (Figure 15.7)

Starting position

a) Start lying on your stomach resting your forehead on the back of your hands.

b) Legs are straight, in a parallel position aligned with the pelvis.

c) Point the feet gently without engaging the *gastrocnemius* or *soleus* muscles.

d) Engage your abdominal muscles to support the spine and lengthen the lower back.

Action

a) Engage the hamstrings and elongate one leg off the floor a few inches.

b) Hold the leg off the floor for a count of 4 and then lower back down to starting position.

c) Complete a full set on one side before you switch to the other side.

Variation

Complete the same exercise as stated above in turn-out.

Repetitions

Complete 8–10 repetitions per set. Based on level of fatigue and muscular control, complete 2–3 sets. If working both in parallel and in turned-out positions, complete one full set of each.

Quick self checks

This exercise is related to a standing back *tendu*. It is important that the hip extensor muscles are engaged to lengthen the leg to the back. If these muscles are weak, and/or you have tight hip flexors, the tendency will be to either rock the hips or overextend the lower back in order to lift the leg. Engage the abdominal muscles for stability of the pelvis and move slowly in order to truly activate the hip extensor muscles. If you find that you are compensating by rocking the hips or extending the lower back, then lower

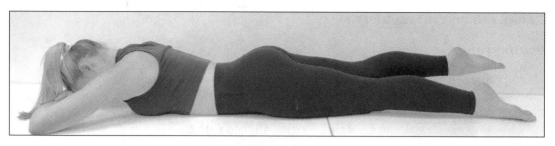

Figure 15.7 Prone leg lifts

the height of the leg until you can efficiently move through this exercise. Work with your breath to help keep the movement flowing. The work should be felt in the back of the upper thigh and buttock. Focus on elongating the muscles at the front of the hip as if the exercise was a stretch for the hip flexors. If you are feeling this in the lower back, then reduce the height of the leg to the back.

KNEELING HAMSTRING AND GLUTEAL MUSCLE WORK (FIGURE 15.8)

Equipment

Exercise mat.

Starting position

a) Begin on hands and knees on the mat.

b) Align your hands under your shoulders and the knees directly under your hips.

c) Straighten and extend your left leg along the floor behind you (Figure 15.8a).

d) Raise your left leg off the floor until the leg is extended and in line with the pelvis.

e) While maintaining a neutral spine and pelvis flex the left knee 90 degrees.

Action

a) Lift the working leg in parallel back *attitude* a few inches. Maintain a feeling of lengthening the leg as you lift. Keep both hip bones parallel to the floor.

b) Return to the starting position with both knees on the mat.

Variation

a) From the starting position c), keep the working leg in an extended parallel *arabesque* position. Lower the foot to the floor and then raise up, achieving as much hip extension as possible without movement in the lower back or pelvis (Figure 15.8b).

b) The extended *arabesque* position can also be completed with an outwardly rotated leg. Especially in the turn-out position, be sure to keep your hips squared to the floor.

Repetitions

8–10 repetitions, repeat on the other side. As long as the quality of the movement is maintained, up to 3 sets is recommended.

Quick self checks

This exercise develops strength and coordination for parallel back *attitude* work. While working through these exercises, pay close attention to the stability of your pelvis and engagement of the abdominal muscles. As the hamstrings are engaging, you want to focus on lengthening across the front of the hip in order to achieve the range of motion purely in the hip joint. High legs here will only stress the back and not work the hamstrings. As with earlier hip extension and knee flexion work, you will feel this in the back of your thigh and lower buttock. Once you have completed the exercises, stand up and work through *tendu* back and see if you can engage the same muscles to make this movement occur.

The anatomy of the hip limits the range of hip extension and this can vary greatly between individual dancers. If the hip extensor muscles are not working efficiently, the tendency is to tip the hips forward into an anterior pelvic tilt or to increase the arch in the lower back. This can lead to compromised movement patterns and injury. Ballet, modern, and jazz

15.8a Start

15.8b End

Figure 15.8 Kneeling variation

dancers should perform this exercise in both the parallel and turned-out leg positions. Working this way will help keep a balance of strength in the muscles that make up the knee flexor / hip extensor group. Remember that achieving muscular balance will help to maintain your range of motion and can help prevent injury.

15.D.2 Flexibility exercises

Dancers need strength in the hip extensors for arabesques, leaps, jumps, and *dynamic balance. If the muscles are tight, they will lose power.*

Sitting hamstring stretch

Starting position

a) Start sitting on the floor with both legs extended in front of you.

b) While keeping the hips square, bend the right knee, bringing the foot to the inside of your left leg, and outwardly rotate the right hip.

Action

a) Slowly walk your hands forward on either side of your stretched leg.

b) Keep your spine straight as you fold over the leg.

c) Once you reach the depth of the stretch, without compromising the alignment of the spine, hold the stretch.

Repetitions

Once the depth of the stretch is reached hold for 30 seconds and repeat three to four times. Repeat on the other side.

Quick self checks

This stretch is not about reaching your nose to your knee. Focus on rotating your pelvis forward away from your hamstrings, creating space in the back of the hips. If you over-curve your spine, the pelvis will not shift and the goal of the stretch will be missed completely. This is a time to remove your ego from the exercise and focus on finding a pure stretch. If you flex your foot, the stretch may be felt more intensely, as this will now include the knee flexors (which also point the foot). If you find that by flexing the foot your back starts to round, relax your foot until you can reclaim the optimal spinal alignment.

15.E Hip abduction

15.E.1 Strength exercises

Strengthening the hip abductor muscles is important for knee tracking and control. By controlling the alignment of the femur *from the hip, the common tendency for the knee to drop inside the line of the foot in* plié *can be addressed.*

PARALLEL LEG RAISE* (FIGURE 15.9)

Equipment

Elastic band, mat or cushioned surface to lay on.

Starting position

a) Lie on your right side on the floor or mat, with your underneath arm stretched or bent under your head. Rest your head on your arm being sure to keep the spine in neutral. Place your left hand in front of the body to stabilize. Keep the abdominal muscles actively engaged to support the spinal alignment.

b) Keep your legs straight, in a parallel position. Flex your feet and glance down to make sure you can just see your toes.

c) Align your shoulders, ribs, and hips on top of each other, avoiding any twisting or rolling of the body forward or backward.

d) Check that your hip bones are stacked directly on top of each other.

Action

a) While maintaining a parallel position lift the top leg (left) toward the ceiling. This will create creases in the side of your hip.

b) Only lift the leg as high as it will go without shifting the entire pelvis or losing the alignment of the waist.

c) Lower the leg back down to the starting position.

Variations (read entire exercise before trying variations)

If you are ready to move on you can add an elastic band tied in a circle and looped around the upper thighs. As you lift the leg the resistance will increase.

Repetitions

10 leg lifts on one side; roll over and repeat on the other side.

Quick self checks

If you have the ability to watch in a mirror, start small to ensure that the movements are isolated to the hip abductors. Also, check that you are breathing with each repetition. The work should be focused directly into the hip abductors. The muscle burn will be felt on the outside of the hip. If you are feeling your quadriceps you are probably leaning back and recruiting the wrong muscles. If you begin to feel a strain in your back you may be leaning too far forward or allowing the pelvis to move as you lift the leg, thus recruiting and compressing the lower back.

Figure 15.9 Parallel leg raise

15.E.2 Flexibility exercises

If the hip abductor muscles are overly tight, then they become weak. They are then not available to control the placement of the femur and this can affect tracking and control at the knee joint.

HIP ABDUCTOR STRETCH—SUPINE (FIGURE 15.10)

Starting position

a)   Lie on your back on a mat or the floor, facing the ceiling.

b)   Legs are straight. Arms open to the side at shoulder height in contact with the floor.

c)   Bend the left knee so the foot is flat on the floor.

Action

a)   Let the left knee fall across the body to the right, allowing the pelvis to roll so that the knee touches the floor.

b)   Stabilize the upper body in a neutral position between the arms so both shoulders are in contact with the floor.

c)   Extend the left knee so that the leg is straight with the hip flexed at 90 degrees.

Repetitions

Hold for 30 seconds. Repeat to the other side.

Quick self checks

Be sure that the underneath leg points straight down in line with the body. Do not allow the spine to arch. Some dancers may feel a stretch in the upper chest area in front of the opposing shoulder. If so, they should use the *pectoralis major* stretch in the shoulder section (Part V). The stretch should be felt in the lateral aspect of the upper hip. Not all dancers will feel the stretch in this position.

Figure 15.10 Hip abductor stretch

Tensor fasciae latae and *gluteus medius* stretch (Figure 15.11)

Equipment

Stable table surface or treatment bench.

Starting position

a)   Lie diagonally across the table surface on your left side with your hips close to the table edge.

b)   Bend the knees and hips to approximately 90 degrees.

c)   Make sure the hips are stacked one on top of the other and that the spine is in neutral.

d)   Place your right hand in front of the body on the table to stabilize. Rest your head on your folded left arm.

Action

a)   Straighten the top leg and take it slightly behind the body so that it clears the edge of the table.

b)   Lower the extended leg down toward the floor, keeping the knee straight.

Repetitions

Hold for 30 seconds. Recover and repeat on the other side.

Quick self checks

Make sure that the spine remains neutral and the hips remain stacked throughout the exercise. The tendency is to allow the top hip to roll outward, but this will negate the stretch. Make sure you position yourself so that the inner thigh of the top leg does not contact the table edge as this

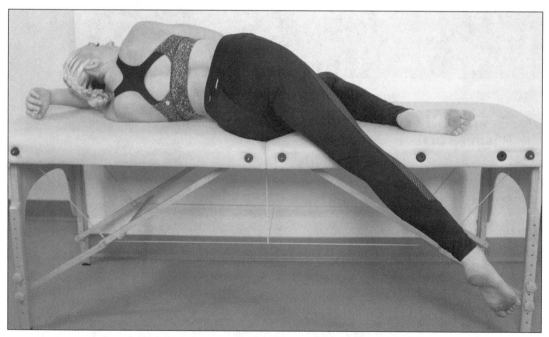

Figure 15.11 TFL and gluteus medius stretch

will limit the adduction movement. It is essential that you choose a very stable surface for this exercise. With the weight toward the edge of the table, it can be prone to tipping.

15.F Hip adduction

15.F.1 Strength exercises

Hip adductor strength is important for standing leg control and also plays a role in turn-out control. This muscle group dominates during the closing phases of leg extensions.

Side lying with chair (Figure 15.12)

Equipment

Mat and chair.

Starting position

a) Lie on your side, head on outstretched arm or arm supporting head, and hips stacked.

b) Place one foot on the seat of the chair and the other foot on the floor under the chair.

Figure 15.12 Side lying with chair

Action

a) Raise the bottom leg up to touch the bottom of the chair and then lower back down to the floor.

b) Avoid pushing the top leg into the chair as the work should be isolated in the bottom leg.

SUPINE WITH A WALL

Starting position

a) Lie on your back with your buttock up against a wall. If a wall is not available you can still complete this exercise, just be aware of keeping your feet pointing directly toward the ceiling.

b) Keep a neutral pelvis and spine position.

c) Outwardly rotate both legs starting with the inner thighs, knees, and heels touching.

Action

a) Outwardly rotate the thighs without tucking the pelvis under and slowly open the legs out to the side like a fan. Do not drop the legs out to the straddle position as this could injure the muscles.

b) Once you have reached your end range externally rotate the thighs a little more and draw the legs back together. Think of trying to wrap the outer thigh around the leg to touch the wall.

SUPINE KNEES BENT WITH A BALL

Equipment

Mat and a small playground ball, cushion, or Magic Circle.

Starting position

a) Lie on your back with your knees bent and feet flat on the floor.

b) Keep a neutral pelvis and spine position.

c) Place a playground ball, cushion, or Magic Circle between your knees.

Action

    a)   In a parallel position with knees bent, squeeze the ball and hold for a count of 3.

    b)   Slowly release the tension but do not drop the ball and then squeeze again.

Repetitions

    For all three adductor exercises complete 8–10 repetitions, rest and repeat. 1–3 sets.

Quick self checks

    For all adductor exercises move at a steady and controlled pace in both the shortening and lengthening contractions of the muscles. In all the adductor exercises be aware of isolating the adductor muscles and keeping the pelvis and spine neutral. It is common for dancers to tuck and recruit other muscles in an attempt to work their adductors. Control the movement in both directions without using momentum. The goal is to develop strength in these under-trained muscles. After completing the adductor exercises, stand and focus on the closing phase of a *tendu* or *dégagé*. Feel the adductors drawing the legs back together and notice if you can more easily maintain your turn-out. The adductors can create the sense of a "third leg" providing stability and balance when you shift onto one leg.

15.F.2 Flexibility exercise

Stretching the adductor muscles can help with hip flexibility for extensions. Releasing excess tension in these muscles will also facilitate their ability to fire for standing leg control.

Stretch the adductors

Equipment

    Exercise mat or cushioned surface to lay on.

Starting position

    a)   Lie on your back on a mat and draw your knees in toward your chest and then extend legs toward the ceiling.

    b)   Turn out your legs. Slowly and carefully open your legs.

    c)   To make this stretch more passive lie with your buttock up against a wall so your feet can rest against the wall in the straddle position.

Action

Hold the stretch for 30 seconds (Figure 15.13). Feel the stretch along your inner thighs, between your knee and hip.

Repetitions

3 to 5 repetitions of the 30 second stretch.

Figure 15.13 Adductor stretch

15.G External rotation with abduction

15.G.1 Strength exercises

The following exercises for strength and flexibility are designed to develop the necessary control of outward hip rotation in various positions including plié, *leg extensions,* arabesque, *and* passé. *These exercises will help to develop the hip abductors and external rotators, which will support your control of turn-out. In addition, strengthening the outside of the hip will help with alignment of the upper leg and the tracking of the knee. The improved control will also help to prevent the tendency to sink into your standing hip.*

Clam shell (Figure 15.14)

Equipment

    Elastic band, mat or cushioned surface to lay on.

Starting position

    a)   Lie on your right side, stretch your right arm on the mat above the head. Rest your head on your arm. Place your left hand in front of the body to stabilize. Keep your abdominal muscles actively engaged to support the spinal alignment.

    b)   With one leg on top of the other, bend at your hips to 45 degrees and the knees at 90 degrees. Your feet will be aligned with your bottom.

    c)   Align your shoulders, ribs, and hips on top of each other, avoiding any twisting or rolling of the body forward or backward.

    d)   Check that your hip bones are stacked directly on top of each other.

Action

    a)   Exhale and stabilize your abdominal muscles as you rotate your upper thigh, allowing your knee to trace an arc toward the ceiling. As the thigh rotates, ensure that the feet are still touching.

    b)   Slowly lower the leg back down to the starting position.

Variation

An elastic band tied in a loop around the upper thigh can be used to increase the resistance. Only attempt this if you have already mastered the alignment and muscle recruitment patterns.

Repetitions

5–10 repetitions on each leg.

Quick self checks

As the top leg is opening, think of the rotation of the greater trochanter down toward your *ischial tuberosity*. A good image to help to find the rotation motion is to envision a candy cane stripe in a spiraling motion around the thigh. As with the previous exercise, keep the hips stacked and focus on isolating the movement as much as possible. Do not focus on how far the leg opens, but instead focus on the precision of the move-ment. Take your time and regulate your breathing. If you are engaging

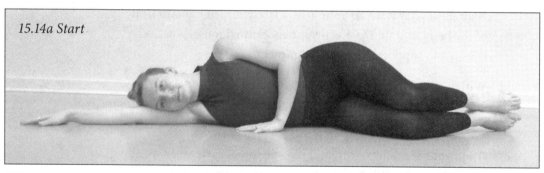

15.14a Start

15.14b End

Figure 15.14 Clam shell

the correct muscles you will feel the area on the side and back of your hip just below the crease of the buttock. If you are not feeling the work in the hip but are feeling a stress in the lower back, then you are likely to be compensating with other muscles. You may be creating the movement either by moving the spine or by shifting the top hip backward as you are opening the leg.

Side leg lifts in turn-out (Figure 15.15)

Equipment

Mat or cushioned surface to lay on.

Starting position

a) Lie on your right side, stretch your right arm on the mat above the head. Rest your head on your arm. Place your left hand in front of the body to stabilize. Keep the abdominal muscles actively engaged to support the spinal alignment.

b) Legs are straight. Keep your bottom leg in a parallel position. Take your top leg into turn-out.

c) Flex your feet and glance down to make sure you can just see your toes.

d) Align your shoulders, ribs, and hips on top of each other, avoiding any twisting or rolling of the body forward or backward.

e) Check that your hip bones are stacked directly on top of each other.

Action

a) While maintaining a stable bottom leg continue to rotate the top leg into outward rotation while lifting toward the ceiling. This will create creases in the side of your hip.

b) Only lift the leg as high as it will go without shifting the entire pelvis or losing the alignment of the waist.

c) The leg will move slightly to the front of the torso.

d) Lower the leg back down to the starting position.

Repetitions

10 leg lifts on one side; roll over and repeat on the other side.

Quick self checks

Less is more! It is common for dancers to compensate with additional muscle recruitment or to compromise the alignment in an effort to kick the leg up higher than required. The key to all the outward rotator exercises is to focus on these small muscles and not recruit the larger, less efficient muscles. If you have the ability to watch in a mirror, start small to ensure that the movements are isolated to the hip abductors. Also, check that you are breathing with each repetition. The work should be focused directly into the deep rotators. The muscle burn will be felt on the outside of the hip under the gluteal crease. If you are feeling your quadriceps, you are probably leaning back and recruiting the wrong muscles. If you begin to feel a strain in your back, you may be leaning too far forward or allowing the pelvis to move as you lift the leg, thus recruiting and compressing the lower back. The deep six external rotators are small muscles and don't need high resistance to be worked.

Figure 15.15 Side leg lifts in turn-out

15.G.2 Flexibility exercises

The following flexibility exercises target the adductors, abductors, and external rotator muscles in various orientations. This highlights the interrelatedness of these muscle groups in movement.

Supine frog stretch

Starting position

Lie on your back with your knees bent and feet together.

Action

a) While maintaining your spinal alignment and neutral pelvis, take several deep breaths and allow gravity to help to open the legs to the frog position.

b) By placing your hands on your upper thighs you can increase the stretch.

Variation

a) Start in a sitting position with the soles of the feet together.

b) While holding the ankles use the forearms to gently push the legs toward the floor.

c) As you push the legs toward the floor, hinge forward from the hips feeling your pelvis rolling forward in between the thighs.

Repetitions

Once depth of stretch is reached, hold the stretch for 30 seconds and repeat three to four times.

Quick self checks

This is a gentle stretch and will not be as valuable if you are a hypermobile dancer. It is important that you maintain the alignment of the spine. Dancers desiring a quick fix will tend to arch their lower backs and tip the pelvis forward in order to get the knees closer to the ground. While this may make it appear that you have a greater range of motion, it will completely negate any benefit from the stretch. The stretch is felt through the upper thigh. If you are feeling any pain in the knee, change the position of the feet by moving them farther from or closer to your bottom. If this does not alleviate the pain then stop this stretch.

Dancers will commonly lie on their stomach in the frog position. This is not recommended unless the alignment is being supervised.

Lying on your stomach often leads to a tendency to arch the back with the bottom in the air, but this is not the correct position. You will be compromising your alignment and potentially hurting your knees or lower back.

CROSS-LEGGED STRETCH (FIGURE 15.16)

Starting position

a) Begin sitting on the floor with your knees bent and your right leg crossed over the left.

b) Bring the right leg over the left until the sole of your right foot is on the floor beside your left thigh; your right hip will be off the floor.

c) Wrap your left arm around your right knee and thigh and pull your right thigh toward your chest.

d) Twist your upper body to face the right side while maintaining the relationship of your thigh to your chest.

e) Pull your right hip back and down until it touches the floor. There should be some space between your right hip and your left heel.

Action

a) Hold the stretch (Figure 15.16). Feel the stretch across the lower portion of the buttock and deep inside the hip.

b) Cross your other leg on top and stretch the other side.

Repetitions

Once you have found a deep sense of stretching in the outward rotators and have relaxed into the stretch, hold for 30 seconds, release, and repeat three to four times.

Quick self checks

Breathe and focus on relaxing the buttock to deepen the stretch. Ensure that both sitting bones are on the floor. If you are feeling a pinching in your hips, adjust the placement of the legs to see if you can create some space and stop the pinching. Once you have found a good stretch, adjust your position slightly and see if you can find an area that is a little tighter. Stay in this new position until the muscles begin to relax. For dancers who are tight in their outward rotators, the stretch will be felt immediately. If the position is a struggle, adjust until you can be as relaxed as possible. If you are fighting to hold a position then the muscles will not stretch. If you are hypermobile you may not feel this stretch. Try the following stretch, which adds the torso.

Figure 15.16 Cross-legged stretch

CROSS LEGGED STRETCH WITH TORSO (FIGURE 15.17)

Starting position

a)   Begin sitting cross-legged on the floor.

b)   If there is no discomfort in the knees continue to cross the top leg farther over the bottom until the foot of the top leg reaches the floor.

c)   Bend forward at your hip joints, being sure to extend the spine as much as possible.

d)   Adjust the space between your ankles and body to the position that provides the best stretch. Some dancers find a better stretch if they place their hands on the floor in front of them. Others prefer to place their hands beside their hips.

Action

a)   Hold the stretch (Figure 15.17). Feel the stretch across the top and lateral aspect of your buttock and thigh.

b)   Cross the other ankle in front and stretch the other side.

Figure 15.17 Cross-legged stretch with torso

Repetitions

Once you have found a deep sense of stretching in the outward rotators and have relaxed into the stretch, hold for 30 seconds, release, and repeat three to four times.

Quick self checks

Check for extra tension or holding patterns in other areas of the body. It is also important to notice if both sides stretch equally or if one side has more mobility than the other. Noticing these small differences can lead to additional discoveries about the balance of your musculature. The stretch should be felt across the top and lateral side of your buttock and thigh and should deepen as you relax into the muscles. Imagine the muscles melting like hot fudge. After you have stretched both sides, stand up and move around to notice the greater freedom obtained in the hip joint.

15.H Internal rotation with abduction

15.H.1 Strength exercise

While many dancers tend to focus all their efforts on improving turn-out at the hips, they fail to recognize the importance of internal rotation. For any joint to work efficiently, it needs to be balanced. Neglecting to exercise the hip in the internal range of motion can lead to imbalances that may predispose you to injury.

SIDE LEG LIFTS WITH INTERNAL ROTATION* (FIGURE 15.18)

Starting position

a) Begin lying on your side with head resting on the bottom arm. Place your top hand in front of the body to stabilize.

b) Bend the bottom leg 90 degrees at the hip and 90 degrees at the knee to create a stable foundation.

c) Engage abdominals to help keep the waist even and the hips stacked throughout the exercise.

d) Extend the top leg straight in alignment with the pelvis and spine.

e) Internally rotate the leg in the hip socket as much as possible without rolling the pelvis forward.

f) Allow the foot to hang in a sickled position letting the toes to point toward the floor.

Action

a) Keeping the inward rotation of the entire leg, raise the leg a few inches. You will be limited in the inwardly rotated position as to how high the leg can move due to bony restrictions.

b) Lengthen the leg back down to the starting position and repeat.

Repetitions

8–10 repetitions and then continue on the other side.

Figure 15.18 Side leg lifts with internal rotation

Quick self checks

For dancers who work in outward rotation most of the time, inwardly rotating the leg in the hip socket without rolling the whole body forward can be a challenge. Take a moment to feel the isolated movement of the hip joint. When in the optimal position, the quadriceps should feel as if they are falling toward the floor and relaxed. Attempt to truly isolate these muscles and avoid using momentum to throw the leg up quickly and then to drop it back down. A slow, even, and steady speed will allow you to monitor the correct activation of the muscle groups. This exercise should elicit a residual burning feeling deep in the hip muscles. Try standing up and balance on one foot. As you balance on one foot feel the deep muscles working to keep you on your leg. Try the balance in parallel and turned-out positions. You may also feel the effect of strengthening these muscles as you work on a single-leg squat, as this will also help with knee tracking.

15.H.2 Flexibility exercises

Stretch the hip abductors. See 15.G.2—Cross-legged stretch (Figure 15.16).

15.I Functional knee stability

While isolated muscle exercises in non-weight-bearing positions have their place in developing strength, muscles also need to learn how to contextualize this strength into weight-bearing movements. They also need to learn how to coordinate and collaborate with other muscles to produce dynamic movement. This exercise works many muscle groups together in a coordinated way to facilitate knee-tracking control.

15.1.1 Single-leg knee bend

Equipment

Full-length mirror.

Starting position

a) Stand on the right leg in parallel and opposite a full-length mirror.

b) Have a wall, *barre*, or chair to your right side in case you need to calibrate your balance at any point.

Action

a) Perform a slow, controlled *demi-plié*.

b) Use the mirror to check that the knee tracks directly over the foot.

c) Recover slowly to a straight leg.

Variation

Only add this variation when you can complete 10 repetitions with control. Wrap an elastic band around the outside of the right thigh. Hold the two ends in your left hand. As you *plié*, apply a pulling action via the band to the right thigh, drawing it toward the midline. This will make the hip abductor muscles on the right work harder against the resistance (Figure 15.19).

Repetitions

Repeat 5–10 times, depending on stability. Repeat on the other leg.

Quick self checks

Weakness in the hip adductors will cause the knee to fall inside the foot. Moderate weakness may cause the knee to take a wandering path to its final position. The aim is for the knee to make a smooth, controlled

descent over the foot. The number of repetitions should be dictated by the level of control. Once the placement has been lost, cease the repetitions. As strength and control improves, add more repetitions, and eventually work up to using the resistance band.

15.1.2 Flexibility exercises

You can use any of the stretch options in section 15.E.2 on page 150.

Figure 15.19 Single-leg knee bend with band

Part IV
The TRUNK and NECK

The trunk is formed by the pelvis, lumbar (lower) spine, thoracic (mid) spine, and rib cage. The neck is formed by the seven bones of the cervical spine. Neck muscles are responsible for moving the head. Trunk muscles move the torso and are either directly or indirectly involved in all dance movement. No matter which movement you execute, the trunk muscles will either produce the movement, or act to control, stabilize, or support it. A strong trunk is a strong "center." When the spine and pelvis are correctly aligned, the muscles of the upper and lower extremities have a stable foundation from which to operate.

While it may be easy to see that you have weak ankles, knees, or arms, it is not so easy to determine weakness in the trunk. There are some weaknesses that are visible and obvious, such as an exaggerated lumbar curve or a depressed chest. Many times, however, a weak trunk will show up as an inability to execute a turn, a fall, a jump, or a leap. For this reason we recommend that every dancer incorporate conditioning exercises for the trunk into their workouts.

The head also plays an important role in dance movement. Correct head alignment contributes to the successful execution of many dance movements, and head position is often used choreographically to convey subtle expression. Unfortunately, the neck muscles that control movement of the head are often ignored in many warm-up sequences. Weak neck muscles are vulnerable to injury and unable to accurately control head alignment. The exercises in Chapter 18 will help to strengthen and stretch the muscles of the neck. Greater range of motion in this area can contribute to many aspects of dance performance.

16
STRUCTURAL ANATOMY

THE MAIN SKELETAL STRUCTURE in the trunk and neck is the spine. The spinal column is made up of 24 vertebrae that are held together by a complex system of ligaments. These vertebrae can be classified into five categories: (1) *cervical*; (2) *thoracic*; (3) *lumbar*; (4) *sacral*; and (5) *coccyx* (Figure 16.1). The cervical vertebrae form the neck, while the other vertebrae form the trunk. The ribs articulate with the thoracic vertebrae, and the pelvis articulates with the *sacrum*.

The vertebrae in each category differ in shape and size. The smallest vertebrae are in the cervical region, and the larger vertebrae are in the lumbar region. The thoracic vertebrae are unique in the fact that they are attached to the ribs. Vertebrae in the sacral region differ greatly from those in the cervical, thoracic, and lumbar categories: the five sacral vertebrae are "fused" together to form the *sacrum*.

Spinal movement results from all the various parts working in flawless harmony. The spine can flex forward, extend backward, side bend to the right and left, and rotate. The unique structural designs of the cervical, thoracic, and lumbar sections of the spine provide specific movement possibilities, and it is important for dancers to be aware of these. The cervical spine has the greatest range of motion in many planes (forward and backward bending, side-bending and rotation). The thoracic spine is more limited in range (especially in extension) due to the relationship to the rib cage. The lumbar spine has more movement in forward and backward bending than the thoracic region, but is limited in rotation. It is not as flexible as the cervical spine, sacrificing movement for its role in stabilization.

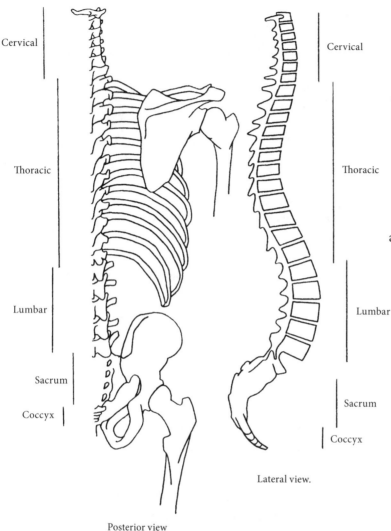

Cervical

Thoracic

Lumbar

Sacrum

Coccyx

Cervical

Thoracic

Lumbar

Sacrum

Coccyx

Lateral view.

Posterior view

Cartilage cushions called *intervertebral discs* separate the vertebrae in the cervical, thoracic, and lumbar areas of the spine. These cushions are made up of a tough, fibrous outer ring surrounding a gel-like center. The intervertebral discs function as shock absorbers for the spine as well as facilitating movement.

The pelvis serves as a link between the spine and legs. It makes up part of the hip joint and forms part of the trunk. The specific bones of the pelvis are discussed in Chapter 13.

Figure 16.1 Posterior and lateral views of the spine

Movements of the trunk and neck

Although the spine and pelvis are both part of the trunk, they can move independently of each other, and their movements are described differently. The spine is capable of *flexion* (bending of the spine forward), *extension* (return of the spine from the flexed position), *hyperextension* (backward bend of the spine beyond 180 degrees), *lateral flexion* (bending the spine to the side), and *rotation* (twisting of the spine).

The pelvis can tilt forward *(ilium* moves forward, *pubis* moves backward). Anatomically this is referred to as an *anterior pelvic tilt*, but in dance it is commonly referred to as "sticking the tail out." The pelvis can also tilt backward *(ilium* moves backward, *pubis* moves forward). Anatomically this is referred to as a *posterior pelvic tilt*, but many dancers refer to this action as "tucking under." Finally, the pelvis can tilt laterally *(ilium* drops down on one side of the body and raises on the other side of the body). Anatomically this is referred to as *lateral pelvic tilt*, and in dance could manifest as "sitting" into one hip, or "hiking" one hip in extensions.

Movements of the spine and pelvis often occur in combination. For example, an anterior pelvic tilt is usually accompanied by hyperextension of the lumbar spine. This combined movement is commonly referred to as "hyperextending" or "over-arching" the back. Posterior and lateral pelvic tilts may also be accompanied by spinal action. A posterior pelvic tilt may be associated with flexion or just a flattening of the spine, while a lateral tilt of the pelvis may involve lateral flexion of the spine.

The neck, or cervical spine, is the most mobile part of the spinal column. It can flex, extend, hyperextend, laterally flex (side bend), and rotate.

Movement of the spine is controlled by muscles of the trunk and neck, while movement of the pelvis is controlled by trunk and hip muscles. The hip muscles are primarily responsible for tilting the pelvis anteriorly. The trunk muscles are primarily responsible for tilting the pelvis posteriorly. The muscles of both the hip and trunk are responsible for tilting the pelvis laterally.

The muscles that move the trunk and neck are generally *bilateral* (located on both sides of the body). When these bilateral pairs contract simultaneously, they produce either flexion, extension, or posterior pelvic tilt, depending upon the muscles involved. If the muscles on only one side of the trunk or neck contract, then lateral flexion is produced. Simultaneous contraction of various combinations of muscles on the right and left sides of the trunk will produce rotation.

Table 16.1 Muscle actions of the pelvis and spine

Movements of the Pelvis and Spine	Dancer Terminology	Muscles
Anterior pelvic tilt and extension of the spine	Sticking the tail out	Iliopsoas Pectineus Erector Spinae
Posterior pelvic tilt and flexion of the spine	Tucking under	Rectus Abdominis External Obliques Internal Obliques
Extension and hyperextension of the spine	Arching the back	Lumbar Erector Spinae Thoracic Erector Spinae Semispinalis Thoracis Semispinalis Cervicis
Lateral flexion of the spine and lateral pelvic tilt	Side-bending and hip hiking	Quadratus Lumborum Erector Spinae Semispinalis Thoracis External Obliques Internal Obliques Rectus Abdominis
Rotation of the trunk	Side twisting	Lumbar Erector Spinae Thoracic Erector Spinae External Obliques Internal Obliques Semispinalis Rotators (deep spinal muscle) Multifidus (deep spinal muscle)

Anterior pelvic tilt and extension of the spine

The primary muscles that tilt the pelvis forward are the *iliopsoas* and *pectineus.* These muscles also flex the hip. They are described in Chapter 13 with the other hip muscles. The *erector spinae* muscles in the lumbar spine may also contribute to the tilt. These are described later.

> ## Find It
> Place your hands on the lower back with the fingers on either side of the spine.
>
> ## Feel It
> Tilt your pelvis so that your "tail" sticks out.
>> Notice the muscles popping up under your fingers. These are the *lumbar erector spinae*.
>
> ## Dance It
> The downward phase of a full-body ripple.

Posterior pelvic tilt and extension of the spine

There are four layers of abdominal muscles, three of which serve to flex the spine and posteriorly tilt the pelvis. These three muscles are the *rectus abdominis*, the *internal obliques*, and the *external obliques*. The *transverse abdominis* (TA) is the fourth abdominal muscle that makes up the central core of the body. This is the deepest and often least understood muscle in the core. While the other three muscles are involved in flexion of the spine, the fibers of the TA wrap around the torso horizontally like a corset keeping the abdominal organs in place and serving as a key core stabilizer. The TA is also the muscle that controls exhalation of the breath, with help from other abdominal muscles.

The abdominal muscles come into play primarily when the spine is being flexed from a lying down position, as in a sit-up. They are most active in the beginning phase of the sit-up before the hips begin to flex. Once the hips flex, the abdominal muscles serve to stabilize the pelvis. These muscles are of particular importance to dancers because of their contribution to optimal alignment. They are crucial in preventing a forward tilt of the pelvis and the resulting hyperextended or swayback posture.

There is some discussion among experts as to the role of the *psoas* muscle in producing movement of the lumbar spine. Research has shown it to be active during both flexion and extension of the lumbar spine, with perhaps more activation in extension. However, this is a complex muscle whose action varies in response to positional change of the hip and spine, so the discussion continues (Park et al. 2013). The *psoas*, part of the *iliopsoas* muscle, is discussed in Chapter 13 as one of the hip flexors (Figure 13.7).

The *rectus abdominis* muscle runs up the front of the body and can be easily palpated on the anterior surface of the abdomen near the midline (Figure 16.2a). It is attached to the *pubic* bone at one end and to the *sternum* and the cartilage that connects some of the ribs to the *sternum* at the other. The *rectus abdominis* is encased in a sheath, or envelope, of connective tissue called *fascia*. In addition to encasing the *rectus abdominis*, this envelope of fascia provides a place for the attachment of the other abdominal muscles.

Parts of the *external obliques* (Figure 16.2b) are attached to the fascia of the *rectus abdominis*. Other parts are attached along the crest of the *ilium*. As a whole, the muscle runs diagonally upward and outward, and at the other end is attached laterally along the lower ribs. The *external obliques* may be palpated on the lateral side of the abdomen.

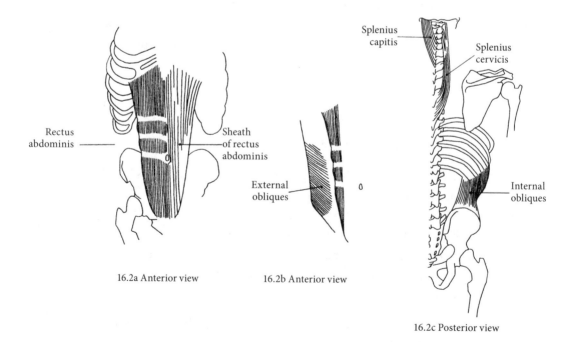

Rectus abdominis

Sheath of rectus abdominis

External obliques

Splenius capitis

Splenius cervicis

Internal obliques

16.2a Anterior view

16.2b Anterior view

16.2c Posterior view

Figure 16.2 Trunk muscles

The *internal obliques* are attached to the crest of the *ilium*, and run diagonally upward and inward to attach to some of the ribs and fascia of the *rectus abdominis* (Figure 16.2c). The *internal obliques* lie beneath the *external obliques*.

Find It
Place the hands on the abdomen.

Feel It
Tilt the pelvis under and curve the lower back while exhaling.

Notice the muscles engaging under your fingers. These are the abdominal muscles.

Dance It
Perform a contemporary/modern dance contraction.

Extension and hyperextension of the spine

Although there are deep posterior muscles that contribute to the extension of the spine, the two major muscle groups responsible for this action are the *erector spinae* muscles and the *semispinalis* muscles. More specifically, the lumbar and thoracic portions of the *erector spinae* work with the thoracic portions of the *semispinalis* to extend the spine.

These muscles are also active when the spine is hyperextended against resistance. If performing back exercises lying on your stomach, you are using the force of gravity as a form of resistance. In order to hyperextend your spine by lifting the chest off the floor you must overcome the resistance of gravity.

The *erector spinae* is a complex muscle system illustrated in Figure 16.3. From its large attachment at the lumbosacral region, it branches as it moves upward, with multiple attachments all along the ribs and vertebrae. A portion of this muscle can be palpated at the lower lumbar region on either side of the spine.

The *semispinalis* is another complex muscle system that runs along the thoracic and cervical vertebrae. It is composed of three sections: the *capitis*, *cervicis*, and *thoracis*. These muscles lie close to the vertebrae beneath the *erector spinae* (Figure 16.3).

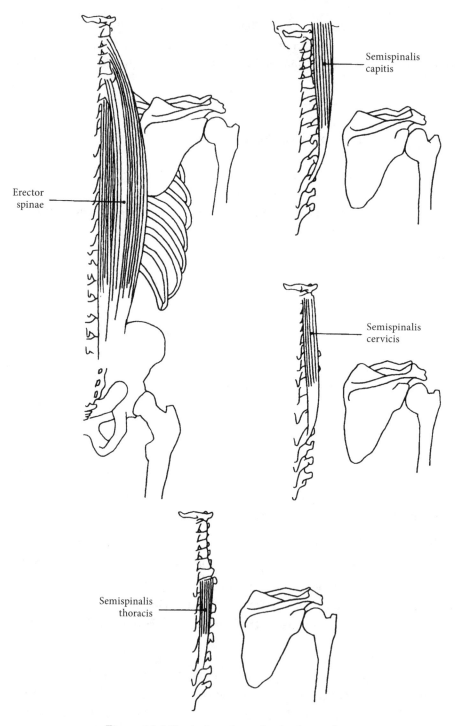

Erector
spinae

Semispinalis
capitis

Semispinalis
cervicis

Semispinalis
thoracis

Figure 16.3 Posterior view of spinal muscles

Find It

Lie face down on the floor. Place the palm and fingers of one hand behind your back, horizontally across the spine.

Feel It

Lift the chest off the floor to arch the spine, keeping the head in line.

Notice the muscles popping up under your fingers. These are the *thoracic erector spinae*.

Dance It

Perform a *cambré* backward or backbend.

Lateral flexion of the spine and lateral pelvic tilt

Lateral flexion is brought about when the muscles on one side of the body contract. Many of the muscles involved in spinal flexion and extension are active during lateral flexion of the spine. When combined with muscles of the hip, they contribute to produce lateral pelvic tilt. The lateral flexors of the trunk include the *erector spinae*, the *internal* and *external obliques*, the *semispinalis thoracis*, the *rectus abdominis*, the deep posterior spinal muscles, and the *quadratus lumborum*. With the exception of the *quadratus lumborum*, all of the muscles have been described.

The *quadratus lumborum* is a relatively short back muscle attached at one end to the iliac crest and at the other end, to the lower vertebrae and twelfth (bottom-most) rib (Figure 16.4).

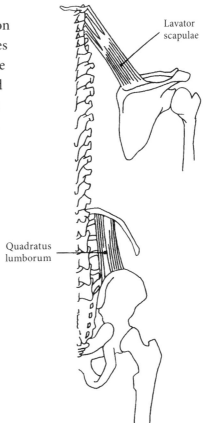

Lavator scapulae

Quadratus lumborum

Figure 16.4 Posterior view of trunk and neck muscles

Find It

Place the fingers on your lower back in the space between the top of your pelvis and the bottom rib.

Feel It

Hitch or hike the hip to the side that your fingers are on.

Notice the muscles popping up under your fingers. These are the *lumbar erector spinae* and *quadratus lumborum*.

Dance It

Perform a side bend.

Rotation of the trunk

Rotation is brought about when certain muscles on one side of the trunk contract simultaneously with certain muscles on the other side. Muscles that produce rotation include the *internal* and *external obliques*, the thoracic and lumbar areas of the *erector spinae*, the *semispinalis*, and the deep posterior spinal muscles. All of these have been described previously.

Find It

Place your hands on your waist with the thumbs contacting the muscles on either side of the spine and the fingers wrapping around to the abdominal muscles.

Feel It

Twist from your waist and look over your shoulder.

Notice the muscles popping up under your fingers. These are the *lumbar erector spinae* at the back and the *oblique* muscles at the front.

Dance It

Perform a body spiral in modern/contemporary.

Table 16.2 Muscle actions of the neck

Movement of the Neck	Dancer Terminology	Muscles
Flexion	Chin to chest	Sternocleidomastoid Scalenus Anterior Scalenus Medius Scalenus Posterior Longus Colli Longus Capitis
Extension	Chin to ceiling	Splenius Capitis Splenius Cervicis Erector Spinae (upper portion) Semispinalis Levator Scapulae Suboccipital Muscles Deep Spinal Muscles
Lateral flexion	Incline of the head or side tilt of the head	Scalenus Anterior Scalenus Medius Scalenus Posterior Sternocleidomastoid Splenius Capitis Splenius Cervicis Erector Spinae (upper portion) Semispinalis
Rotation	Turning the head	Sternocleidomastoid Scalenus Anterior Scalenus Medius Scalenus Posterior Splenius Cervicis Splenius Capitis Erector Spinae (upper portion) Suboccipital Muscles

Flexion of the neck

The primary neck flexors are the *sternocleidomastoid* and the three *scalenes*. They are located on the anterior and side of the spine.

The *sternocleidomastoid* has two heads, one attached to the *sternum* and the other to the *clavicle* (Figure 16.5). They come together and attach to the skull just behind the ear. To feel these muscles in action, place your fingers on your neck from the ear down to the center front of the neck, then flex your neck against resistance (use your other hand under the chin to provide the resistance).

The *scalenus anterior* and *medius* are attached to the first rib, just behind the collarbone, and the *scalenus posterior* is attached to the second rib. At the other end, they all attach to the cervical vertebrae (Figure 16.5).

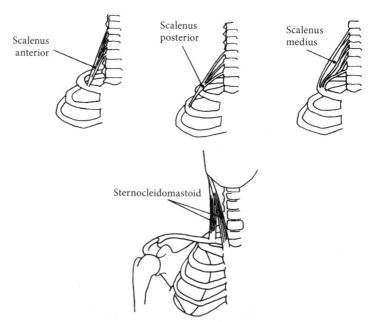

Figure 16.5 Anterior view of neck muscles

Extension and hyperextension of the neck

Many muscles work together to produce extension of the neck. These include the *splenius capitis* and *cervicis*, the upper portions of the *erector spinae* and *semispinalis*, the *levator scapulae*, the deep posterior spinal muscles, and the *suboccipital* muscles. These muscles are also active whenever the neck is hyperextended against resistance. The *erector spinae* and *semispinalis* muscles have already been described, and the *levator scapulae* is illustrated in Figure 16.4. It will be further described in Part V. The *suboccipital muscles*, like the deep posterior muscles, will not be described in further detail. All of these muscles are located on the posterior aspect of the spine.

The *splenius capitis* is attached at one end to some of the thoracic and cervical vertebrae and at the other end, to the skull (Figure 16.2). The *splenius cervicis* is also attached at one end to some of the thoracic vertebrae and at the other end to some of the cervical vertebrae (Figure 16.2). You can feel both these muscles in action by placing your fingers on the back of your neck, just behind the *sternocleidomastoid* muscle, while you extend the neck against resistance.

Lateral flexion of the neck

The primary muscles that produce lateral flexion have all been described. They are the *splenius capitis* and *cervicis*, the upper portions of the *erector spinae* and *semispinalis*, the three *scalenes*, and the *sternocleidomastoid*. Lateral flexion is produced when the muscles on one side of the neck contract.

Rotation of the neck

The *sternocleidomastoid, scalenes, splenius, erector spinae*, and *suboccipital* muscles have all been discussed. They are all active in producing neck rotation.

Neutral alignment

When viewed from the front or back, a plumb line should pass through the center of the head, chest, abdomen, and buttocks. The shoulders, shoulder

Figure 16.6 Plumb line alignment

blades, and hips will be horizontally level unless a structural deviation, such as a difference in leg length or lateral curvature of the spine, precludes this. When viewed from the side, a plumb line will fall through the ear lobe, through the center of the shoulder joint, and hip joint (Figure 16.6). The anterior superior iliac spines, or "hip bones," will be in the same vertical plane as the *symphysis pubis*, or juncture of the pubic bones. The spinal curves will also be apparent.

There are four natural curves in the spine (Figures 16.7). The forward curve in the neck is called the *cervical lordosis;* the backward curve in the middle back is called the *thoracic kyphosis;* the forward curve in the lower back is called the *lumbar lordosis;* and the backward curve in the *sacrum* is called the *sacral kyphosis* (the *sacrum* is fused into this position). These curves are formed by the architecture of the vertebrae and the intervertebral discs. They serve both to strengthen the spine so that it can support the body's weight and to act as shock absorbers by distributing the forces of gravity and of our own movements. Balance is achieved when the curves of the lumbar spine and cervical spine are relatively equal and when the curves of the thoracic spine and sacrum also mirror each other. Compensation patterns will occur when one of these curves moves from neutral. For instance, an increase in lumbar lordosis will lead to a similar increase in cervical lordosis that will result in a forward head alignment.

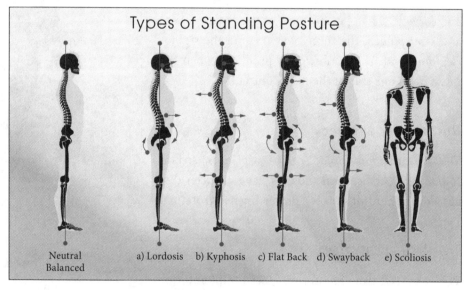

Figure 16.7 Spinal curves

17

QUESTIONS and ANSWERS: The TRUNK and NECK

The questions and answers that follow concern improvement in technique and prevention of injuries to the trunk and neck.

1. What are some of the most common issues related to spinal and pelvic alignment?

When the spinal curves are either increased or decreased through postural adaptations, the weight of the body will no longer be transmitted through the center of the vertebrae and the intervertebral discs. Depending on the alignment issue, the weight of the body will fall toward the front, back, or sides of the vertebrae. This will increase the stress on the vertebrae, spinal ligaments, and surrounding soft tissues. If the discs are being loaded asymmetrically, this can cause weakening of their outer fibrous layer, thus increasing the risk of injury. The issue will be compounded by jumping and landing when the increased forces fall on structures that are placed in a compromised alignment.

The spinal muscles will also be affected. When the natural curves are altered, spinal muscles will contract or stretch as they respond and adjust to the new alignment. This makes them less efficient and more vulnerable to injury. The change in muscle recruitment may also serve to reinforce or even exaggerate the altered alignment.

The lumbar spine is particularly susceptible to injury for several reasons. The accumulated weight of the head, cervical spine, shoulder girdle, arms, rib cage, and thoracic spine pass through the lumbar spine, while ground reaction forces are being transmitted upward from the feet and legs. When the dancer is

Figure 17.1 Increased lumbar lordosis

partnering, the added weight of another body will also be transmitted to the lumbar spine. While the thoracic spine has the rib cage to help support its alignment, the lumbar spine has no such assistance. Finally, the joint between the fifth (lowest) lumbar vertebra and the *sacrum* is particularly vulnerable as it has to provide a stable base for the spine while also allowing for bending and twisting movements. Whenever you flex, extend, or hyperextend the spine, the *lumbosacral joint* is involved and it is at particular risk in hypermobile individuals.

Injuries to the lumbar spine include *disc injuries*, *stress fractures*, *facet joint irritation*, and *vertebral subluxation* (partial sliding out of alignment). This area is also susceptible to muscle spasms, chronic aches, and ligament sprains.

Alignment issues in the spine do not happen in isolation; the ramifications will be apparent throughout the kinetic chain. For instance, an increased *lumbar lordosis* will often be accompanied by hyperextended knees, an anterior tilt of the pelvis, and a high chest and head position (Figure 17.1).

Figure 17.2 Forward head

Figure 17.2 illustrates another example of an increased *lumbar lordosis*. In this case the upper torso is leaning back, accentuating the lumbar curve. In an effort to compensate, the head is thrust forward placing increased forces on the cervical spine and neck musculature.

A hyperextended lumbar curve may also hinder the successful performance of some dance movements. For example, it can limit leg extension to both the front and back, as well as causing difficulty in maintaining turn-out in side extensions. Sometimes dancers intentionally assume an anterior pelvic tilt and hyperextended back posture in order to increase their turn-out. Tilting the pelvis does relax the *iliofemoral* ligament at the front of the hip, and this results in a slight increase in turn-out. However, this strategy causes many other issues, so should not be used. Part III contains further information on turn-out and alternative ways to improve this motion.

To address a hyperextended lumbar curve and anterior pelvic tilt, it will be advantageous to strengthen the trunk flexors and stretch the trunk extensors. At the same time, the hip extensors should be strengthened and stretched, while the hip flexors should be stretched. Exercises to do this are listed below.

Some dancers mistakenly think that their back is supposed to be straight or flat. In an attempt to minimize their *lumbar lordosis*, they resort to "tucking" the pelvis under (Figure 17.3). This posterior tilt of the pelvis will decrease the lumbar curve, but there will be resulting compensations in the knees and chest. The loss of *lumbar lordosis* will also make the spine more vulnerable to the shock forces traveling up from the feet and legs.

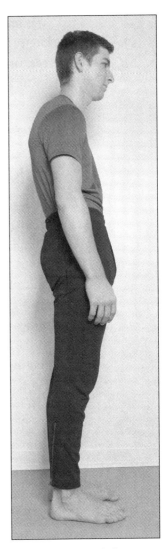

Figure 17.3 Tucking the pelvis

Another manifestation of the attempt to achieve a straight spine occurs in the thoracic region. Dancers often display little or no thoracic kyphosis and can even tend toward hyperextension of some vertebral segments. This can become exaggerated if they push the rib cage and chest forward in an effort to "pull up". This will shift the whole body weight forward and will encourage the knees to hyperextend.

It is important to identify and address alignment issues as soon as possible. The longer they are allowed to continue, the more difficult it becomes to make changes. In some cases, alignment issues that begin with muscular imbalances and postural habits can cause structural changes that may become permanent.

2.　I feel like I have several alignment issues, and that one affects another. How do I know which one to address first?

As we saw from the answers to Question 1, the body is a highly integrated system and no alignment issue exists in isolation. First, take stock of all the areas of concern and see if you can draw connections among them. For instance, are you over-rotating your feet, causing you to tilt the pelvis anteriorly to help you to balance in this position, and is this leading to an increase in your lumbar curve? Alignment issues may be addressed from the top down (e.g., from the spine down into the legs) or from the bottom up (e.g., starting at the feet). Beginning at the feet and working your way up is often a good way to ensure that no contributing factors are missed out. Once a firm base of support has been established at the feet, this can facilitate changes in the legs, pelvis, spine, head, and arms. However, some people may prefer to address the spinal alignment first, as when the center of the body is in neutral, it can facilitate changes in the legs, arms, and head.

Whichever choice you make, it is key to remember to evaluate the entire body, sensing how one alteration affects another area. Changes in torso alignment will not be completely successful if placement issues in the feet, ankles, arms, or head are left unrecognized. Similarly, issues in the feet and knees will not be satisfactorily resolved until the alignment of the torso, arms, and head are addressed.

It is also important to remember that some alignment issues are structural in nature and cannot be changed. Examples may be a limited *demi-plié* due to inherent bone architecture, tibial torsion, and differences in leg length. These may require technique modifications to ensure that the anatomy is being safely used to its maximal advantage. You should seek the guidance of your teacher or dance medicine professional for help with any of these issues.

3.   I want to improve my backbends and back *port de bras*, but worry about hurting my spine. What is the best way to safely approach this movement?

When the back is arched, the curve primarily takes place in the cervical and lumbar regions of the spine. Recall from Chapter 16 that the shape of the cervical and lumbar vertebrae permit hyperextension, while the anatomical structure of the thoracic vertebrae allows very little hyperextension to occur. This limited hyperextension in the thoracic spine does not seem apparent when one first looks at a back *port de bras*. This is because the forward curve of the rib cage completes the visual line. In reality, however, an arched back primarily occurs in the cervical and lumbar regions of the spine.

When you bend back, it is important that the arch be properly controlled in order to protect the cervical and lumbar structures. Question 1 on page 185 explains the vulnerability of the lumbar spine and some of the injuries that can occur in that area. Bending back can stress the lumbar area if appropriate muscular control and spinal alignment are not engaged. This places the vertebrae, discs, nerves, and ligaments at risk of injury.

Injuries to these areas can also occur if the weight of the head or body is allowed to fall into the cervical and lumbar curves. To avoid injury to the cervical region, the head position should be controlled by the neck flexors in an eccentric muscle action. The head should appear to be an extension of the spine, rather than look as if it has fallen back. To avoid injury to the lumbar region, the position of the torso should be controlled by the trunk flexors in an eccentric muscle action. The torso should be "lifted" before starting to bend, and the "lift" should continue throughout the movement. This will engage the appropriate muscles and keep the weight of the body from sinking into the lower back.

Some dancers cheat when they perform a back *port de bras*. Instead of using the trunk muscles, they achieve the arched appearance by tilting the pelvis forward. This will not produce the appropriate aesthetic line, and will create stresses in the structures of the lower back, particularly at the *lumbosacral joint*.

As for improving this movement, it is important to realize that there are anatomical factors that ultimately determine hyperextension of the spine. These factors differ from one dancer to another and help to explain the wide range of back flexibility seen among individuals. Some of the structural factors that affect hyperextension include the shape of the vertebrae, as well as the laxity or looseness of the ligaments. Exercise cannot change an individual's spinal architecture, so dancers must work within the limits of their own anatomy.

Another factor that affects hyperextension is the strength and flexibility of the anterior trunk muscles. When you bend back, the trunk flexors function in an eccentric muscle action to produce the movement. This means they must be strong enough to control the movement and flexible enough to accommodate the hyperextended position. Conditioning these muscles will help improve the position of your back when you arch backward.

Exercises that stretch the trunk flexors must necessarily hyperextend the spine. While hyperextension is a natural spinal movement, care must be taken to protect the vertebrae, discs, nerves, and ligaments from increased stress. As explained above, the shape of the thoracic vertebrae limits hyperextension, while the shape of the lumbar vertebrae favors hyperextension. Because the lumbar spine is particularly susceptible to injury, it is important that hyperextension in that area be wisely controlled. The exercises in the next chapter will help to develop this control.

4.   I have been told I have an anterior pelvic tilt. I am not sure really what this means or what to do about it.

In evaluating an anterior pelvic tilt, it is important to remember that the natural curve in the lower back varies widely among individuals, as does the shape of the gluteal muscles. If the appearance of the lumbar curve is the only factor considered, it is possible to make mistakes in evaluating pelvic placement. The pelvis of someone whose natural curve is slightly greater than the "norm" may appear to be tilted, even though the spine and pelvis are correctly aligned for that body structure. The shape of the gluteal muscles can also make a lumbar curve appear more exaggerated. In these instances, dancers should not be told to tuck in the pelvis in an attempt to decrease the lumbar curve. While the visual result may represent a more neutral curve, these dancers will be compromising their natural alignment and potentially stressing the underlying structures.

There is another way of evaluating pelvic placement that can help safeguard against these misjudgments. This requires an assessment of the relationship between the "hip bones" and the *symphysis pubis*. Recall from the anatomy section that when the pelvis is correctly aligned, the *anterior-superior iliac spines*, or "hip bones," are in the same vertical plane as the *symphysis pubis*. In an anterior pelvic tilt, the *ilium* is moved forward and the *symphysis pubis* is moved backward. As a result, the vertical plane through the *anterior-superior iliac spines* is forward of the vertical plane through the *symphysis pubis*. Using these bony landmarks as reference points is more accurate than using the lumbar spine itself as a guide.

5. When my teacher says to "lift up" and stand up straight, my ribs stick out. I can't seem to lift up without sticking out my rib cage. What can I do to correct this?

Recall from the previous chapter the location and function of the trunk flexors and extensors. The trunk flexors are attached to the ribs and pelvis on the front of the body. When the pelvis is stationary, the trunk flexors act to pull down on the ribs. The attachment of the trunk extensors on the back of the body means that a contraction here will cause the ribs to lift and stick out. When a dancer pulls up correctly, the trunk flexors and extensors work in a balanced partnership. This gives the dancer a lifted or elongated appearance without projecting the ribs forward.

Some dancers find it difficult to lift up correctly. The problem begins when they attempt to lift up by contracting the trunk extensors alone, as this causes the ribs to stick out. This will be compounded if they try to correct the rib position by contracting the trunk flexors with a force greater than that of the trunk extensors. While this action pulls the ribs into better alignment, it leaves the dancer trapped in a tight corset of muscle contraction. Movement of the torso will then be inhibited and breathing will be restricted.

A better solution is to lift up by using both the trunk flexors and extensors. Should the ribs still protrude, a partial relaxation of the trunk extensors will help. It is particularly important to restore a balance between the two muscle groups without excessive muscular tension. The use of imagery can help facilitate the alignment of the ribs over the pelvis: Imagine the ribs are a hot air balloon floating over the pelvis with tethers connecting the balloon to the entire pelvic girdle. This will keep a balance between the flexors and extensors of the spine. This balance permits a lift of the torso in addition to freedom of movement and ease in breathing.

If a dancer habitually stands with the ribs protruded, the trunk extensors can become shortened and tight while the trunk flexors become weak. When this happens, additional conditioning work is needed to restore a balance between the two muscle groups.

6.　What can I do to improve the line of my *arabesque* and back *attitude*?

When the leg is lifted to *arabesque* or back *attitude*, the spine is hyperextended. Question 3 discusses the structural limitations that determine hyperextension of the spine. These factors must be considered when evaluating the line of your *arabesque* or back *attitude*. Individual dancers with varying spinal anatomies will achieve different lines in *arabesque*. This does not mean that the line of your *arabesque* cannot be improved, but it must be achieved within your anatomical parameters. If you push the body beyond its inherent capacities, you risk causing injury, as well as distorting the aesthetic line.

To protect the spine, it is important to be aware of the alignment of the upper torso and hip. The upper torso should be allowed to move or lean slightly forward to accommodate the movement of the leg behind. If it is held too straight and upright, the spine may be harmfully hyperextended. The hip should not be lifted or allowed to twist. If the hip is allowed to twist, rotary forces can compromise the integrity of the spine. To avoid this, the hip should be kept down, parallel with the shoulder.

Conditioning work can also help to improve your *arabesque* and back *attitude*. Exercises to strengthen the trunk extensors will help the position of the back. The trunk flexors should also be conditioned. They must be strong enough to maintain a lift in the front of the body and flexible enough to accommodate the hyperextended position. Well-conditioned muscles at the hip will also improve the position of the leg. Exercises for the muscle groups acting on the hip are shown in Chapter 15.

7.   Although I am performing sit-ups every day I still don't feel I have enough strength in my "core." I am not sure if I am doing my abdominal muscle exercises correctly.

Dancers often spend a considerable amount of time in and out of the dance studio working on their abdominal muscles to find their elusive "core." However, they have often been taught to do crunches, oblique work, and full sit-ups without having a clear understanding of how these exercises should be performed to ensure optimal abdominal muscle recruitment for core stability.

In the initial stages of the sit-up, the abdominal muscles are active in flexing the spine. However, in the last part of a full sit-up, the hip flexors act as the primary movers and the abdominal muscles act as stabilizers. Many dancers don't realize the dynamic role the abdominal muscles play and develop poor habits. During technique classes, the abdominal muscle series given tends to be performed to music at a quick tempo, which encourages using momentum and activation of the hip flexors without the stability of the abdominal muscles. It is important to use a partial sit-up to increase the isolated strength of the abdominal muscles. By adding movement of the legs during partial sit-ups, you will increase the workload of your abdominal muscles as they have to work to flex the torso and stabilize the lumbar spine. If you add a body twist to this partial sit-up, you will also strengthen the oblique abdominal muscles.

The progression of difficulty with abdominal muscle work is very individual and one of the most important considerations is the stability of the lumbar spine. As the legs are extended in exercises like double-leg raises, there is a potential to injure the lower back. Double-leg raises can cause the lower back to hyperextend, unless the person performing them already has very strong abdominal muscles. This stresses the lower back and can lead to injury. This exercise should only be considered when adequate abdominal muscle control has been acquired.

If you are struggling with your core, you should evaluate the activation of the hip flexors and if your lower back is hyperextending. If these are both issues then focus on partial sit-ups until you can build your strength. In abdominal muscle work, increasing repetitions is not the key to success. The key to your abdominal core is your focus on how you are moving: avoid overcompensating with the hip flexors, slow down to avoid using momentum, and use your breath.

8.   Can a stress fracture occur in the spine?

Yes. During childhood and adolescence, a condition called *spondylolysis* can occur, most often in the fourth and fifth lumbar vertebrae. This condition is more common in dancers and gymnasts than in the general public. Some experts believe it may be caused by repetitive flexion and extension of the spine. Others believe the problem may be precipitated by weak abdominal muscles and a hyperextended spinal posture. In either case, dancers are cautioned against hyperextending the back in order to increase turn-out.

Spondylolysis is often identified by chronic low-back pain, particularly on one side of the spine. This pain becomes acute when executing a back *arabesque* or back *attitude* on the injured side. The treatment for this condition usually includes rest and possibly immobilization. After the stress fracture is healed, a conditioning program to strengthen the abdominal muscles is usually recommended, along with exercises to correct any other muscular imbalances.

If a stress fracture is bilateral (on both sides) and goes untreated, other complications can result. One problem is vertebral subluxation, where a vertebra can partially slide out of place. This is known as *spondylolisthesis*. This most commonly occurs at the fifth lumbar vertebra, where it slides forward on the *sacrum*. It can also occur at the fourth lumbar vertebra, where it slides forward over the fifth lumbar vertebrae. The symptoms are often not particularly dramatic. They can include low-grade back pain, similar to that associated with muscle strain, that is worse during exercise but relieved by rest. Symptoms may also be exaggerated by hyperextending the spine and relieved by forward bending. Any back pain that persists for more than a few days should be assessed by a dance medicine professional. If you are also experiencing symptoms of numbness or pins and needles in one or both legs, you should seek help as soon as possible as this can indicate pressure on the spinal nerve roots or spinal cord.

9.   I have been told by my doctor that I have scoliosis. How might this impact my dance career?

Scoliosis (Figure 17.4) is a sideways curvature of the spine that may be congenital, developmental, or of unknown origin (*idiopathic scoliosis*). It may manifest as a simple C-shaped curve or with two curves causing an S-shape. It is important to note that a *scoliosis* may be very mild, causing no symptoms or notable restrictions. In more extreme cases, back pain may be experienced, along with difficulty in achieving some dance positions, such as *arabesque.*

If the *scoliosis* is significant, then it can produce bilateral asymmetry. This can manifest as an uneven horizontal line in the shoulders, shoulder blade asymmetry, and uneven arm hang. It should be noted, however, that almost everyone has a slight degree of asymmetry, sometimes owing to the dominance of one hand and overuse of the muscles on the dominant side. These deviations should not be confused with *scoliosis.* The asymmetry caused by *scoliosis* is far more pronounced and is commonly a result of a difference in leg lengths. In the standing position, the floor places the feet at the same level, so a discrepancy in leg lengths will manifest in an uneven line at the pelvis where the longer leg will push one *ilium* upward. As the *sacrum* is held between the two *ilia*, the spinal alignment will be initiated at an angle causing compensatory curves above.

Dance teachers are often the first to spot the beginnings of *scoliosis.* One way to check is to have the dancer bend forward as if to touch their toes. This may reveal a misalignment in the vertebrae and may result in a "rib hump" where one side of the rib cage remains more prominent. Other clues are if one shoulder blade is more pronounced, if the rib cage looks higher on one side, or if the muscles of the lumbar spine are more developed on one side. However, caution

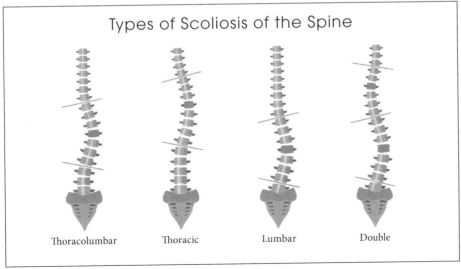

Figure 17.4 Scoliosis

should be noted that just because there may be an asymmetry present, this does not necessarily represent a problem. If the dancer is pain free and coping well with the technical demands of dance, then he or she may have compensated well for any apparent asymmetries. However, if the dancer is experiencing back symptoms or notable restrictions in technique, then a medical professional should be consulted for further evaluation.

10. Lifts and partnering in all styles of dance are demanding. My back sometimes hurts after partnering. What do I need to be aware of to prevent back injuries?

Optimal alignment of the spine is critical in partnering to ensure that the increased forces and loads are transmitted through the weight-bearing structures while being supported by the appropriate muscles. The most common issue that can lead to back pain is hyperextension of the lumbar spine when lifting. When this happens, the full weight of the partner is transmitted to the facet joints rather than the vertebral bodies. The facet joints are not designed to be weight-bearing structures and so can become damaged and painful when being loaded in this way. The hyperextended position will also result in reduced availability of the abdominal muscles for the appropriate spinal support.

The mechanism of lifting the partner from the ground into the air also requires detailed consideration in order to protect the spinal discs—particularly if the lift is initiated while in motion. The intervertebral discs are particularly vulnerable when loaded in a rotated position. This can compromise the outer fibrous ring that contains the gel-like fluid inside. Repeated loading in a rotated position can weaken the outer structure, eventually leading to a protrusion of the inner fluid that can press on the spinal nerves, causing radiating pain and other complications. Attention should therefore be paid to aligning the pelvis to the vertical axis of the lift to maintain the neutral position of the lumbar vertebrae and discs. The partner should also be lifted as close to the body as possible. The farther one has to reach forward to lift, the greater the strain on the discs. Breath also plays an important role. Exhaling at the initiation of the lift will engage the natural spinal stabilizing effect of the *transversus abdominis* muscle, thus affording the spine some protection.

In addition to alignment, another protection for the back is to develop strength and flexibility in the upper torso, shoulders, and arms. Dance technique classes usually concentrate on building strength in the legs but do not generally develop sufficient upper-body strength for partnering. Chapter 21 includes conditioning exercises to prepare the shoulder girdle and arms for partnering work.

Partnering is a complex skill that depends on timing as much as strength. In many instances, the timing can be off and the lift can "go wrong." When this happens, quick reactions are essential to protect both partners from the risk of injury. To cope safely with these situations requires strength, flexibility, and the ability to react and adapt quickly. We recommend that dancers involved in partnering follow a conditioning program designed to develop strength and flexibility throughout the entire body, and focus on coordinating timing and breathing patterns for each lift combination.

11. My back always aches after dance class. Should I be concerned about this?

While some degree of muscle fatigue is common after a strenuous class, it is not wise to accept repeated pain in the same area of the body. If your lower back aches, you should speak with your teacher or see a physician. Ask your teacher to help you to assess your alignment. It is not always possible for dancers to see alignment issues that occur as they are moving. Sometimes a dancer will be optimally placed during the warm-up or *barre*, but slip into sub-optimal patterns when engaged in more complicated movement sequences.

In addition to working with your teacher to identify possible issues in technique, you should also consider seeking medical advice. Many serious injuries start with chronic back ache as the first warning sign. Pain is something to be evaluated and alleviated, not ignored.

12. Sometimes after modern or jazz technique classes, my neck is stiff, restricted, and painful. What can I do about this?

The average person's head weighs about twelve pounds and is heavier than many people realize. The neck is a highly mobile structure that must balance and carry this weight. Additionally, the cervical spine is surrounded by many vital structures such as nerves, arteries, veins, and lymph vessels that are running to and from the head and brain, as well as down into the arms. Injury in this area can therefore go beyond just an issue with joints and muscles.

Some modern and jazz styles involve vigorous head and neck movements such as head rolls and flicks. With many dancers having some degree of hypermobility, these movements can become quite exaggerated, placing the delicate structures of the neck at risk of injury. When the underlying joints are moved through a potentially dangerous range of motion, the surrounding muscles can be triggered into a spasm to limit the movement and prevent further injury. This can result in a stiff and painful neck and is a sign that the neck was placed at risk. Recall that rotational movements place the spinal discs at particular risk of injury. Damaged discs can press on the spinal nerves causing both local pain and symptoms such as numbness or tingling into the arms and hands. Particular care should be taken with backward head rolls. If you tip your head back and find it difficult to talk, or if you feel tingling or pins and needles in either the neck, arms, or hands, you have allowed the head to go too far and may be damaging the spinal nerves. Head movements to the back also place the load onto the facet joints, which can also become painfully irritated. If you experience any symptoms of dizziness or headaches associated with neck movements, you should seek immediate medical attention. Concussion is a condition that is usually associated with a blow to the head, but it can also be caused by vigorous head movements. This is a serious medical issue that should not be ignored.

Strong and flexible neck muscles are needed to control head movements like spotting when you turn, as well as head circles or head rolls. Exercises for neck control are shown in the next chapter.

18

STRENGTH and FLEXIBILITY EXERCISES:
The TRUNK and NECK

THIS SECTION PROVIDES STRENGTH, FLEXIBILITY, and integration exercises for the trunk and neck. Where appropriate, injuries are also discussed. Each section will provide the exercise name, any equipment needed, and starting positions. Step-by-step descriptions of the action of the exercise, and suggestions for self checks and comments on what you might feel are offered.

(Pilates-based exercises are denoted by an *.)

The exercises in this section target what is commonly referred to as the *core*. However, there are various interpretations of what the term *core* actually refers to, so we will just say a few words about that here. When a dance teacher refers to pulling up or engaging "the core," dancers often tend to think only of their abdominal muscles. While the abdominal muscles discussed earlier are major players, of equal importance are the spinal muscles located on the back of the body. Here we have both large muscles that extend the spine and smaller intrinsic muscles that stabilize local segmental areas between specific vertebrae. While executing the exercises in this section, you need to divide your attention equally between both the actions of the abdominal muscles and the stabilizing role of the spinal muscles. To help you to achieve this, it was worth reviewing the section on maintaining neutral spine alignment in a supine position (Chapter 3) and the exercises for spinal extension in Chapter 18, section 18.B. Also of relevance is the Plank exercise, which you can find in Chapter 21, section 21.A

Note: Be sure to read Part I before performing any of the following exercises.

Table 18.1 Roadmap

Action	Strength Exercises	Flexibility Exercises
Individual Movements		
Trunk flexion	18.A.1	18.A.2
Trunk extension	18.B.1	18.B.2
Trunk rotation	18.C.1	18.C.2
Trunk side-bending	18.D.1	18.D.2
Deep neck muscles	18.E.1	18.E.2
Combination Movements		
Spinal articulation	18.F	

18.A Trunk flexors

While there are numerous exercises to address the abdominal muscles, these exercises have been selected to build awareness, breath, coordination, and challenge. The names will be familiar to those who know Pilates work, however many of these exercises exist under different names depending on the specific trainer or working environment. When approaching the abdominal exercises, bear in mind that you should be focusing on developing dynamic strength and coordination, not an externalized view of how these muscles should look. A deeper awareness will facilitate the development of an integrated and stable core that lends itself to efficient movement and the prevention of injury. As discussed earlier, flexion of the trunk involves contracting the abdominal muscles. This creates a bending movement of the spine like a forward contraction in modern dance. Using your breathing efficiently and increasing your awareness of the muscles that you are engaging will be more beneficial than increasing your repetitions.

Equipment

For all abdominal muscle exercises, the use of a mat is suggested (if available) to provide some padding for the spine—especially for those of you with bony spines. All exercises can also be performed on the dance floor or carpet.

18.A.1 Strength exercises

This is a progression of exercises aimed at challenging the abdominal muscles. These will help to increase stability for the lower back and pelvis.

CHEST LIFT (FIGURE 18.1)*

Starting position

a) Lie on your back, knees bent and hip-width apart, with the feet flat on the floor.

b) Place your hands behind your head, and keep the elbows wide.

c) Maintain a neutral pelvic position and elongated spine.

Action

a) Inhale and become aware of your body on the floor.

b) Exhale and draw in the abdominal muscles. Focus on lengthening the spine and dropping your ribs toward your hips. As you engage the abdominal muscles, allow this to curve your upper spine, lifting your head, chest, and shoulders off the mat.

c) Inhale and hold this contracted position. Continue to deepen the curve.

d) Exhale while lowering and lengthening the upper body back to the mat.

Repetitions

5–10 repetitions.

Quick self checks

This is an introductory abdominal muscle exercise and should be used to bring focus to how you are recruiting these muscles. Be careful to avoid using momentum and pulling on your neck in the upward phase—this is a common error during a typical "crunch." Check in with your hips and see if you are gripping either your gluteal muscles or your hip flexors. There is no rush here as the *chest lift* should move with full and complete breaths.

Figure 18.1 Chest lift

THE HUNDRED (FIGURE 18.2)*

Starting position

    a)   Lie on your back, knees bent at a table top position (90 degrees at the hips and knees). Ideally your inner thighs, knees, and inside of the feet will be touching.

    b)   Reach your hands toward the ceiling with palms facing toward your feet. Keep your arms straight throughout the exercise.

    c)   Maintain a neutral pelvic position and elongated spine.

Action

    a)   Inhale and become aware of your body on the floor.

b) Exhale and draw in the abdominal muscles as practiced in the *chest lift*. Raise your head and shoulders off the mat and reach the fingertips toward the feet.

c) Alternate inhaling and exhaling for 5 counts each as you pulse the arms by your hips. Connect the pulse with the breathing pattern. 5 pulses = 5 count inhale, 5 pulses = 5 count exhale.

d) Exhale while lowering and lengthening the upper body back to the mat.

Variation

To increase the intensity of this exercise you can extend your legs straight toward the ceiling. When you have good control, the next challenge will be to start lowering the legs toward the floor while maintaining a stable lower back and pelvis.

Repetitions

Pulse the arms for a total of 10 sets or 100 pulses.

Quick self checks

The Hundred exercise is a core exercise in the work of Joseph Pilates. This exercise is a great warm-up for the body as well as serving to strengthen the abdominal muscles. It teaches stability of the torso and lower back, and actively involves your breathing. As the arms pulse by the sides of the body, they should only be moving about 6 inches up and down and should be kept close to the side of the body. Continue to lengthen your fingertips toward the feet while pulsing to encourage the shoulders to lengthen away from the neck.

Figure 18.2 The Hundred

SINGLE-LEG STRETCH (FIGURE 18.3)*

Starting position

a)   Lie on your back, knees bent at a table top position.

b)   Raise your head and shoulders off the mat and place your left hand on your right bent knee and your right hand on your right ankle.

c)   Extend the left leg straight at a 45-degree angle to the floor.

d)   Maintain the lifted position throughout the entire exercise.

Action

a)   Using quick breaths, alternate the legs and hand positions without changing the height of the torso off the mat.

b)   Exhale as the knee comes into the chest, deepen the abdominal contraction, and stabilize the torso.

c)   Inhale as you are in the transition phase of switching the leg position.

d)   Once you have completed the exercise, exhale while lowering the torso and head back to the mat and bring the knees into the chest.

Figure 18.3 Single leg stretch

Repetitions

8–12 sets. A set is one cycle of the legs coming into the chest.

Quick self checks

This exercise (or ones similar to it) is performed in technique classes on a regular basis. Many times these are done with fast music to keep everyone on a quick pace. When speed and momentum is used to throw the legs into extension, the control of the abdominal muscles is lost. Abdominal muscle exercises involve adding the movement of the legs to challenge their ability to stabilize the lower back. The abdominal muscles are not moving your legs, this action is produced by your hip flexors as described in Part III. If you are feeling pain or snapping in your hips, take your legs higher and slow down. As you gain control and coordination you will be able to increase the speed.

SINGLE-STRAIGHT-LEG STRETCH*

Starting position

a)   Lie on your back, knees bent at a table top position.

b)   Raise your head and shoulders off the mat and extend the right leg to the ceiling and the left leg, at a 45-degree angle to the floor.

c)   Gently touch the back of the right knee with both hands.

d)   The head and shoulders will stay off the mat throughout the exercise.

Action

a)   Using quick breaths, alternate the legs without changing the height of the torso off the mat.

b)   Exhale as the straight leg comes toward the chest. Deepen the abdominal muscle contraction while stabilizing the torso.

c)   Inhale as you are in the transition phase of switching the leg positions.

    d)   Once you have completed the exercise, exhale while lowering the torso and head back to the mat, and bring the knees into the chest.

Repetitions

8–12 sets. A set is one cycle of the legs coming into the chest.

Quick self checks

Extending the legs adds an additional challenge for the stability of the lower back. As the hip flexors work to bring the leg toward the chest and then control the lowering of the opposite leg toward the floor, the lower back will tend to increase its lumbar curve. Once the lower back is in an arched position the abdominal muscles are not doing their job to support the action of the legs. An example of this in dance can be seen when doing *battements* or leg extension work: if the alignment of the spine is compromised due to a lack of abdominal muscle support, the hip flexors will become overworked. Be precise and work slowly and thoughtfully until you have a strong sense of the abdominal muscle support.

DOUBLE STRAIGHT-LEG STRETCH (FIGURE 18.4)*

Starting position

    a)   Lie on your back, legs extended straight to the ceiling.

    b)   Raise your head and shoulders off the mat and place your hands behind your head with the elbows open to the sides.

    c)   The head and shoulders will stay off the mat throughout the exercise.

Action

    a)   Exhale and lower both legs together toward the floor while maintaining the position of the torso.

    b)   Inhale as you bring the legs back to the starting position.

    c)   Once you have completed the exercise, exhale while lowering the torso and head back to the mat and bring the knees into the chest.

Repetitions

5–10 repetitions.

Quick self checks

Lowering both straight legs toward the floor will create an intense challenge for the abdominal muscles in controlling the pelvis. As the legs begin to lower toward the floor, the lower back will begin to lift up as soon as the abdominal-muscle control is lost. If you are feeling any strain in the lower back, limit the range of motion or stop the exercise completely. Some dancers will quickly drop the legs to the floor and then try to bring them back up using momentum. This is not recommended unless you have excellent control: by using momentum in place of a lack of abdominal muscle control, you will be likely to overwork and tighten your hip flexors.

Figure 18.4 Double straight leg stretch

18.A.2 *Flexibility exercise*

Release of trunk flexor muscles after conditioning.

ABDOMINAL MUSCLE STRETCH (FIGURE 18.5)

Starting position

a) Lie on your stomach with your forehead on the floor.

b) Place your hands up by your ears and let your forearms rest on the floor close to your shoulders.

Action

a) Lift your chest off the floor. Move your forearms toward the midline until they are under your shoulders and can comfortably support your weight. Look up, but do not let your head tip back so far that you are looking directly up at the ceiling.

b) Use the abdominal muscles to prevent the weight from sinking into the lower back.

c) Hold the stretch. Feel the stretch along the front of the body between the *sternum* and *pubic* bone. Many people feel compression, but not pain, in the back.

Variation

Straighten your elbows, but do not let your thighs lose contact with the floor (Figure 18.5). You can walk your hands slightly forward if you need to. The difficulty can be further increased by walking your hands in, toward your chest, until they are under your shoulders. Your upper thighs should not lose contact with the floor.

Repetitions

Hold the stretch for 30 seconds and repeat 3 times.

Quick self checks

Think of the spine as a strand of pearls: when in the hyperextended position you are trying to maintain equal space between each vertebrae to avoid compression. It is also important to focus on the stability of the

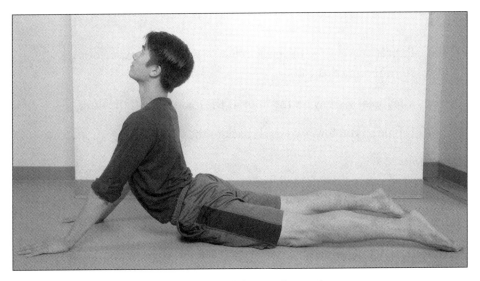

Figure 18.5 Abdominal stretch

shoulders. The tendency in hyperextension or trunk stretches is to allow the shoulders to come up to the ears. Just like a back extension in technique class, you want the line of the stretch to be fully supported without crunching the spine.

18.B Trunk extensors

18.B.1 Strength exercises

Building strength in the trunk extensors will help with the support for backbends and for facilitating the arabesque *line.*

BASIC BACK EXTENSION (FIGURE 18.6)

Starting position

a) Lie on your stomach with elbows bent at a 90-degree angle and hands on the floor.

b) Legs are extended long and can be slightly turned out.

c) Keep your head in line with the spine.

Action

    a)   Exhale and engage the back extensor muscles to raise your sternum up off the floor.

    b)   The forearms stay on the floor as the torso lifts off the floor.

    c)   Inhale as you lower yourself back to the floor.

Repetitions

    8–10 repetitions.

Quick self checks

Think of maintaining space between all the vertebrae as you extend the spine. Although the work is coming from the contraction of the back extensor muscles you need to think of elongating the front of the body. This includes lengthening the front of the hips and keeping the abdominal wall engaged to protect the lower back.

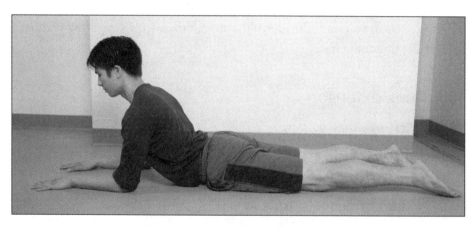

Figure 18.6 Basic back extension

SWIMMING (FIGURE 18.7)*

Starting position

    a)   Lie on your stomach with arms reaching above the head and legs elongated straight along the floor.

    b)   Engage your abdominal wall to create length and stability in the lower back.

Action

    a)   On an exhale reach the right arm and the left leg off the floor while extending the spine.

    b)   Switch to the other side without relaxing back down to the floor.

    c)   While alternating sides, work with your breath: exhale 4 counts, inhale 4 counts.

Repetitions

15–25 sets. A set is one breath cycle.

Quick self checks

Find the diagonal stretch through the body connecting the opposite arm to leg with each reach. Be aware that you are equally engaging both sides of the body and keeping a smooth transition between sides. Dancers will often sacrifice their alignment in order to feel that they are extending the spine farther than everyone else. This exercise is not about the height but is about the activation of the spinal muscles while keeping the shoulders down into the back.

Figure 18.7 Swimming

18.B.2 Flexibility exercises

These exercise both target flexibility in the spinal joints and also stretch the muscles of back extension. A more flexible spinal column will facilitate backbends and leg extensions to the back. Releasing tension in the back extensor muscles can help to relieve the postural issues associated with an over-arched spine.

CAT/COW (FIGURE 18.8)

Starting position

a) Start on your hands and knees. Stack the shoulders over the hands and the pelvis over the knees.

b) Find a neutral spine and keep the neck and head in line with the rest of the spine.

Action

a) Exhale and begin by tucking your tailbone under and then sequentially curve the spine until you are in a catlike curve (Figure 18.8a).

b) Inhale at the top of the curve.

c) Leading with the tailbone, exhale as you move to an arched spine and try to articulate each vertebra as you go (Figure 18.8b).

Figure 18.8a Cat

Figure 18.8b Cow

Repetitions

5–8 repetitions.

Quick self checks

Work to articulate the entire spine. It is common to have areas that are tight or lack the ability to articulate through movement. Use the breath to encourage the articulation and stop in areas that feel stuck.

Child's pose (Figure 18.9)

Starting position

a)   Kneeling with the knees together on a mat or other comfortable surface.

b)   Bend your torso forward to rest on your thighs.

c)   Keep your sitting bones in contact with the feet.

Action

a)   Exhale and walk the fingers away from the body until the arms are stretched above the head.

b)   Continue to breathe into the stretch, softening with each exhale.

Figure 18.9 Child's pose

Repetitions

Hold for 30 to 60 seconds.

Quick self checks

Make sure that the shoulders are relaxed. If necessary, widen the arms to a high V-shape to facilitate this. Do not allow the sitting bones to rise off the heels as the arms move forward. Some dancers may find this position uncomfortable for the knees or the feet. This can be a result of tight thigh muscles or ankle dorsiflexor muscles. If so, these should be assessed and addressed.

18.C Rotating the trunk

18.C.1 Strength exercises

In dance, we rarely stay with the torso purely facing the direction of movement for prolonged periods. Every time we move through space, the torso needs to rotate to counter the motion of the legs, and achieving many arm lines requires body rotation. Therefore the muscles of the torso need to be able to facilitate this rotation while keeping us stable. The following exercises target these complex motions.

OBLIQUE REACH

Starting position

 a)   Lie on your back, knees bent and hip-width apart, with the feet flat on the floor.

 b)   Place your hands behind your head, and keep the elbows wide.

 c)   Maintain a neutral pelvic position and elongated spine.

Action

 a)   Inhale and become aware of your body on the floor.

 b)   Exhale and draw in the abdominal muscles. Focus on lengthening the spine and dropping your ribs toward your hips. As you engage the abdominal muscles, allow this to raise your head and shoulders off the mat on the diagonal.

c) As you contract along the diagonal bring your left chest toward your right hip.

d) Inhale and bring the torso to the center in the *chest lift* position.

e) Exhale and rotate to the other diagonal, bringing the right chest toward your left hip.

f) Repeat by traveling back through the center to the other side without dropping the torso back down to the floor.

Repetitions

10 sets. A set is contracting to the left, center, right, center.

Quick self checks

As with most abdominal muscle work, when the hands are behind the head you should keep the elbows wide. Try to maintain a light touch of the hands behind the head so you are not pulling on the head to come up. You will notice that the action description did not say to bring the elbow to the knee. It is important to focus on the movement in order to truly access the oblique muscles.

SINGLE-LEG STRETCH WITH TWIST (FIGURE 18.10)*

Starting position

a) Lie on your back, knees bent at a table top position.

b) Raise your head and shoulders off the mat and place both hands behind your head with the elbows wide.

c) Extend the left leg straight at a 45-degree angle to the floor.

d) Rotate your left shoulder toward your bent right knee.

e) Maintain the lifted position throughout the entire exercise.

Action

a) Using quick breaths, alternate the legs and the direction of the torso rotation without changing the height of the torso off the mat.

b)   Exhale as the knee comes into the chest, deepen the abdominal contraction, and stabilize the torso.

c)   Inhale as you are in the transition phase of switching the leg position and rotating the chest to the other side.

d)   Once you have completed the exercise, exhale while lowering the torso and head back to the mat and bring the knees into the chest.

Repetitions

8–12 sets. A set is one cycle of the legs coming into the chest.

Quick self checks

This is essentially a combination of the *single-leg stretch* and the *oblique reach* exercises. This exercise is another common abdominal muscle exercise performed at gyms and in dance classes. Typically this exercise is done quickly and with momentum swinging the body down to the floor and then pulling the elbow across to the knee. To find the full benefit of this exercise, slow down the tempo and avoid the use of momentum. As the legs switch, use the same energy or stretch that usually accompanies a *fondu* movement. You can also think of having a pile of cotton balls under your shoulder blades and that you are trying not to fall back and squash them.

Figure 18.10 Single leg stretch with twist

18.C.2 Flexibility exercise

Stretching the muscles of trunk rotation helps to increase rotational capacity and to relieve tension that might affect the muscles' efficiency to react in movement.

Oblique muscle stretch (Figure 18.11)

Starting position

    a)   Sitting on a mat or floor. Legs either extended or crossed, as comfortable.

    b)   Place the left hand on the floor by your side to stabilize.

Action

    a)   Inhale and raise your right arm in a sideways arc to the side of the head.

    b)   Exhale and continue the arc into a side-bend to the left.

Variation

Once in the side-bent position, rotate the torso so that the upper shoulder moves backward and the lower shoulder forward.

Repetitions

Hold for 30 seconds. Recover to the start position and repeat to the other side.

Quick self checks

Be sure not to elevate the shoulder of the raised arm. Check that your spine is in neutral alignment and that you are not "popping" the rib cage forward. Ensure that both sitting bones remain in contact with the floor, resisting the temptation to tilt the pelvis to the side.

Figure 18.11 Oblique muscle stretch

18.D Trunk side-bending

18.D.1 Strength exercises

Strengthening the muscles of trunk side bending is important for stability in off-balance positions. These muscles also provide stability in upper body, weight-bearing positions and help to provide support for arm movements and lifts.

SIDE LIFTS (FIGURE 18.12)*

Starting position

    a)   Lie on your left side with legs extended and head resting on the extended left arm.

    b)   Peak down toward your feet and make sure you can just see your toes.

    c)   Stack your feet, pelvis, ribs, and shoulders.

    d)   Your right hand can be used as a support in front of the body or, as a challenge, can reach along the side of the body toward the feet.

Action

    a)   Inhale and lift both legs off the floor while keeping the inner thighs together.

    b)   Exhale as you lower the legs back to the floor.

Variation

    a)   On the inhale as you lift both legs off the floor, reach the bottom arm up off the floor along with the torso. This creates an elongated crescent shape.

    b)   Exhale as you lower the legs, arm, and torso back to the floor.

Repetitions

    8–10 repetitions. Repeat on the other side.

Figure 18.12 Side lifts

Quick self checks

With all side work, the key is to truly stay in lateral flexion. If you over-work your back extensors you will fall forward and feel the work in the lower back. If you overwork your hip flexors and abdominal muscles, the tendency is to fall backward and not feel the work in the waist. This is not a large movement. Be minimal and focus on core support throughout.

SIDE PLANK (FIGURE 18.13)

Starting position

a) Begin on your side, supported on one elbow with hips, knees, and feet stacked.

b) Stabilize the shoulder joint and girdle and engage the abdominal wall.

Action

Lift the body to a side plank position—feet, pelvis, torso and head aligned. Hold the side plank position for 30 seconds to a minute maintaining alignment through the entire spine.

Repetitions

Alternate sides and complete 1–3 repetitions. As the work becomes easier, you can increase the time of each repetition.

Figure 18.13 Side plank

Quick self checks

Stabilizing the shoulder and keeping the body aligned from head to toe is the primary focus. Engage the abdominal wall, narrowing the waist to support the spine. Careful attention to the front of the supporting shoulder joint is important to avoid risk of a shoulder injury. In addition, if your knees feel strained you can bend the bottom knee to alleviate any pain.

18.D.2 Flexibility exercise

While these side-bending exercises recruit many of the core stabilizing muscles (stretches for which have already been shown), they also activate the quadratus lumborum *muscle. The following exercise should be done in conjunction with the oblique muscle stretches shown on page 217.*

QUADRATUS LUMBORUM STRETCH (FIGURE 18.14)

Starting position

a) Stand with the feet in a parallel second, slightly wider than hip-width apart.

b) Bend the knees, tuck the pelvis under, and curve the spine as in the cat position on page 212 (Figure 18.8a).

Action

a) Exhale as you deepen the *plié*, and draw the right arm diagonally across the body until it is above the left shoulder.

b) Deepen the tuck of the pelvis to focus the stretch between the crest of the *ilium* and the lowest (twelfth) rib.

Variation

Begin in a seated position and execute as above (without using the *plié*). Be sure to still tuck the pelvis.

Repetitions

Hold for 30 seconds breathing naturally. Repeat to the other side.

Quick self checks

Be sure not to tense the shoulders as the arms elevate. Some dancers may feel this stretch focused into the rib cage. If so, deepen the pelvic tuck and increase the curve of the spine. If the intercostal muscles between the ribs are tight, these may need to soften before the stretch is felt lower down into the *quadratus lumborum*. This stretch will target both these muscle groups.

Figure 18.14 Quadratus lumborum stretch

18.E The neck

The dancer's neck can be vulnerable to injury for a variety of reasons. In modern, jazz, and commercial dance techniques, the neck can be put through rapid changes of position, and in styles such as hip hop it can also be playing a weight-bearing role. In classical ballet technique, the quest for an elongated neck line can lead to a loss of the natural cervical lordosis (curve)—a loss that can place the underlying structures at risk. Typically, there is a tendency for over-dominance of the external neck musculature (the sternocleidomastoid *and the* scalene *muscle group at the*

front and sides, and the levator scapulae *and* trapezius *muscle group at the back).
It is also key to note that many issues from the neck may arise from a weakness
in the core trunk-stabilizing muscles. In the absence of dynamic strength here, the
neck muscles will need to over-recruit in order to stabilize the weight of the skull,
which can be up to twelve pounds in the average person. Therefore, any neck issues
need to be looked at in the context of the potential predisposing factors and com-
parative strength of the core trunk musculature. Also key is the use of electronic
devices, such as phones and laptops, that cause us to round the shoulders and
hyperextend the neck. You may need to look outside your dance training to view
the cause of any neck symptoms.*

18.E.1 Strength exercises

*The deep neck muscles provide core control for the neck and can become weak if
the external muscles have become dominant. These exercises involve very subtle
movements. Any large movements will necessarily recruit the external muscles
and negate the purpose of the exercise.*

STRENGTHEN THE DEEP NECK FLEXOR MUSCLES (FIGURE 18.15)

Starting position

    a)   Lying face up on a floor mat or stable surface with the knees bent.

    b)   Ensure that the spine is in neutral (Figure 18.15a). Place a small
         towel under the head if needed.

Action

    a)   First, lift the whole head off the floor and notice the muscles at the
         front of the neck engaging. These are NOT the muscles you will
         be targeting.

    b)   Now gently nod your head downward without lifting it off the
         floor, as if to look at your toes. Feel the deeper muscles working
         (Figure 18.15b).

Variation

Stand with your back and head against a wall, feet 3 inches from the wall.
Repeat the same nodding movement with the head looking down toward

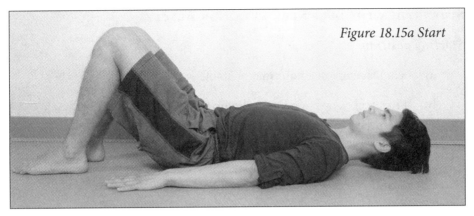

Figure 18.15a Start

Figure 18.15b End

Figure 18.15 Strengthen deep neck flexors

your toes. Keep the head in contact with the wall. This contextualizes the exercise into a more dance-specific position.

Repetitions

Hold the position for 5 seconds. Rest, then repeat 5 times.

Quick self checks

If at any time you feel the external neck muscles engaging (as they did when you first lifted the head off the towel), stop the exercise. Make sure you are not squeezing the neck downward—just activating the deep flexor muscles. You should be aware of the deep neck flexor muscles (*longus capitis* and *longus colli*) that lie behind the *sternocleidomastoid* and *scalene muscles*. Your airway should still be open. If it is not, you are pushing too far.

STRENGTHEN THE DEEP NECK EXTENSOR MUSCLES

Starting position

a) Lying face up on a floor mat or stable surface with the knees bent.

b) If the neck is not in neutral alignment, use a small towel or book under the head.

Action

Exhale and push the head back into the floor, towel, or book.

Repetitions

Hold for 5 seconds. Rest, then repeat 5 times.

Quick self checks

Be sure that you are not recruiting the outer shoulder muscles (*trapezius* and *levator scapulae*). Do not crunch the airway—your breath should be easy and free. Make sure you are initiating from a neutral spinal position before initiating the neck movement. You should be aware of the deep extensor muscles (*semispinalis*, *splenius*, and *longus capitis* and *cervicis* groups). You should not feel the outer *trapezius* or *levator scapulae* doing the work. If you do, stop the exercise and seek the advice of a dance medicine professional.

18.E.2 Flexibility exercises

These stretches target both the deep and superficial muscles. Stretches for the deep neck flexors have not been included as they require the neck to be placed in a vulnerable position. Any persistent problems should be examined by a medical professional.

STRETCH FOR THE DEEP NECK EXTENSORS (FIGURE 18.16)

Starting position

a) Lying face up on a floor mat or stable surface with the knees bent.

b) Lace fingers behind the base of the skull, elbows wide.

Action

a) Allowing the weight of the head to fall into the hands, exhale and use the arms to tilt the head forward as if looking at the toes.

b) Bring the elbows together as you tilt, being careful not to tense the shoulders.

Variation

Repeat the above motion in a standing or sitting position.

Repetitions

Hold the stretch for 30 seconds. Rest and repeat 3 times.

Quick self checks

Be sure that you are not actively lifting the head off the table. The neck muscles should be completely relaxed with the effort being produced by the arm muscles. Check that you are not tensing the shoulders up toward the neck. Use the out-breath to help to relax the neck. The airway should remain open and clear. You should feel the neck muscles on either side of the spine stretching in this exercise. Depending on where you hold your tension, this may also be felt down into the thoracic spine. You should not feel any tension at the front of the neck or any reduction in your capacity for breathing.

Figure 18.16 Stretch for deep neck extensors

STRETCH THE LATERAL NECK FLEXOR MUSCLES (FIGURE 18.17)

Starting position

    a)   Standing or sitting in a chair.

    b)   Laterally tilt your right ear toward your right shoulder.

    c)   Place your right hand over the left side of the head.

    d)   Have your left arm extended downward by your left side.

Action

    a)   Use gentle over-pressure with the right hand to draw the right ear toward the right shoulder.

    b)   At the same time, walk the fingers of your left hand down the side of your right leg in opposition to the head movement.

Figure 18.17 Stretch for lateral neck flexor muscles

Variation

When sitting, the lower arm can be dropped off the side of the chair toward the ground, or can hold on to the chair seat to facilitate the opposing movement of the neck stretch. This can also be performed lying down on a mat, walking the fingers down the side of the leg toward the feet.

Repetitions

Hold the stretch for 30 seconds. Rest and repeat to the other side.

Quick self checks

Be sure not to "crank" the head over to one side; use only gentle over-pressure. Pay attention to the shoulder of the arm providing the pressure—do not allow it to rise up in an effort to create more force. Feel the shoulder blade on the other side of the direction of the stretch drawing down into the back. Keep the chin in a neutral position, face forward: do not allow it to rotate toward the armpit. If executed correctly, you should feel a stretch in the *scalene* muscle group on the side of the neck. You may additionally feel a stretch into some of the fibers of the *upper trapezius* muscle.

STRETCH FOR THE *UPPER TRAPEZIUS* AND *LEVATOR SCAPULAE* MUSCLES (FIGURE 18.18)

Starting position

a)   Standing or sitting in a chair.

b)   Turn your head a quarter turn to the right.

c)   Place your right hand over the crown of the head to the back of the skull.

d)   Extend your left arm downward by your left side.

Action

a)   Use gentle over-pressure with the right hand to draw the chin toward the right armpit.

b)   At the same time, walk the fingers of your left hand down the side of your left leg in opposition to the head movement.

Variation

When sitting, the lower arm can be dropped off the side of the chair toward the ground, or can hold on to the chair seat to facilitate the opposing movement of the neck stretch. This can also be performed lying down on a mat, walking the fingers down the side of the leg toward the feet.

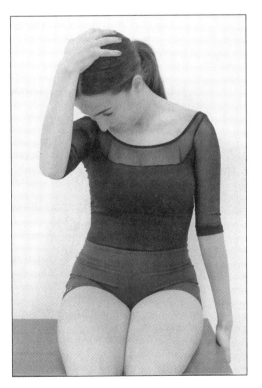

Figure 18.18 Stretch for upper trapezius and levator scapulae

Repetitions

Hold the stretch for 30 seconds. Rest, and repeat to the other side.

Quick self checks

Be sure not to "crank" the head down toward the armpit; use only gentle over-pressure. Pay attention to the shoulder of the arm providing the pressure: do not allow it to rise up in an effort to create more force. Feel the shoulder blade on the other side of the direction of the stretch drawing down into the back. If executed correctly, you should feel a stretch in the *levator scapulae* and *upper trapezius* muscles at the back of the neck.

ANTERIOR FASCIA AND PLATYSMA STRETCH (FIGURE 18.19)

Starting position

a) Standing or sitting in a chair.

b) Place palm of the left hand on the right chest just below the collar bone, fingers pointing toward the armpit.

c) Gently press the surface tissue down toward the underlying rib cage and away toward the armpit.

Action

a) Holding the pressure with the left hand, exhale and gently rotate the neck in the opposite direction (left).

b) Gently raise the chin up toward the ceiling, keeping the jaw relaxed.

c) To deepen the stretch, close the lower jaw so the teeth meet.

Variation

This exercise can also be performed lying down with the knees bent to 90 degrees. The lying position is optimal as the underlying muscles will be active in a sitting or standing position.

Repetitions

Hold the stretch for 30 seconds. Rest, then repeat to the other side.

Quick self checks

Do not use too much pressure with the hand on
the chest—just enough to trap the superficial
layer of fascia between your palm and the underlying bone. Avoid hyperextending the neck when
raising the chin. Use the jaw position rather than
the neck to deepen the stretch. Keep breathing normally throughout the stretch. As this is
a stretch for the fascia, it will be felt across the
area of several muscle groups. A general stretching sensation should be apparent from the point
of contact with the hand on the chest up to the
jawline.

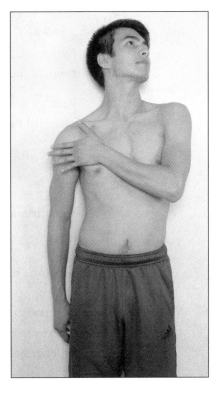

*Figure 18.19 Anterior fascia
and platysma stretch*

18.F Spinal articulation

*These exercises facilitate segmental movement and control of the spine. As dancers,
we require the spine to be both flexible and dynamically stable. These exercises
help with both mobility and control.*

BRIDGING (FIGURE 18.20)*

Starting position

a) Start lying on your back with the knees bent and feet flat on the
    floor.

b) Check that the placement of your feet is directly opposite your
    ischial tuberosities.

c) In order to maintain the knee alignment while bridging, you can
    place a small playground ball or foam pad in between the knees to
    align the knees with the hips and feet.

d) Arms are resting palms down on the floor by your side.

Action

a)   Exhale, tuck your pelvis and then roll the spine one vertebra at a time off the floor.

b)   Reach a bridge position where the shoulders, ribs, hips, and knees are all in one line.

c)   Inhale on the way back down to the starting position.

Repetitions

8–10 repetitions.

Quick self checks

Pelvic lifts or bridging are geared toward activating the gluteal muscles and finding spinal articulation. However, many dancers do not reach a final neutral position, typically finishing in an anterior pelvic tilt that encourages hyperextension of the lower back. Work to keep your pubic bone higher than your hip bones while focusing on the lengthening in the lower back.

Figure 18.20 Bridging

Roll ups*

Starting position

a) Start lying on your back with the legs extended and arms overhead.

b) Legs are parallel, inner thighs touching; feet are flexed.

c) When taking the arms overhead, only go as far as you can while maintaining a neutral spine.

Action

a) Inhale and bring your arms from overhead down toward your side as you roll your head and chest off the floor.

b) Exhale as you hit the transition from the abdominal muscles to the hip flexors to bring your body to a sitting position.

c) Inhale as you stretch over your legs.

a) Exhale and roll your body back down to the floor one vertebra at a time.

b) End with the arms overhead ready for the next repetition.

Repetitions

8–10 repetitions.

Quick self checks

The focus should be on articulating the spine and finding length between each segment. If you find it difficult to make a smooth transition either to sitting or back down to the floor, hold on to an elastic band wrapped around the feet to provide support allowing you to work on the control. Over time you will find this exercise becomes easier.

Part V

The SHOULDER and ARM

The arms are very important in dance movement. They contribute to the success of many turns, falls, leaps, and lifts. The arms also communicate feeling as well as adding to the quality and style of movement. Even if the rest of the body is moving well, the movement can appear stiff and awkward if the arms are not positioned optimally and moving gracefully or dynamically.

The positions of the elbow and wrist are particularly crucial in producing a fluid, aesthetically pleasing line. While audiences, choreographers, or teachers may forgive a structurally unaesthetic foot, a misplaced arm line will draw the eye and disrupt the flow of expression, and will always be noticed.

In most technique classes, much time is spent exercising the lower limbs and, to a lesser extent, the torso. However, comparatively little time is spent training the upper limbs. For some dancers, the arm exercises performed in class are sufficient to develop strength and control, but others find that class work is not sufficient to correct issues with arm placement. These dancers may struggle with issues such as drooping wrists, unsupported elbows, and tense shoulders. Specific conditioning exercises for the shoulders and arms can help these dancers.

Partnering requires a great deal of strength and flexibility in the arms, shoulders, and upper torso of both men and women. The average dance technique class, with its emphasis on the legs and torso, does not adequately prepare a dancer for partnering. In Chapters 20 and 21, specific exercises are recommended to help dancers prepare for partnering work.

19
STRUCTURAL ANATOMY

THE SHOULDER CAN BE DIVIDED INTO TWO PARTS, the shoulder joint and the shoulder girdle. The one bone that both parts have in common is the *scapula*, or the shoulder blade (Figure 19.1).

The right *scapula* forms part of the shoulder joint and shoulder girdle on the right side of the body. The left *scapula* forms part of the shoulder joint and the shoulder girdle on the left side of the body.

The plural form of the word *scapula* is *scapulae*. This term is used whenever reference is made to both the right *scapula* and the left *scapula*. For example, if a dancer pinches her shoulder blades together, it can be said she is pinching her *scapulae*.

The *scapula* is a triangular bone lying on top of the ribs at the back of the torso. It has two projections, found near the shoulder and called the *acromion process* and the *coracoid process*. The former is found at the most lateral (side) aspect, and the latter projects forward into the chest area. The *scapula* also has a shallow cup or dish formation called the *glenoid fossa*. These features allow the shoulder blade to articulate with other bones in the shoulder.

The shoulder joint is comprised of the *scapula* and the *humerus* or upper arm bone (Figure 19.1). The round head of the *humerus* fits into the *glenoid fossa* of the *scapula*. The articulation is called the *glenohumeral joint*. The shallow nature of the *glenoid fossa* allows for the great range of movement we have available at this joint.

The shoulder girdle is comprised of the *scapula*, the *clavicle* (collar bone), and the *sternum* (breast bone; Figure 19.1). The acromion, the lateral projection of the *scapula*, articulates with the *clavicle*. This articulation is called the

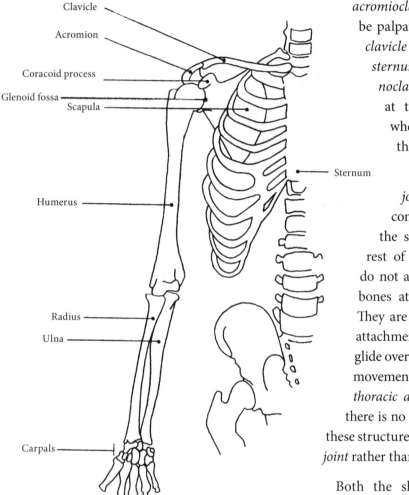

Clavicle
Acromion
Coracoid process
Glenoid fossa
Scapula
Humerus
Radius
Ulna
Carpals
Sternum

Figure 19.1 Anterior view of right shoulder girdle and arm bones

acromioclavicular joint, and can be palpated at the shoulder. The *clavicle* also articulates with the *sternum;* this is called the *sternoclavicular joint.* It is located at the base of the throat where the rounded ends of the *clavicles* can be felt.

The *sternoclavicular joint* is the only joint that connects the three bones in the shoulder girdle with the rest of the body. The *scapulae* do not articulate with any other bones at the back of the body. They are held in place by muscle attachments alone. The *scapulae* glide over the posterior ribs during movement, forming the *scapulothoracic articulation.* However, as there is no joint capsule connecting these structures it is known as a *pseudojoint* rather than a *true joint.*

Both the shoulder joint and the shoulder girdle are stabilized by ligaments and muscles. A description of the most important muscle groups is included in the material that follows.

Movements of the shoulder joint

Movements at the *glenohumeral joint* include the following: *flexion* (from resting at the side, the arms move in a forward, upward direction until they reach fifth position); *hyperflexion* (the arms move from fifth position in a backward direction behind the head); *extension* (return from flexion); *hyperextension* (from resting at the side, the arms move in a backward, upward direction); *abduction* (from resting at the side, the arms move through second position and up to fifth position); *adduction* (return from abduction); *outward rotation* and *inward rotation* of the upper arm; *horizontal adduction* (the arms move from second position toward the front of the body); *horizontal abduction* (return from horizontal adduction); and *circumduction* (full circle of the arms).

Movements of the shoulder girdle

Some of these movements include *elevation* of the *scapulae* (shrugging the shoulders); *depression* (return from elevation); *abduction* (pulling the *scapulae* away from the midline of the back, as when stretching the arms forward); and *adduction* (pulling the *scapulae* toward the midline of the back, as when "pinching" the shoulder blades together). The *scapulae* will also rotate upward to facilitate abduction of the arm and rotate downward on the return to neutral. Other movements of the *scapulae* are not included in this discussion.

Interaction of the shoulder joint and the shoulder girdle

The movements of the shoulder joint and the shoulder girdle are closely interwoven. Recall, from the discussion of anatomy, that the head of the *humerus* articulates with the *glenoid fossa* of the *scapula*. Whenever the arm moves, the *scapula* on that side of the body also moves. This movement of the *scapula* positions the *glenoid fossa* in such a way that the *humerus* can have full range of movement. If the *scapula* was unable to move, the *humerus* would be greatly limited in its range of motion.

Movements of the shoulder joint involve the interaction of 18 different muscles. Some of these muscles position the *scapula* while others move the *humerus*. Studying these muscles need not be overwhelming if you first identify the muscles that control the position of the *scapula*. These muscles are called the shoulder girdle muscles.

Once you understand the shoulder girdle muscles, you will be ready to study the movements of the shoulder joint. For each movement of the shoulder joint, the muscles that move the *humerus* will be presented first. Then the muscles that position the *scapula* will be identified.

Table 19.1 Muscle actions of the scapula

Movement of the Scapula	Dancer Terminology	Muscles
Depression	Pulling shoulders down	Subclavius Lower Trapezius
Elevation	Shoulder tension or hiking	Levator Scapulae Rhomboid Major & Minor Upper Trapezius
Adduction (retraction)	Pinching the shoulder blades	Levator Scapulae Rhomboid Major & Minor Trapezius (all sections)
Abduction (protraction)	Round shoulders	Serratus Anterior Pectoralis Minor
Upward rotation	When lifting the arms to the side, the scapulae will follow by rotating upward	Middle Trapezius Lower Trapezius Serratus Anterior
Downward rotation	When lowering the arms, the scapulae will rotate downward	Rhomboid Major Rhomboid Minor Pectoralis Minor

Shoulder girdle muscles

There are seven muscles that change the position of the *scapula* (Figures 19.2 and 19.3). These include the *subclavius* and *pectoralis minor* on the anterior aspect of the shoulder girdle; the *serratus anterior* on the lateral aspect of the shoulder girdle; and the *levator scapulae, rhomboids major* and *minor*, and the *trapezius* on the posterior aspect of the shoulder girdle.

The *subclavius* is a small muscle band. It is attached at one end to the cartilage of the first rib, and the other end is attached to the *clavicle* (Figure 19.2). It is active in depressing the *scapula*.

The *pectoralis minor* is attached to the anterior surface of the third through fifth ribs and to the *coracoid process* of the *scapula* (Figure 19.2). It draws the *scapula* forward and downward (as in the rounded-shoulder position).

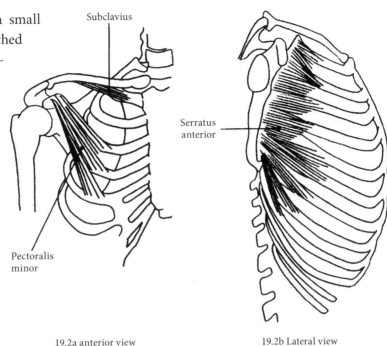

Subclavius

Serratus anterior

Pectoralis minor

19.2a anterior view

19.2b Lateral view

Figure 19.2 Anterior and lateral views of shoulder girdle muscles

The *serratus anterior* is attached at one end to the lateral surface of the first eight or nine ribs. At the other end it is attached to the anterior surface of the *scapula* (Figure 19.2). This muscle abducts the *scapula* and also pulls it forward.

The *levator scapulae* is attached on one end to the upper four cervical vertebrae. At the other end it is attached to the *scapula* (Figure 19.3). It is responsible for elevating the *scapula* and assists in adduction.

The *rhomboid major* and *rhomboid minor* muscles form a wide band that is attached to the last cervical and the first five thoracic vertebrae. The other end of this muscle band is attached to the *scapula* (Figure 19.3). These muscles adduct the *scapulae* as well as elevate them.

The *trapezius* is attached to the base of the skull, the posterior ligaments of the cervical spine, as well as to the seventh cervical vertebra and all the thoracic vertebrae (Figure 19.3). The other end of this large muscle is attached to the back of the *scapula*, the *acromion process*, and the *clavicle*. It is convenient

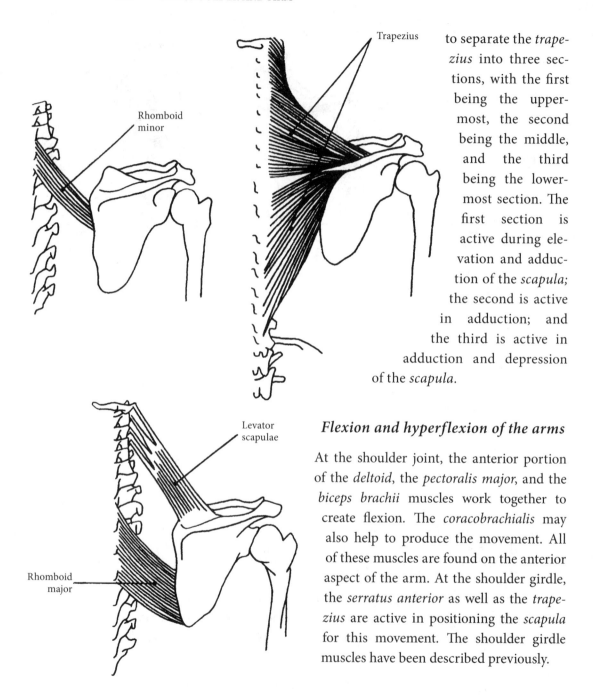

to separate the *trapezius* into three sections, with the first being the uppermost, the second being the middle, and the third being the lowermost section. The first section is active during elevation and adduction of the *scapula*; the second is active in adduction; and the third is active in adduction and depression of the *scapula*.

Flexion and hyperflexion of the arms

At the shoulder joint, the anterior portion of the *deltoid*, the *pectoralis major*, and the *biceps brachii* muscles work together to create flexion. The *coracobrachialis* may also help to produce the movement. All of these muscles are found on the anterior aspect of the arm. At the shoulder girdle, the *serratus anterior* as well as the *trapezius* are active in positioning the *scapula* for this movement. The shoulder girdle muscles have been described previously.

Figure 19.3 Posterior view of shoulder girdle muscles

Table 19.2 Muscle actions of the shoulder joint

Movement of the Shoulder Joint	Dancer Terminology	Muscles
Flexion	Raising the arm to the front (devant)	Anterior Deltoid Pectoralis Major Biceps Coracobrachialis
Extension	Extending the arms behind the body	Latissimus Dorsi Teres Major Posterior Deltoid Pectoralis Major (some fibers extend the flexed arm)
Abduction	Raising the arm sideways to second	Deltoid Supraspinatus
Adduction	Returning the arm sideways from second	Latissimus Dorsi Pectoralis Major Teres Major Teres Minor (assists weakly) Posterior Deltoid (may assist)
Internal rotation	Inverted arm line	Subscapularis Latissimus Dorsi Pectoralis Major Anterior Deltoid
External rotation	Outwardly rotating arms	Infraspinatus Teres Minor

The *deltoid* is a muscle that covers the shoulder joint like a cap sleeve. It is attached to the *clavicle*, the *acromion*, and the back of the *scapula* at one end (Figure 19.4). On the other end it is attached to the lateral aspect of the *humerus*. This muscle can be palpated at the shoulder and upper arm. The anterior muscle

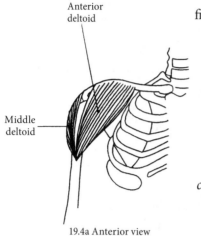

19.4a Anterior view

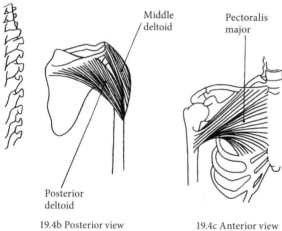

19.4b Posterior view   19.4c Anterior view

Figure 19.4 Anterior and posterior views
of shoulder muscles

fibers are active in all forward movements of the arm as well as the inward rotation of the arm. The posterior fibers can produce extension with outward rotation. The entire muscle functions to produce abduction. This muscle is commonly used in any lifting movement. Indeed, any movement of the *humerus* will generally involve some part of the *deltoid* muscle.

The *pectoralis major* is attached at one end to the *clavicle*, the *sternum*, and the anterior cartilage of the upper ribs. Its attachment at the other end is to the *humerus* (Figure 19.4). The *pectoralis major* can easily be palpated as the large muscle of the chest region. When different portions of the *pectoralis major* contract, a variety of movements are produced. These include flexion, adduction, horizontal adduction, and inward rotation of the *humerus*, and extension against resistance. This muscle is important in partnering, especially during lifts.

The *biceps brachii* is a two-joint muscle crossing both the shoulder joint and the elbow joint (Figure 19.5). The *biceps brachii* has two heads: one is attached to the *coracoid process* of the *scapula*, and the other to the *glenoid fossa* of the *scapula*. At the other end, the muscle is attached to the lower arm. Although its main action is at the elbow, it also flexes and abducts the shoulder joint against resistance when the elbow is straight. It may also be active in horizontal adduction. This muscle can easily be palpated on the anterior aspect of the upper arm.

The *coracobrachialis* is a small muscle that is found on the anterior aspect of the arm. It is attached to the *coracoid process* of the *scapula* at one end and to the medial aspect of the *humerus* at the other end (Figure 19.5). The *coracobrachialis* flexes and adducts the *humerus* as well as moving the arm through horizontal adduction.

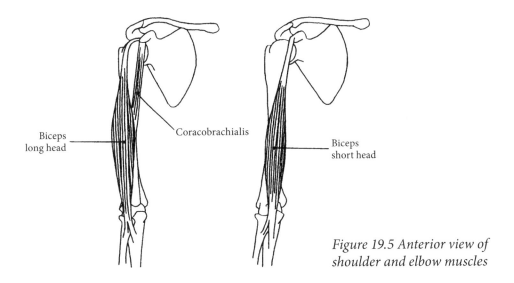

Figure 19.5 Anterior view of shoulder and elbow muscles

Find It

Place the fingers of your left hand horizontally across to the far side of your right chest, just below the collar bone.

Feel It

Raise your right arm to the front.

Notice the muscles popping up under your fingers. These are the *pectoralis major* on top, and the tendons of the *biceps brachii* and *coracobrachialis* beneath.

Dance It

Perform a port de bras from *bras bas* to fifth position.

Extension of the arms

Muscles responsible for arm extension include portions of the *pectoralis major* (described previously), the *latissimus dorsi*, the *teres major*, and the posterior *deltoid* (described previously). The long head of the *triceps* may also be involved. At the shoulder girdle the *pectoralis minor*, the *subclavius*, the *rhomboids*, and the *trapezius* are active in positioning the *scapula* for this movement. These shoulder girdle muscles have been previously described.

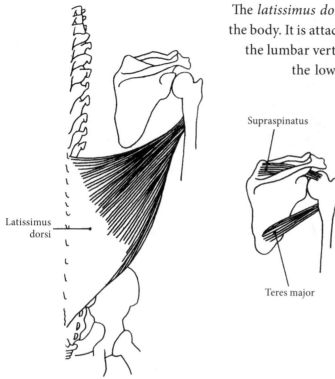

The *latissimus dorsi* is located on the posterior aspect of the body. It is attached at one end to the *sacrum*, the *ilium*, the lumbar vertebrae, the lower thoracic vertebrae, and the lower ribs (Figure 19.6). At the other end, it is attached to the anterior aspect of the *humerus*, with an additional attachment to the inferior angle of the *scapula* (not shown). This muscle covers the lower and middle portions of the back. It can be palpated on the lateral aspect of the torso below the armpit. Contraction of the *latissimus dorsi* results in extension and adduction of the arm against resistance. It also produces inward rotation of the arm.

Figure 19.6 Posterior view of shoulder joint muscles

The *teres major* is a muscle also located on the posterior aspect of the body. It is attached at one end to the *scapula* and at the other end to the anterior aspect of the *humerus* (Figure 19.6). It functions to extend and adduct the arm. It can also rotate the *humerus* inward. Because this muscle has similar functions as the *latissimus dorsi*, it is sometimes referred to as the *latissimus dorsi*'s "little helper."

The *triceps brachii* muscle (Figure 19.7), found on the posterior aspect of the arm, has three heads. The long head is a two-joint muscle that crosses both the shoulder joint and the elbow joint. The long head is attached to the *scapula* at one end and to the fascia (connective tissue) of the forearm at the other end. This fascia connects it to the *ulna*, one of the bones in the lower arm. The lateral and medial heads originate on the *humerus* and insert on the fascia and *ulna*. The *triceps brachii* can easily be palpated on the posterior aspect of the upper arm. Although its primary function is to extend the elbow, the long head assists in adduction, extension, and hyperextension of the shoulder joint.

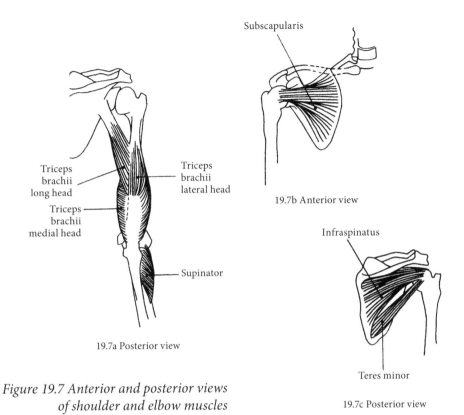

Triceps
brachii
long head

Triceps
brachii
lateral head

Triceps
brachii
medial head

Supinator

19.7a Posterior view

Subscapularis

19.7b Anterior view

Infraspinatus

Teres minor

19.7c Posterior view

*Figure 19.7 Anterior and posterior views
of shoulder and elbow muscles*

Find It

Stand with your right arm by your side, palm forward, and the back of
the hand against a firm surface, such as a pillar, door jamb, or heavy
piece of furniture.

Pass your left hand under your right arm-pit and place the fingers
onto the soft-tissue crease between the arm and the back of the shoulder.

Feel It

Press the back of your right hand, with the elbow straight, into the firm
surface.

Notice the muscles popping up under your fingers. These are the
posterior deltoid, *teres major*, and *latissumus dorsi*.

Dance It

Perform a reverse *port de bras* from *bras bas* to fifth position.

Hyperextension of the arms

At the shoulder joint, the *posterior deltoid*, the *latissimus dorsi*, and the *teres major* produce hyperextension of the arms. At the shoulder girdle, the *pectoralis minor* causes an adjustment in the position of the *scapula*. All these muscles were previously described.

Abduction of the arms

At the shoulder joint, the *deltoid* and the *supraspinatus* abduct the *humerus*. At the shoulder girdle, the *serratus anterior* and the first and third portions of the *trapezius* cause a change in the position of the *scapula*. With the exception of the *supraspinatus*, all these muscles have been described.

The *supraspinatus* is a small muscle attached to the top of the *scapula* and at the other end to the top of the *humerus* (Figure 19.6). Although its main action is to stabilize the head of the *humerus* in the *glenoid fossa* so that the *deltoid* can abduct, it also assists in flexion and horizontal abduction.

Find It
Place the fingers of your right hand across the body onto the cap of muscle at the top of the left arm—where the sleeves of a T-shirt would sit.

Feel It
Lift the left arm to the side.

Notice the muscle popping up under your fingers. This is the *deltoid* muscle.

Dance It
Lift your arm sideways from *bras bas* to fifth position.

Adduction of the arms

When arm adduction is performed against resistance, the *latissimus dorsi, teres major, pectoralis major* and possibly the *posterior deltoid* function to produce the movement. At the shoulder girdle the *rhomboids, pectoralis minor,* and *levator scapulae* are active in positioning the *scapula*. All these muscles have been described.

Find It

Sit on a chair with your right arm hanging down beside the seat. Cup your left hand under your right armpit leaving the thumb just below the collar bone at the front and the finger pads in the soft-tissue crease between the arm and the shoulder at the back.

Feel It

Press your right arm inward against the resistance of the chair seat.

Notice the muscles popping up under your fingers. These are the *pectoralis major* at the front and the *posterior deltoid, teres major,* and *latissimus dorsi* at the back.

Dance It

Return the arm sideways from fifth position to *bras bas*.

Inward rotation of the arms

At the shoulder joint, the muscles responsible for inward rotation of the *humerus* are the *subscapularis*, the *latissimus dorsi*, the *anterior deltoid*, and the *pectoralis major*. At the shoulder girdle the *serratus anterior* and the *pectoralis minor* are the primary muscles acting to position the *scapula*. With the exception of the *subscapularis*, these muscles were all described above.

The *subscapularis* is attached at one end to a large area of the anterior surface of the *scapula*. At the other end it is attached to the anterior aspect of the *humerus* (Figure 19.7). The *subscapularis* stabilizes the *glenohumeral joint*. Its primary action is to produce inward rotation of the upper arm. This muscle is very difficult to palpate due to its position on the undersurface of the *scapula*.

Outward rotation of the arms

At the shoulder joint, the *infraspinatus* and the *teres minor* produce outward rotation of the *humerus*. At the shoulder girdle, the *rhomboids* and the *trapezius* are active in positioning the *scapula*. These shoulder girdle muscles have been described previously.

The *infraspinatus* and *teres minor* are muscles located on the posterior aspect of the body, attached to the *scapula*. At the other end they are attached to the *humerus* (Figure 19.7). They are active during outward rotation of the *humerus* and are also important in stabilizing the joint.

Find It

Keep your left arm by your side, palm facing backward, and reach across under the arm-pit with your right hand to place the fingers on the soft-tissue crease between the arm and the back of the shoulder.

Feel It

Rotate the whole left arm from the shoulder so that the palm faces forward.

Notice the muscles popping up under your fingers. These are the *infraspinatus* and *teres minor*.

Dance It

Move the arms from first position to the *demi-bras* or *presenté* position.

Horizontal abduction of the arms

At the shoulder joint, the *posterior deltoid*, the *infraspinatus*, the *teres minor*, and the long head of the *triceps* are active in horizontal abduction of the arms. At the shoulder girdle, the *rhomboids* and the *trapezius* muscles position the *scapula*. All of these muscles were described previously.

Horizontal adduction of the arms

At the shoulder joint, the *pectoralis major*, the *anterior deltoid*, and *coracobrachialis* are the chief muscles producing horizontal adduction of the arms. At the shoulder girdle, the *serratus anterior* and *pectoralis minor* are active in positioning the *scapula*. All of these muscles have previously been described.

Structure of the elbow joint

The elbow actually contains two joints. The first consists of the articulation of the *humerus* with the two forearm bones, the *ulna* and *radius*. The second consists of the articulation of the *ulna* with the *radius*. For our purposes we will use the term *elbow joint* to refer to both of these (Figure 19.1).

Movements of the elbow joint

Movements of the elbow are usually described from a starting position in which the palm of the hand is facing forward. These movements include *flexion* (moving the hand toward the shoulder), and *extension* (return from flexion). With the elbows bent to 90 degrees we can inwardly rotate the forearm (palms facing downward) known as *pronation*, and outwardly rotate the forearm (palms facing upward) known as *supination*.

Table 19.3 Muscle actions of the elbow

Movement of the Elbow	Dancer Terminology	Muscles
Flexion	Bending at the elbow	Biceps Brachii Brachialis Brachioradialis (mid-pronation flexion)
Extension	Straightening the elbow	Triceps Brachii Anconeus
Inward rotation of the forearm (pronation)	Turning palms downward	Pronator Teres Pronator Quadratus
Outward rotation of the forearm (supination)	Turning palms upward from pronation	Supinator Biceps Brachii

Elbow flexion

The chief muscles that produce elbow flexion are the *biceps brachii* (described previously), the *brachialis*, and the *brachioradialis*.

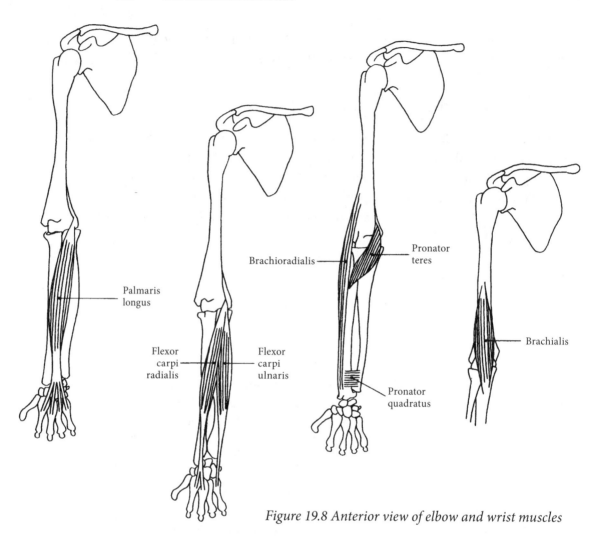

Palmaris
longus

Brachioradialis

Pronator
teres

Flexor
carpi
radialis

Flexor
carpi
ulnaris

Pronator
quadratus

Brachialis

Figure 19.8 Anterior view of elbow and wrist muscles

The *brachialis* is attached to the anterior aspect of the *humerus* at one end and at the other end, to the anterior aspect of the *ulna* (Figure 19.8). Since this muscle is located beneath the *biceps brachii*, it is difficult to palpate, but contributes to much of the bulk of the *biceps brachii*.

The *brachioradialis* is attached at one end to the lateral aspect of the *humerus* and at the other end, to the lateral aspect of the *radius* (Figure 19.8). It can be felt by placing your hand on the anterior and lateral surfaces of the forearm near the elbow. It is mainly involved in flexion of the elbow from the mid-pronation position (when the palm of the hand is oriented midway between pronation and supination).

Find It

Place your right arm by your side, palm facing forward. Place the fingers of your left hand onto the middle of the right upper arm.

Feel It

Bend the right elbow.

Notice the muscles popping up under your fingers. These are the *biceps brachii* on top and *brachialis* below.

Dance It

Any arm movement where the elbow bends in toward the body

Elbow extension

The chief muscles that produce elbow extension are the *triceps brachii* (described previously) and the *anconeus*. They are located on the posterior aspect of the elbow.

The *anconeus* is a small muscle attached at one end to the lateral aspect of the *humerus* (Figure 19.9). At the other end it is attached to the posterior aspect of the *ulna*. Because it is so small, this muscle is difficult to palpate.

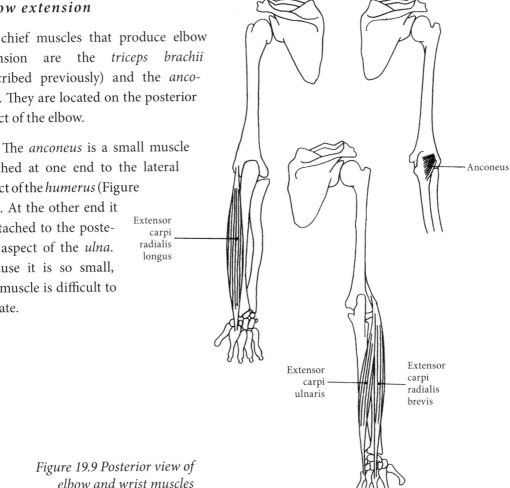

Anconeus

Extensor carpi radialis longus

Extensor carpi ulnaris

Extensor carpi radialis brevis

Figure 19.9 Posterior view of elbow and wrist muscles

Find It

Place your left arm straight out in front of you, level with the shoulder and with the elbow bent to 90 degrees. Place the fingers of your right hand on the back of the left upper arm.

Feel It

Straighten the left elbow.

Notice the muscle popping up under your fingers. This is the *triceps brachii*.

Dance It

Any arm movement where the elbow moves from a bent to straight position.

Inward rotation of the forearm

The muscles that produce inward rotation of the forearm are the *pronator teres* and the *pronator quadratus*. They are found on the anterior aspect of the arm and were shown in Figure 19.8.

The *pronator teres* is attached at one end to both the *humerus* and *ulna* and on the other end to the lateral aspect of the *radius*.

The *pronator quadratus* is a small muscle attached to the *ulna* on one end and to the *radius* at the other end.

These muscles are difficult to palpate.

Outward rotation of the forearm

The muscles that produce outward rotation are the *biceps brachii* (already described) and the *supinator* (Figure 19.7).

The *supinator* is a short muscle attached to the lateral aspect of the *humerus* and to the *ulna*. At the other end, it is attached to the lateral aspect of the *radius*. This muscle is also difficult to palpate.

Structure and movements of the wrist joint

The wrist joint consists of the *radius, ulna,* and two rows of *carpal* bones (Figure 19.1). Movements of the wrist are usually described from a starting position in which the palm of the hand is facing forward. These movements include *flexion* (moving the palm of the hand toward the lower arm), *extension* (return from flexion), *hyperextension* (moving the back of the hand toward the lower arm), *abduction* (moving the hand away from the body), *adduction* (moving the hand toward the body), and *circumduction* (moving in a circle).

There are many muscles that contribute to the performance of these movements. Some of these are considered wrist muscles and others are muscles of the hand and fingers. Only the muscles that are considered wrist muscles will be described.

Table 19.4 Muscle actions of the wrist

Movements of the Wrist	Dancer Terminology	Muscles
Flexion	Bending the wrist toward the palm	Flexor Carpi Radialis Flexor Carpi Ulnaris Palmaris Longus (when present)
Extension of the wrist and hand	Lifting the wrist upward	Extensor Carpi Radialis Longus Extensor Carpi Radialis Brevis Extensor Carpi Ulnaris
Abduction	Angle wrist toward thumb	Extensor Carpi Radialis Longus Extensor Carpi Radialis Brevis Flexor Carpi Radialis
Adduction	Angle wrist toward little finger	Flexor Carpi Ulnaris Extensor Carpi Ulnaris

Flexion of the wrist

Some of the muscles that produce flexion of the wrist are the *flexor carpi radialis*, the *flexor carpi ulnaris*, and the *palmaris longus*. The *palmaris longus* may be absent in some people, and may even be present on one hand but not on the other. These muscles are located on the anterior aspect of the arm and are shown in Figure 19.8.

The *flexor carpi radialis* is attached to the medial aspect of the *humerus* at one end and at the other end, to the palmar aspect of the second and third *metacarpals*.

The *flexor carpi ulnaris* is also attached to the medial aspect of the *humerus*. At the other end, it is attached to some of the wrist bones as well as to the fifth *metacarpal*.

The *palmaris longus*, as the *flexor carpi radialis* and *ulnaris*, is attached at one end to the medial aspect of the *humerus*. At the other end, the attachment is to the middle hand bones. The *palmaris longus* is located between the *flexor carpi ulnaris* and the *flexor carpi radialis*. As you flex your wrist against resistance, you can see the prominent tendon of this muscle on the inside of your wrist, although it is not always present.

Find It

Place your right arm out with the palm facing upward. Place the fingers of your left hand onto the uppermost surface of the right forearm.

Feel It

Bend the wrist upward.

Notice the muscles popping up under your fingers. These are the wrist flexors.

Dance It

Jazz arm position with the arm straight up and the wrist flexed over.

Extension and hyperextension of the wrist

Some of the muscles that produce extension and hyperextension of the wrist are the *extensor carpi radialis longus*, the *extensor carpi radialis brevis*, and the *extensor carpi ulnaris*. These muscles are located on the posterior aspect of the arm and are shown in Figure 19.9.

The *extensor carpi radialis longus* is attached at one end to the lateral aspect of the *humerus*. At the other end it is attached to the back of the second *metacarpal*.

The *extensor carpi radialis brevis* is also attached to the lateral aspect of the *humerus*. At the other end it is attached to the back of the third *metacarpal*.

The *extensor carpi ulnaris*, like the other two extensor muscles, is attached to the lateral aspect of the *humerus*. At the other end, it is attached to the back of the fifth *metacarpal*.

Find It

Extend your left arm forward, palm facing down and the wrist dropped. Place the fingers of your right hand on the uppermost surface of the left forearm.

Feel It

Extend the wrist upward from the dropped position through 180 degrees.

Notice the muscles popping up under your fingers. These are the wrist extensors.

Dance It

The push-up or handstand position of the wrist.

Abduction of the wrist

Abduction is produced by the *extensor carpi radialis longus* and *brevis* and the *flexor carpi radialis*. Each of these muscles has already been described.

Adduction of the wrist

Adduction is produced by the *extensor carpi ulnaris* and the *flexor carpi ulnaris*. Both of these muscles have been described.

Neutral alignment of the shoulder and arm

Viewed from the front, the shoulders should be aligned horizontally and be open, rather than rounded. Viewed from the back, the *scapulae* should also be horizontally aligned and should not "wing" or be pinched together. Viewed from the side, a plumb line should pass through the ear lobe, through the center of the shoulder, and through the center of the hip (Figure 19.20). The arms should hang freely, and the hands should align with the center of the hip.

While there may be structural causes, such as *scoliosis*, that may alter this alignment, asymmetries are often caused by muscular imbalance. Round shoulders, tense or elevated shoulders, and "winged" *scapulae* are some of the more common alignment deviations caused by muscular imbalance. These are discussed in the answers to the questions that follow.

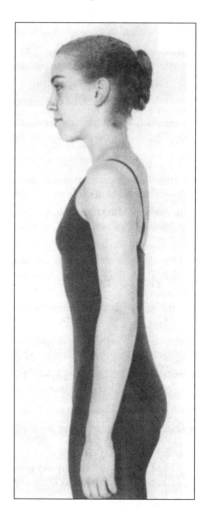

Figure 19.10 Optimal alignment of shoulder and arms.

20

QUESTIONS and ANSWERS:
The SHOULDER and ARM

The questions and answers that follow concern improvement of dance technique and prevention of injuries in the shoulders and arms.

1. My teacher is always telling me to correct my arms when they are in second position. What can I do to improve my arm placement in second?

In second position, the arm should slope gently downward from the shoulder to the elbow and on to the hand. The inner surface of the elbow joint should be pointing forward and diagonally downward, and the palm of the hand should also be facing the front. The arm should describe a gentle curve with the fingers extending the line outward.

A common observation in second position is that the elbow is slightly dropped and the line of the wrist is broken, often due to fatigue of the arm muscles. Rather than just trying to address this locally at each of those joints, if you begin by supporting the arm from the torso, most of these "kinks" will disappear. Dancers often think of the arm line as beginning at the shoulder joint. However, this is not helpful as it leads to a reliance on recruiting the small, dynamic muscles of the shoulder and arm to play the supporting role when they are not really designed for this. The large muscles that stabilize the *scapulae* and the torso are much better suited to the task of supporting the weight of the arm. They are designed for power and endurance in ways that the smaller arm muscles are not. A useful image is to see the arm as the trunk of a tree that has large roots that spread all the way through the torso to the lumbar spine. Engaging these "roots" will result in recruitment of the large *latissimus dorsi* muscle as well as the muscles that stabilize the *scapulae*. Once the supporting role for the arm has been transferred to these larger muscles, the arm will naturally follow the desired line, and will not tire as easily and begin to droop.

2.   My shoulders seem to round forward and my teacher is always telling me to pull them back. Are there exercises that can help me to correct this issue?

In many cases, round shoulders are caused by an imbalance of the muscles on the front and back of the chest. These muscles work as paired groups—tension in the muscles at the front will draw the shoulders forward and lead to weakness in the balancing muscles at the back as they are stretched out. In today's technological age, the use of mobile phones, tablets, and laptops encourages us to round the shoulders forward and drop the head down, while holding the device up in space with the arms. This all represents an enormous amount of load into the neck and shoulder muscles and can significantly contribute to the aforementioned imbalances. The main muscles that maintain the forward shoulder posture are the *pectoralis major, pectoralis minor,* and *subscapularis.* The muscles that will be stretched and weakened by this alignment are the *rhomboid major* and *rhomboid minor.* In a neutral position, the distance between the right and left shoulders, as measured across the chest, should be equal to the distance between the two shoulders as measured across the back. In the rounded-shoulder posture, the distance at the front will be notably shorter than that at the back. When this muscular pattern has become ingrained, simply trying to "push" or "pull" the shoulders back in response to a teacher's cue will likely be a fruitless exercise. First, the tight *pectoralis* and *subscapularis* muscles must be addressed; then second, the *rhomboid* and other scapular stabilizing muscles need to be strengthened. This can take time and patience to address. To effect a lasting change, you need to be mindful of your shoulder alignment and muscle recruitment during all of your daily activities, not just those in the dance class. This involves checking your alignment when you are using your phone or computer, driving, or even just watching television! By combining awareness of your habitual shoulder alignment with an appropriate stretching and strengthening routine, a neutral shoulder position can be found and maintained. Exercises for this can be found in Chapter 21 below.

3.   I have shoulder blades that protrude or "wing." I have trouble actively controlling their placement. What can I do to address this?

"Winged" or protruding *scapulae* may be caused by an imbalance in the muscles that control their position (Figure 20.1). It is not usually a painful condition, but it can lead to weakness in arm and shoulder movements, and can be a particular issue for lifting or weight-bearing on the arms. It is commonly, but not exclusively, seen in hypermobile dancers. The main cause of this issue is weakness in the *serratus anterior* muscle. This muscle covers the undersurface (closest to the rib cage) of the *scapula* and attaches to the top eight or nine ribs at the

front of the torso. It serves to stabilize the *scapula* against the back of the rib cage and thus prevents winging. It also moves the *scapula* laterally and forward to facilitate arm movements and is particularly active during a forward punching motion.

In rare cases, particularly if the winging occurs on one side only, this condition can be caused by damage to the nerve that serves the *serratus anterior*. However, this is usually secondary to shoulder trauma so an obvious link can be made. For this scenario, medical help should be sought, but for all other cases, a strengthening program can be useful in addressing this issue.

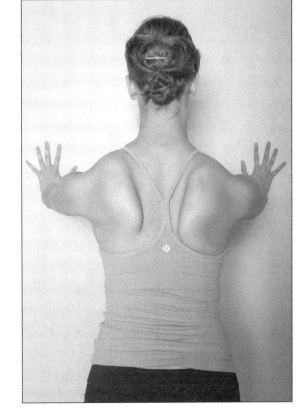

Figure 20.1
Winged scapulae

4.   I am required to do a lot of inversions and struggle finding the ability to control the movement when upside down (Figure 20.2). What are things I could think about to improve this type of movement?

In commercial and concert dance choreography there is a greater demand for dancers to be able to weight-bear on their hands in upside-down positions. Dancers with extensive gymnastics or hip hop training have an advantage for this work as those techniques naturally incorporate the placing of weight on the hands and being supported by the muscles of the upper body. In dance technique classes requiring these types of movements the discussion typically revolves around the mechanics of the movement, set up, and follow through. With the exception of a few push-ups or planks incorporated as part of a technique class, very little physical training is typically offered in the studio setting to improve these skills.

In today's dance world, movements that involve going upside down are much more complex than just performing a cartwheel, which relies heavily on momentum. To help to develop your skills in this area, there are several factors that you can address to improve your inverted work. The first is to focus on developing coordinated strength and flexibility between the arms, shoulders, and trunk. In addition to strength, you need to have an adequate range of mobility in your shoulders in order to get your arms into the optimal placement above the head without impacting the alignment of your spine. Exercises in Chapter 21 will address these issues. You should specifically focus on the scapular stabilization exercises provided in 21.A, as the ability to control the movements is greatly dependent upon the stability of the *scapulae* on the back of the ribs. Incorporating core work will also help with the control of the inverted movements and will increase the amount of time you can maintain the given position. The last item to take note of is the alignment of the head and neck when in an upside-down position. Not all dancers are comfortable going upside down and will tend to lift their heads. However, this will throw off the entire alignment of the spine making control of the movement more difficult. If the shoulders, arms, and trunk have a balance between flexibility and strength you will feel more confident and secure when upside down, then giving you the confidence to let go of the weight of the head.

It is also important to note that performing movements with the body inverted and the head pointing downward creates significant changes in the vestibular mechanism that is crucial for balance. When you are new to these movements, you may find yourself feeling dizzy or disoriented, and lacking balance control. This system needs to be trained in addition to the torso and upper-body strength work. A good way to start is to begin by using slow movements into inversion and taking the time to calibrate your balance into this new orientation without weight-bearing. Addressing your breathing patterns is also key. Holding your breath in the inverted position is not advisable due to the increases in pressure in the circulatory system. Using an exhale to initiate movements helps to balance the pressure increases, and also activates the deep abdominal muscles that are key to stabilizing the body.

Figure 20.2 Inversion

5. **My elbows and wrists hyperextend and I find it really uncomfortable when doing upper-body, weight-bearing moves. What should I do?**

Joint laxity at the elbow and wrist is common among hypermobile dancers and can present a challenge for upper-body, weight-bearing movements. Hyperextension at the elbow is similar to hyperextension at the knee, where the joint does not fall through the center of the plumb line. Weight-bearing on the arms with the elbows in the hyperextended position will therefore stress the joint surfaces and surrounding ligaments and is not advised. As we saw in Question 1, the strength for the arms should be generated from the torso muscles that are much better suited to supporting body weight. A lack of strength and control centrally will result in greater forces of body weight being directed into the joints of the arm and wrist. Therefore, strength training for the core and for the scapular stabilizers should be the focus before upper-body weight-bearing is attempted. Dancers with hyperextended elbows need to find a neutral elbow-joint alignment, which would allow the forces to be directed linearly through the bones and down into the floor. This will feel like they are flexing the elbow slightly, but building muscular strength around this neutral position will be protective of the joint structures.

A hyper-flexible wrist joint can represent quite a problem for upper-body weight-bearing. The muscles that control wrist movement are located in the forearm with only their thin, cable-like tendons crossing the joints of the wrist. So there is very little inherent stability locally at the wrist. Loading a hypermobile wrist with body weight will force some of the small carpal bones together, creating inflammation and pain. For the push-up or plank positions, a modification can be made to avoid hyperextending the wrist. By making a fist with the hand and placing the flat surface of the proximal *phalanges* against the floor, the wrist can be "splinted" into a neutral position, thus eliminating the issue of hyperextension (Figure 20.3).

By following all the guidelines for building torso, shoulder, and arm strength for upper-body weight-bearing, as well as reeducating the elbow into a neutral position, hypermobile dancers will be afforded the best protection for this type of movement. However, particularly with the wrist joints, weight-bearing on the arms may have to be limited or excluded altogether for vulnerable individuals.

Figure 20.3
Splinted wrists

21

STRENGTH and FLEXIBILITY EXERCISES: The SHOULDER and ARM

This section provides strength, flexibility, and integration exercises for the shoulder and arm. Where appropriate, injuries are also discussed. Each section will provide the exercise name, any equipment needed, and starting positions. Step-by-step descriptions of the action of the exercise, and suggestions for self checks and comments on what you might feel are offered.

21.A Scapular stabilization

21.A.1 Strength exercises

The scapular stabilizing muscles provide an anchoring force that is the basis for any arm movements. Whether just holding the arm in second position or placing the whole body weight onto the hands, the scapular stabilizing muscles provide the roots for arm support. These exercises are designed to engage these muscles in contextualized positions that involve coordination between several muscle groups.

WALL PLANKS WITH SCAPULAR PRESS

Starting position

    a)   Stand facing a wall. Place your hands on the wall at shoulder width and height.

    b)   Stand with your feet aligned under your hips.

Note: Be sure to read Part I before doing any of the following exercises.

Table 21.1 Roadmap

Action	Strength Exercises	Flexibility Exercises
Combination Movements—*Scapula*		
Scapular stabilization	21.A.1	21.A.2
Individual Movements—*Glenohumeral Joint*		
Flexion	21.B.1	21.B.2
Extension	21.C.1	21.C.2
Abduction	21.D.1	
Adduction	21.E.1	
External rotation	21.F1	
Internal rotation	21.G.1	21.I.2
Combination Movements—*Scapulae* and *Glenohumeral Joint*		
Arm opening	21.H	21.A.2
Dips	21.H	21.J.2
Reverse plank	21.H	21.J.2
Individual Movements—Elbow Joint		
Flexion	21.I.1	21.I.2
Extension	21.J.1	21.J.2
Pronation/ supination	21.K.1	
Individual Movements—Wrist Joint		
Flexion	21.L.1	21.L.2
Extension	21.M.1	21.M.2

c) Stand just far enough away from the wall to allow your body weight to lean into the wall.

d) Focus on drawing the lower part of the *scapulae* down and together as if you are trying to place them in your back pockets.

e) Keep the front of the shoulders wide.

Action

a) Hold the wall plank position.

b) With straight elbows allow the *scapulae* to glide around your rib cage toward your spine, by contracting the *rhomboids* and *middle and lower trapezius* muscles. Your body will move closer to the wall as you adduct the *scapulae*.

c) Next push your hands into the wall and draw the *scapulae* apart gliding them around the rib cage using the *serratus anterior*. The body will move away from the wall slightly and your upper back may round slightly.

Variation

After holding the wall plank and completing a full set with the scapular press, stabilize the *scapulae* and complete a set of wall push-ups.

Repetitions

Hold wall plank for 30 seconds. 8–10 repetitions of scapular press. 8–10 wall push-ups.

Quick self checks

Technique class alone typically will not address the strength needs of the shoulder region. Beginning with stabilization exercises on the wall allows you to focus specifically on the stability of the *scapulae* without adding the additional challenge of the full weight of the body. Focus on the *scapulae* lying flat on the back of the rib cage. Keep the neck long and aligned with the spine.

PLANKS (FIGURE 21.1)

Starting position

a) Plank variation can either be done on the knees or with legs extended.

b) Align the hands under the shoulders.

c) Engage the abdominal muscles to support the alignment of the spine.

Action

a) Hold the plank position either on the knees or with legs extended.

b) Focus on drawing the bottom of the *scapulae* down and together as if you are trying to place them in your back pockets.

c) Keep the front of the shoulders wide.

Variation

Once you can maintain a stable position add a complete push-up.

Figure 21.1 Plank

Repetitions

> Hold for 30 seconds then rest and repeat again. Follow with 8–10 repetitions of a full push-up.

Quick self checks

> Weight-bearing in a kneeling or full plank position challenges the core as much as it challenges the stability of the *scapulae*. When holding the plank position or doing a full push-up, it is important to engage the muscles of the abdominal wall and the hip extensor muscles in order to maintain alignment of the entire body. As your strength increases, you can increase the duration of the hold and the number of push-ups.

21.A.2 Flexibility exercise

The following stretch is a generic one that targets several muscle areas. The stretch will be felt in the tightest spot on each individual dancer. This can include the back of the shoulder blade, the back of the upper arm, and the space between the shoulder blades.

ARM PRETZEL STRETCH FOR POSTERIOR SHOULDER MUSCLES (FIGURE 21.2)

Starting position

> a) Standing or sitting.
>
> b) Stretch the arms out in front of the body. Cross left arm over right arm above the elbow.
>
> c) Loop forearms around each other until the palms meet in the "prayer" position.
>
> d) Keep the upper arms in line with the shoulders, flex the elbows to 90 degrees, and point the fingers straight up to the ceiling.

Action

> Following the trajectory of the fingers toward the ceiling, exhale and lift the elbows upward.

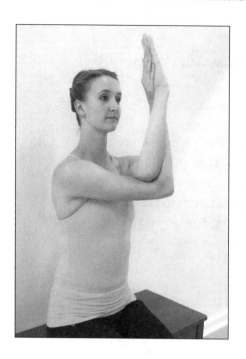

Repetitions

Hold for 30 seconds. Rest, then repeat crossing the other arm on top.

Quick self checks

Be sure that the shoulders remain relaxed at all times. This is a generic stretch for all the structures on the back of the shoulders. Each dancer will feel the stretch where he or she holds the most tension. For some this will be between the shoulder blades, while others may feel the stretch at the back of the shoulder joint.

Figure 21.2 Arm pretzel

21.B Shoulder flexion

21.B.1 Strength exercise

This is a resistance exercise to promote strength in the upward motion of the arm when in front of the body (from bras bas *to fifth position).*

RESISTED SHOULDER FLEXION (FIGURE 21.3)

Starting position

   a)   Stand with legs in parallel with the feet aligned under the pelvis.

   b)   Place the end of the elastic band under your right foot.

   c)   Hold the band near the right thigh with the right hand facing back and keep the arm in line with the shoulder.

Action

   a)   While stabilizing the shoulder girdle reach your right arm forward in a fluid motion to about the height of the shoulder.

   b)   Slowly lower the arm back down to your side.

Repetitions

8–10 repetitions on each side.

Quick self checks

The height of the arm reach is dictated by how well you can maintain the stability of the *scapula* while keeping the shoulder slightly depressed. As soon as the shoulder lifts up you have gone too far.

Figure 21.3 Resisted shoulder flexion

21.B.2 Flexibility exercise

This exercise will facilitate shoulder flexibility and is particularly useful for those who have a tendency toward a round-shoulder posture.

STRETCH FOR THE *PECTORALIS MAJOR* (FIGURE 21.4)

Starting position

a) Find a wall, door jamb, or pillar. Stand facing the structure an arm's width away.

b) Extend the arm at shoulder height and place the fingertips onto the structure.

Action

Turn the feet and hips 90 degrees away from the wall, door jamb, or pillar.

Figure 21.4 Stretch for pectoralis major

Variation

Place the palm of the hand against a wall with the arm at shoulder height with the body facing parallel to the wall. Extend forward into a lunge position, placing the foot furthest away from the wall in front (Figure 21.4).

Repetitions

Hold for 30 seconds. Rest, and repeat with the other arm.

Quick self checks

Be sure that the shoulder of the extended arm remains relaxed. As you turn away or lunge, maintain a neutral spine—do not allow the spine to extend or arch. Make sure that the hips and feet are aligned, focusing the rotation into the upper chest. You should feel the stretch across the chest in the area of the *pectoralis major* muscle.

21.C Shoulder extension

21.C.1 Strength exercise

This will strengthen the arm and shoulder for movements behind the body. It also contributes to scapular stability.

LATISSIMUS DORSI PULL

Equipment

Elastic band and *barre* or door with a knob.

Starting position

a)   Wrap an elastic band around the *barre* or a door knob (be sure the door is closed!).

b)   Hold an end of the band with each hand.

c)   Stand far enough away to create some tension in the band while arms are reaching forward at a 45 degree angle in front of the body.

Action

a)   With straight arms and palms facing toward each other draw the arms down and back toward your sides.

b)   As the hands move back past the hips a few inches draw your *scapulae* down and back toward your waist.

c)   Slowly allow your arms to return to the starting position.

Repetitions

8–10 repetitions.

Quick self checks

If the shoulder extensors are weak, the elbows will tend to bend as the body recruits the *biceps brachii* to help with the pull. As the arms travel back think of driving your hands down toward the floor and keeping the elbows straight. Keeping the elbows straight will also work the *triceps brachii*.

21.C.2 Flexibility exercise

This is a stretch for the muscles of shoulder extension. This can improve shoulder mobility and facilitate power availability for weight-bearing on the arms.

STRETCH FOR *TRICEPS BRACHII* AND *LATISSIMUS DORSI* (FIGURE 21.5)

Starting position

a)   Standing or sitting.

b)   Elevate the right arm up to the side of the head.

c)   Flex the elbow so that the forearm drops behind the head.

d)   Grasp the right elbow with the left hand.

Figure 21.5a Stretch
for triceps brachii

Figure 21.5b Stretch
for latissimus dorsi

Action

Using the left hand, apply gentle over-pressure to the right elbow, pulling it farther behind the head (Figure 21.5a).

Variation

Holding the above position, continue the stretch into a side-bend to the left. This will include the *latissimus dorsi* into the stretch (Figure 21.5b).

Repetitions

Hold for 30 seconds. Rest, and repeat to the other side.

Quick self checks

Be sure that the shoulders remain relaxed at all times. Do not allow the spine to hyperextend (arch). In the first variation, the stretch should be felt in the area of the *triceps brachii* on the back of the upper arm. In the second variation, the stretch should be felt lower into the side of the torso.

21.D Shoulder abduction

21.D.1 Strength exercise

Raising the arm to the side involves the coordination of several muscles, including the supraspinatus—*one of the* rotator cuff *muscles. The four* rotator cuff *muscles need to be in balance to ensure good alignment of the* humerus *in the shoulder socket. The three exercises that follow this one address each of these muscles in conjunction with others.*

Resisted side arm raise (Figure 21.6)

Equipment

Elastic band.

Starting position

a) Standing in parallel.

b) Place an elastic band under the right foot.

c) Hold the band in the right hand, palm facing the body.

d) The band is slightly slack when the arm is in the starting position.

Action

a) Raise the right arm directly to the side, stopping when the hand is at shoulder height.

b) Return the arm back to the starting position.

Repetitions

8–10 repetitions. Switch the elastic band to the other side and repeat.

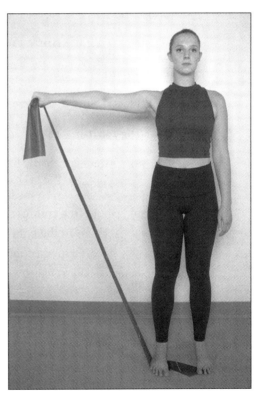

Figure 21.6 Resisted side arm raise

Quick self checks

> If the shoulder begins to rise while the arm is lifting, lower the height of
> the arm until you can maintain the placement of the shoulder. Through-
> out the exercise keep the weight evenly distributed between both feet,
> and your torso and hips, stacked. You want to avoid leaning your body to
> compensate for weak abductors.

21.E Shoulder adduction

21.E.1 Strength exercise

This is the return of the arm from abduction back to neutral. This works several muscles (see Table 19.2). Adding resistance here increases strength for the downward motion of the arm but also creates added strength for supported arm positions.

RESISTED ARM ADDUCTION (FIGURE 21.7)

Equipment

> Elastic band and *barre* or door with a knob.

Starting position

> a)   Attach an elastic band to a *barre* or a door knob (be sure the door
>   is closed!).
>
> b)   Stand in a comfortable parallel position far enough away to create
>   tension in the band while the arm is reached directly out to the
>   side in a low second position.

Action

> a)   With the palm holding the elastic band facing toward the floor
>   engage the adductor muscles under the armpit to pull the band
>   toward the side of the leg.
>
> b)   Return the arm to the starting position.

Repetitions

> 8–10 repetitions on each arm.

Quick self checks

This exercise is designed to train the adductor muscles of the arm. However, if they are weak, the tendency will be for the shoulder to lift up in an attempt to pull the hand to the hip. If you struggle to maintain the placement of the shoulder, you can lessen the tension on the band or not pull the band all the way to the hip.

Figure 21.7 Resisted arm adduction

21.F External rotation

21.F.1 Strength exercise

This exercise targets the muscles that rotate the humerus *outward. Included in these is the* infraspinatus—*one of the four* rotator cuff *muscles.*

RESISTED EXTERNAL ROTATION (FIGURE 21.8)

Equipment

Elastic band and *barre*, door with a knob, or heavy piece of furniture.

Starting position (Figure 21.8a)

a) Attach an elastic band to a *barre*, door knob (with door shut), or heavy piece of furniture.

b) The band needs to be adjusted to the height of your elbow whether you are standing or sitting.

c) In either a standing or sitting position keep the spine in a neutral position with the torso stacked over the pelvis. Legs are kept in an easy parallel position.

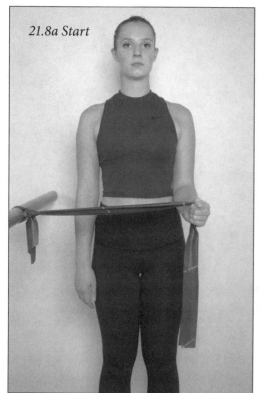 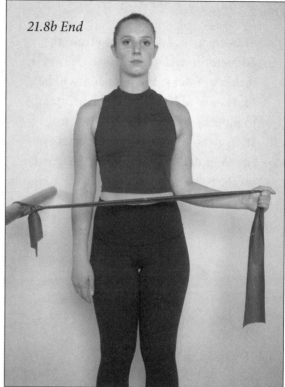

21.8a Start

21.8b End

Figure 21.8 Resisted external rotation

d) Flex your left elbow 90 degrees and bring your left forearm across your torso. Your left upper arm should touch your left side and your right arm should be straight.

e) Hold the elastic band with the left hand and adjust your distance from the attached end of the band so there is some tension in the elastic.

Action (Figure 21.8b)

a) Keep your left upper arm held against your side and your left wrist straight, and move your left hand away from the midline of your body. Your left palm will face the right diagonal at the completion of the movement.

b) Return to the starting position.

c) If you do not feel a strong resistance from the elastic, sit or stand farther from where the band is attached.

d) Complete all repetitions on the first side before changing sides.

Repetitions

8–10 repetitions on each side.

Quick self checks

It is important that you have attached your elastic band to a secure item that won't be pulled over in the exercise. Focus on isolating the movement of the shoulder joint in pure external rotation. If the shoulder begins to fatigue, stop and take a rest before continuing.

21.G Internal rotation

21.G.1 Strength exercise

The muscles of internal rotation include the subscapularis—*the last of the four* rotator cuff *muscles. All the above four muscles need to be addressed to ensure shoulder balance.*

Resisted internal rotation (Figure 21.9)

Equipment

Elastic band and *barre*, door with a knob, or a heavy piece of furniture.

Starting position (Figure 21.9a)

a) Attach an elastic band to a *barre*, door knob (with door shut), or a heavy piece of furniture.

b) The band needs to be adjusted to the height of your elbow whether you are standing or sitting.

c) In either a standing or sitting position keep the spine in a neutral position with the torso stacked over the pelvis. Legs are kept in an easy parallel position.

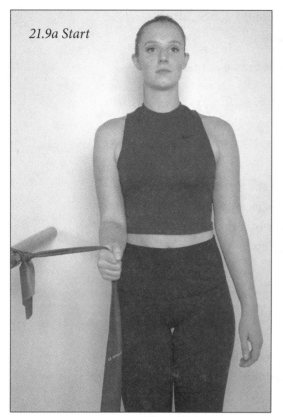

21.9a Start

21.9b End

Figure 21.9 Resisted internal rotation

d)   Flex your right elbow 90 degrees. Your upper arm should be held
     against your right side. Your wrist should be straight and your
     palm should be facing the left wall.

e)   Hold the elastic band with the right hand and adjust your dis-
     tance from the attached end of the band so there is some tension
     in the elastic.

*Action (**Figure 21.9b**)*

a)   Keep your upper arm held against your side and your wrist
     straight, and pull your hand across your body. Your forearm will
     touch your torso (Figure 21.9b).

b)   Return to the starting position.

c) If you do not feel a strong resistance from the elastic, sit or stand farther from where the band is attached.

d) Complete all repetitions on the first side before changing sides.

Repetitions

8–10 repetitions on each side.

Quick self checks

It is important that you have attached your elastic band to a secure item that won't be pulled over in the exercise. Focus on isolating the movement of the shoulder joint in pure internal rotation. Try not to pull your entire arm across the body. As soon as your elbow begins to lift away from your waist stop the motion and return to the starting position.

21.G.2 Flexibility exercises

It is not possible to stretch the subscapularis *muscle itself due to its anatomical location. Problems here require the attention of a physical therapy professional who can use manual techniques to release this muscle. However, the* pectoralis minor *muscle is usually also implicated in issues of internal rotation, so the stretch found at 21.I.2 can also be helpful.*

21.H Combined movements of the *scapulae* and *glenohumeral joint*

While isolated shoulder movement exercises have their place, it is also key to include exercises that contextualize these movements into the varying combinations that we encounter in normal dance movement. This teaches the muscles to coordinate with others to produce smooth, integrated movement.

ARM OPENINGS (FIGURE 21.10)

The action of taking the arms from first to second works shoulder horizontal abduction and scapular adduction.

Equipment

Elastic band.

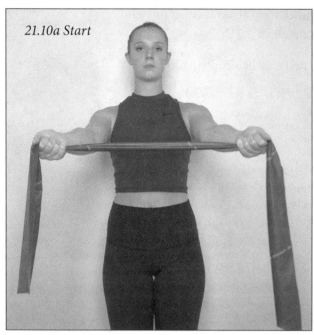

21.10a Start

Starting position (Figure 21.10a)

a)   Stand with feet hip distance apart and make sure the spine is in a neutral position.

b)   Hold the elastic band in the hands with elbows straight. Keep the palms of the hands facing the ceiling.

c)   Raise the arms in front of the body just below shoulder height.

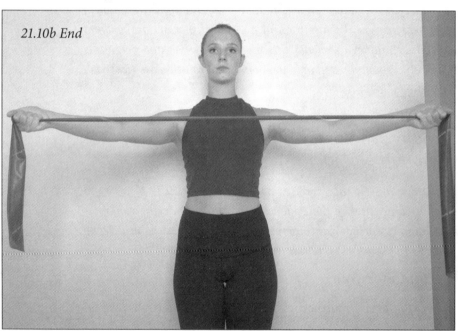

21.10b End

Figure 21.10 Arm openings

d)   Start with the arms shoulder width apart and only a slight tension on the elastic band.

Action (Figure 21.10b)

a)   Engage the muscles between the shoulder blades and on the back of the arms to draw the hands apart, stretching the band.

b)   Take the arms to a second position and then slowly return to the starting position.

Repetitions

8–10 repetitions.

Quick self checks

Focus on expanding the front of the chest while engaging the muscles at the back of the arms and in between the *scapulae*. Avoid thrusting the chest forward and elevating the rib cage.

Dips

These are best performed on a chair or bench but can also be done sitting on the floor.

Starting position

a)   Place the palms on the edge of a chair on either side of the hips.

b)   Hold the weight of your body with your arms and shift the feet forward on the floor.

c)   Stabilize your *scapulae* and draw your shoulders away from your ears.

Action

a)   Bend your elbows lowering the body toward the floor.

b)   Extend your elbows and return to the starting position.

Repetitions

8–10 repetitions, 1–3 sets.

Quick self checks

Be sure to focus the movement in the elbows and not the legs. Only bend as far as you can without losing the control of the *scapulae*. When at full extension of the elbows, lengthen the spine, neck, and shoulders.

REVERSE PLANK (FIGURE 21.11)

Starting position

a)   Sit on the floor with legs stretched out in front of the body.

b)   Place your hands on either side of the hips with fingertips pointing toward your feet.

c)   Keep your shoulders aligned over your wrists.

Action

a)   Press the torso and pelvis up engaging the elbow and shoulder extensors and scapular adductors.

b)   Strive to align the entire body from head to toe.

c)   Hold the position for a count of 10.

Figure 21.11 Reverse plank

d) Lower the pelvis back to the floor.

Repetitions

1–5 repetitions.

Quick self checks

Along with the upper body, the abdominal muscles and the muscles that extend the hips need to engage to maintain the alignment of the body in the reverse plank. Do not allow your elbows or knees to hyperextend. If you are feeling pressure in the back of the knees try bending them and placing the feet flat on the floor. Dancers with tightness across the front of the shoulders may struggle with this exercise until more width is created to open up the shoulders.

21.1 Elbow flexion

21.1.1. Strength exercise

While this exercise is typically referred to as a biceps curl, *it equally targets the* brachialis *muscle that lies beneath the* biceps brachii *and is a pure elbow flexor. The* biceps brachii *muscle splits its focus between elbow flexion and the additional movements of elbow supination and shoulder flexion.*

RESISTED *BICEPS* CURL (FIGURE 21.12)

Equipment

Elastic band.

Starting position (Figure 21.12a)

a) Standing in parallel.

b) Place an elastic band under the right foot.

c) Hold the band in the right hand, palm facing forward.

Action (Figure 21.12b)

a) Keep the right elbow by the side of the body throughout the exercise.

b) Draw your hand up to your shoulder in a bicep curl.

c) Lower back down to the starting position.

Repetitions

10 repetitions, 1–3 sets on each side.

Quick self checks

Once the elbow reaches about 90 degrees continue to keep the elbow at the side of the body. Keep your weight even on both feet and shoulders squared as you complete each set. If you need more resistance shorten the length of the elastic band.

21.12a Start   21.12b End

Figure 21.12 Resisted biceps curl

21.I.2 Flexibility exercise

The biceps brachii *has both a long head and a short head. This stretch targets the short head and also the* pectoralis minor *muscle that can affect scapular positioning. The long head of the* biceps brachii *can be targeted by using the* pectoralis major *stretch in section 21.B.2 on page 269.*

STRETCH FOR *BICEPS BRACHII*—SHORT HEAD (FIGURE 21.13)

Starting position

a) Find a door jamb, pillar, or wall. Stand facing the structure half an arm's length away.

b) Extend the upper arm to the side at shoulder height with the elbow bent at 90 degrees.

a) Place the vertically oriented forearm along the line of the structure.

Action

Turn the feet and hips 90 degrees away from the door jamb, wall, or pillar.

Repetitions

Hold for 30 seconds. Rest, and repeat with the other arm.

Quick self checks

Figuer 21.13 Stretch for biceps brachii

Be sure that the shoulder of the extended arm remains relaxed. As you turn away, maintain a neutral spine—do not allow the spine to extend or arch. Make sure that the hips and feet are aligned, focusing the rotation into the upper chest. The stretch should be felt just in front of the shoulder joint and down into the belly of the *biceps brachii* muscle in the upper arm.

21.J Elbow extension

21.J.1 Strength exercise

This is a resistance exercise to strengthen the triceps brachii *muscle. If you have any stiffness in your shoulder joints and neck, you may find it difficult to achieve the starting position for this exercise comfortably. You may find it useful to use the stretch series from the previous chapter, found in section 18.E.2 before attempting this exercise.*

RESISTED *TRICEPS* EXTENSION (FIGURE 21.14)

Equipment

Elastic band.

Starting position (Figure 21.14a)

a)   In a sitting or standing position hold the elastic band between both hands.

b)   The right arm is bent above the head, palm facing forward, with the hand stopping behind the head.

c)   The left arm is inwardly rotated and bent behind the back with the hand stopping in the middle of the mid-back.

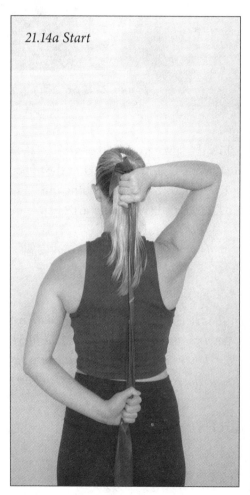

21.14a Start

21.14b End

Figure 21.14 Resisted tricep extension

Action (Figure 21.14b)

While maintaining the placement of the left arm, extend the right hand toward the ceiling increasing tension on the elastic band.

Repetitions

10–15 repetitions on each arm.

Quick self checks

Maintain the position of the top arm. The elbow should stay pointing toward the ceiling. Work to keep the position of the top wrist neutral with palm facing forward throughout the exercise.

21.J.2 Flexibility exercise

Stretching the triceps brachii *will help with shoulder mobility and ensure that the muscle is tension-free and able to fire optimally.*

STRETCH FOR *TRICEPS BRACHII*

Starting position

   a)   Standing or sitting.

   b)   Elevate the right arm up to the side of the head.

   c)   Flex the elbow so that the forearm drops behind the head.

   d)   Grasp the right elbow with the left hand.

Action

Using the left hand, apply gentle over-pressure to the right elbow, pulling it farther behind the head.

Repetitions

Hold for 30 seconds. Rest, and repeat to the other side.

Quick self checks

Be sure that the shoulders remain relaxed at all times. Do not allow the spine to hyperextend (arch). The stretch should be felt in the area of the *triceps brachii* on the back of the upper arm.

21.K Elbow pronation and supination

22.K.1 Strength exercises

Strength in the forearm muscles is essential for upper-body weight-bearing to ensure that the body weight does not fall unsupported into the delicate wrist joints. These muscles are also important for partnered lifts.

Palms up / palms down

Equipment

Chair or bench, hand weights.

Starting position

a)   Begin sitting and hold a hand weight in each hand.

b)   Rest your elbows on your thighs with your palms facing up. Your forearms should extend beyond your knees.

Action

a)   Rotate your forearms so your palms face down. Keep your wrist straight.

b)   Return to the starting position.

Repetitions

10–15 repetitions on each arm.

Quick self checks

Holding the weights will help to strengthen your hand muscles. Keep the movement isolated in the forearms and shoulders down.

21.L Wrist flexion

21.L.1 Strength exercise

These muscles are important for wrist support and for facilitating expressive movements through the hands and fingers. They are also important for upper-body weight-bearing.

Wrist curls with hand weights

Equipment

Chair or bench, hand weights.

Starting position

a) Sit with a hand weight in each hand.

b) Place your forearms on your knees with your hands extending beyond your knees, your palms facing up.

c) Relax your wrists so your palms face forward.

Action

a) Flex your wrists.

b) Return to the starting position.

Repetitions

10–15 repetitions on each arm.

Quick self checks

Holding the weights will help to strengthen your hand muscles. Move at a steady speed to flex your wrists and return to the starting position so you work the muscles both in a concentric and eccentric contraction.

21.L.2 Flexibility exercise

Flexibility in these muscles ensures optimal movement at the wrist and into the fingers. It will also help to facilitate extended wrist positions in both weight-bearing and non-weight-bearing movements. While there are some standard stretches for the wrist flexor muscles, these can place stress on the wrist joint (which is particularly an issue for hypermobile individuals). Additionally, such stretches often do not focus the stretch into the muscle bellies but just pull on the tendons. For these reasons we suggest some active release techniques in place of stretches.

Active release for wrist flexor muscles

Equipment

Chair and table.

Starting position

a) Sit on the edge of a desk or table.

b) Extend the arm in front of you with the elbow flexed at 90 degrees so that the forearm rests on the table surface (palm up) with the wrist clear of the edge.

Action

a) With the wrist flexed, place the heel of the opposite hand onto the bellies of the wrist flexor muscles.

b) Press gently downward toward the underlying bone, and upward toward the elbow.

c) Maintaining this pressure, slowly extend the wrist downward off the edge of the table.

Repetitions

Repeat 3 times. To cover the whole muscle area, move the opposing hand farther up the flexor muscle bellies with each repetition .

Quick self checks

Do not use too much pressure onto the muscle bellies. You need just enough pressure to trap the muscles against the underlying bone. Too much pressure may cause bruising. Be sure the shoulders remain relaxed throughout. If you find it awkward to achieve this motion without shoulder tension when sitting, stand and place your center of gravity over the direction of pressure. This will minimize any tendency for shoulder tension.

21.M Wrist extension

21.M.1 Strength exercise

These muscles are important for wrist support and for facilitating expressive movements through the hands and fingers. They are also important for upper-body weight-bearing.

WRIST EXTENSION WITH HAND WEIGHTS

Equipment

Chair or bench, hand weights.

Starting position

a) Sit with a hand weight in each hand.

b) Place your forearms on your knees with your hands extending beyond your knees, your palms facing down.

c) Relax your wrists until your palms face your shins.

Action

a) Extend your wrists.

b) Return to the starting position.

Repetitions

10–15 repetitions on each arm.

Quick self checks

Holding the weights will help to strengthen your hand muscles. Move at a steady speed to flex your wrists and return to the starting position so you work the muscles both in a concentric and eccentric contraction.

21.M.2 Flexibility exercise

While there are some standard stretches for the wrist extensor muscles, these can place stress on the wrist joint (which is particularly an issue for hypermobile individuals). Additionally, such stretches often do not focus the stretch into the muscle bellies but just pull on the tendons. For these reasons we suggest some active release techniques in place of stretches.

ACTIVE RELEASE FOR THE WRIST EXTENSOR MUSCLES

Equipment

> Chair and table.

Starting position

> a) Sit on the edge of a desk or table.
>
> b) Extend the arm in front of you with the elbow flexed at 90 degrees so that the forearm rests on the table surface (palm down) with the wrist clear of the edge.

Action

> a) With the wrist extended, place the heel of the opposite hand onto the bellies of the wrist extensor muscles.
>
> b) Press gently downward toward the underlying bone, and upward toward the elbow.
>
> c) Maintaining this pressure, slowly flex the wrist downward off the edge of the table.

Repetitions

> Repeat 3 times. To cover the whole muscle area, move the opposing hand farther up the extensor muscle bellies with each repetition.

Quick self checks

> Do not use too much pressure onto the muscle bellies. You need just enough pressure to trap the muscles against the underlying bone. Too much pressure may cause bruising. Be sure that the shoulders remain relaxed throughout. If you find it awkward to achieve this motion without shoulder tension when sitting, stand and place your center of gravity over the direction of pressure. This will minimize any tendency for shoulder tension.

Part VI

PUTTING IT ALL TOGETHER

Now that you have viewed the individual exercises that can contribute to a dancer's health and fitness, it may seem like an overwhelming amount of information. It is key to understand that not all of those exercises may be appropriate or useful to you as an individual. They may apply only at certain times, depending on an injury you may have encountered—or perhaps they would apply to a particular choreographic repertoire that you are involved with at a given time.

This section will offer some compilation programs that draw together specific groups of exercises to target particular issues such as technique challenges, injury recovery and prevention, alignment choices, specific joint instability, and physically demanding movements. It will also offer options for cardiovascular fitness and balance training.

While not all these combinations will suit the needs of every dancer, the examples should give you an idea of how training prescriptions can be built and developed to keep you dancing longer and stronger. Looking toward the bigger picture of your training needs, this section will also explore alternative training modalities such as Pilates, Gyrotonics, and yoga. The aim of this book is to provide you a firm foundation for building and expanding upon your training choices.

22

TRAINING the ENTIRE DANCER

Cardiovascular fitness

Research has shown that although dancers perform slightly better than non-dancers in terms of their cardiovascular fitness, they lag significantly behind other athletes (Rodrigues-Krause, Krause, and Reischak-Oliveira 2015). Dance classes typically have a stop/start nature involving short exercises with rests in between. This primarily works the body *anaerobically* and trains it for short bursts of activity—the equivalent of being a short-distance sprinter. However, the choreographic demands of performance often require dancers to sustain activity for 15 to 20 minutes, or perhaps even longer. This requires *aerobic* fitness—the equivalent of being an endurance athlete. If this is not being trained during a dance class, then it is essential to have a supplemental training routine that provides *aerobic* training. Fatigue is a significant risk factor for injury. Therefore, having a cardiovascular system that can meet both the *aerobic* and *anaerobic* requirements of a dance career means that you will have improved endurance, will not tire as easily, and will have a reduced risk of injury. Cardiovascular fitness also plays an important role in injury recovery—the fitter you are, the quicker you will heal.

To improve your aerobic fitness capacity, it is recommended that you undertake exercise that elevates your heart rate to 70–90 percent (depending on your fitness levels) of its maximal capacity for 20–30 minutes, 2 to 3 times a week (Wyon 2005). To calculate your maximal heart rate (MHR), you use the simple equation of 220 beats per minute (bpm) minus your age. Then calculate 70 percent of this to find your target heart rate (THR) for starting these exercises. Here is an example for an 18-year-old dancer:

220 – 18 = 202 bpm (MHR)

202 x 0.70 = 141 bpm (THR)—70 percent of your MHR

202 x 0.90 = 182 bpm (THR)—90 percent of your MHR

You may want to start your aerobic training program at the 70 percent end of the range, so for the first week, work at a heart rate of 141 bpm; then the next week, move up to 75 percent and so on until you reach the 90 percent mark.

There are many options you can choose for your *aerobic* training. These include a static exercise bike, elliptical machine, swimming, skipping, or running on a treadmill. You may want to take into consideration the impact on your joints of some of these activities. For instance, you may wish to choose cycling, elliptical machine, or swimming to avoid loading the joints of the feet, knees, and spine. You can measure your heart rate using a fitness-tracker watch or by using one of the free heart-rate apps available for smartphones. Additionally, some exercise equipment in gyms, such as static bikes and elliptical machines, have built-in heart-rate monitors on the handlebars.

While supplemental cardiovascular training is recommended, it is also considered good practice to include some dance-specific endurance training into dance class itself. Teachers could design this into the class perhaps once a week so that the dancers only need to undertake supplemental training another two times outside of class. This could involve either a high intensity warm-up that is continuous over 20–30 minutes or a center combination that is learned incrementally, then performed for the purpose of continuous repetition over a similar time period (Rafferty 2010). In this way, the endurance requirements for a dancer's fitness can be addressed within the artistic environment of a dance setting, and not just relegated to a supplemental training routine in a more athletic environment.

Nutrition

As you undertake a supplemental cardiovascular training program, another important consideration is how this will affect your nutritional requirements. Remember that food is fuel, and if you are significantly increasing the fuel demands for your body through fitness training, you will need to address this in terms of an increase in nutritional intake. You also need to ensure that you are adequately hydrated; cardiovascular training will result in fluid loss that needs to be replaced. If you are in any doubt about the best way to fuel yourself appropriately for performance, consult a nutritionist or dietician who has experience in working with dancers or athletes. They can help you to create a nutritional plan that complements your physical requirements (Challis 2016).

Caution

Before starting any cardiovascular fitness training, you must be sure that you are in good health. If you have any unexplained shortness of breath, heart racing, dizziness, persistent headaches, abnormal fatigue, or are just feeling unwell, you should consult your doctor before you begin an exercise program. Even if you are generally fit and well, you should be mindful of tailoring your cardiovascular fitness exercise to your current energy levels. If you are feeling particularly fatigued, perhaps after an intensive class or rehearsal, then it is not a good idea to add a cardio workout that day. Remember that fatigue is a major risk factor for injury. When you are tired, the best recipe is rest. You should never undertake cardio training when you are suffering from any kind of infection, such as a cold, virus, or even a wound infection. Similarly, if you are on any kind of prescribed medication, you should consult your doctor before beginning cardio training. The increased metabolic demands may alter your dosage requirements, so changes in training should always be done under medical advisement.

Three-minute step test

If you want to assess your current level of *aerobic* cardiovascular fitness against the normative data for your age group, you can complete the *Three-Minute Step Test* below (Bronner and Rakov 2014).

Equipment

A stopwatch or clock with a second hand (available on most smartphones).

A metronome (there are free metronome apps for smartphones).

A bench or step that is 12" (30cm) high.

A chair or place to sit.

A heart-rate monitor (there are free heart-rate monitor apps for smartphones).

Sneakers or athletic shoes.

Set-up

Set the metronome to 112 beats per minute (males and females the same). As an alternative, you can find a piece of music that has a tempo of 112 beats per minute to use.

In a seated position, take your resting heart rate and make a note of the figure.

Step test

1. You will step up onto the bench with one foot (1st beat), step up with the second foot (2nd beat), step down with one foot (3rd beat), step down with the other foot (4th beat).

2. Continue this for 3 minutes, being sure your steps are in time with the metronome or music.

3. At the end of three minutes of stepping "up, up, down, down," record your heart rate while standing. Take a note: this figure is your maximal heart rate (MHR).

4. Immediately after, sit in the chair for one minute of sitting rest.

5. At the end of one minute, record your heart rate again. This is your one-minute recovery heart rate (RHR).

Use your one-minute recovery heart rate to see where you register on Table 22.1. Find your age bracket, then find your RHR number in the column beneath. Check to the left to see the rating for your RHR score. If you score in the 3–6 (average to very poor categories) then you need to undertake supplemental cardio training. Note that there are separate charts for males and females.

Table 22.1 Step test

ADAM Center Interpretation:
NORMS FOR 3-MINUTE STEP TEST (Metronome: 112 beats/min)
(Based on 1-minute recovery HR)

Fitness category	18–25	26–35	36–45	46–55	56–65
Men					
0 Excellent	<79	<81	<83	<87	<86
1 Good	79–89	81–89	83–96	87–97	86–97
2 Above average	90–99	90–99	97–103	98–105	98–103
3 Average	100–105	100–107	104–112	106–116	104–112
4 Below average	106–116	108–117	113–119	117–122	113–120
5 Poor	117–128	118–128	120–130	123–132	121–129
6 Very poor	>128	>128	>130	>132	>129
Women					
0 Excellent	<85	<88	<90	<94	<95
1 Good	85–98	88–99	90–102	94–104	95–104
2 Above average	99–108	100–111	103–110	105–115	105–112
3 Average	109–117	112–119	111–118	116–120	113–118
4 Below average	118–126	120–126	119–128	121–126	119–128
5 Poor	127–140	127–138	129–140	127–135	129–139
6 Very poor	>140	>138	>140	>135	>139

Balance and proprioceptive training

If you recall from Chapter 5, a dancer's balance involves a complex interaction between many body systems. Just as any other aspect of the dancer's physiology, these systems will also benefit from additional training outside the dance studio in order to hone the speed and accuracy of the balance mechanisms. While this should form part of your basic supplemental training program, it is of particular importance in the recovery phase from injury. As we saw, many of the balance receptors that feed the brain vital information about where we are in space are contained within the muscles, tendons, ligaments, and joint capsules. If any of these structures are damaged as a result of injury, then this can affect the messaging system to the brain. Part of any injury rehabilitation program should therefore pay attention to this system. Any deficit in the balance mechanisms can lead to an increased risk of recurrent injury.

A basic test for a dancer's level of balance ability is to stand on one leg (the raised leg must not be touching the standing leg as this gives the body additional feedback information) and then to close the eyes. A dancer should be able to remain on balance with the eyes shut for a minimum of 30 seconds. If you wobble, touch the raised foot to the standing leg, or put the foot down, the test is over and you should stop the timer. You should try this on both sides as it is common for one leg to be more stable than the other. If you have had a foot, ankle, or knee injury, this may dramatically affect your ability to achieve the 30-second goal, even if the injury was some time ago and is apparently healed.

If you have had an injury, then your doctor, physical therapist, or dance rehabilitation professional should give you some specific exercises to target the balance and proprioceptive systems. However, there are some general exercises that should be a part of your training program, whether you are injured or not, and these are basic and simple to do.

The following balance exercise can be performed on any of these options, ranging from easy to challenging:

Pillow or sofa cushion.

Balance disc.

Rocker board.

Wobble board.

Standing on any of the above equipment options will pose a challenge to the body's balance mechanisms. Beginning with a pillow or sofa cushion, place the item on the floor then stand on it with two feet. (It is best to have a wall or chair nearby on which you can place a steadying hand should you lose your balance.) You will notice that your feet will be making numerous small adjustments to keep you balanced. Once you have a sense of the unsteady surface, try balancing on one foot at a time. The constant small corrections are representative of a flow of data running from your feet to your brain and back down to the muscles. This will be exercising the balance system.

As you improve your ability to remain steady on the surface on one foot, try closing your eyes to challenge the balance systems further. By removing one of the important components of the balance mechanism (the eyes), the information processing from the other structures will become enhanced. You can progress to the more challenging options of a balance disc, rocker board, and wobble board. To enhance and contextualize the exercise to be more dance specific, you can begin to try *tendu en croix*, *rond de jambe*, *retiré*, and *développé en croix* movements on the challenging surface.

Another development for these balance exercises is to add some coordination and interaction components to your balance training. These are particularly useful to dancers who may also need to handle props in a performance or have to interact with other performers. While performing the above balance exercises on the challenging surface, try throwing and catching a ball, either against a wall or with a partner. To further enhance the experience, you can add a cognitive distraction element such as counting backward from 100 in multiples of three while performing the balance and ball-throwing exercise. By distracting your cognitive focus from the balance exercise, you encourage the action to become more automatic.

The above exercises can help to speed up your reaction times, improve your balance adaptation mechanisms, and thus reduce the risk of injury. They should therefore be included in your supplemental training program (Batson 2008).

Psychological health

Another key component in the quest for health and fitness is to explore our psychological attitude to training. It is not uncommon for dancers to have perfectionistic tendencies that can affect how they approach the construction of a training routine. While setting goals and targets for training is useful and necessary in order to gauge one's progress, these have to be realistic and manageable. Trying to reach too far too quickly can adversely affect the results and even lead to potential injury. A perfectionist may be driven to believe that "more is better" and try to fill every spare moment with supplemental training that could eventually lead to burnout. Just as a balanced pose in dance requires numerous small adjustments to achieve, the same approach is true for our thought processes. Setting yourself a stringent program and then adhering to it rigidly, regardless of changes in external circumstances, is not helpful. Your program should adapt to your physical needs of the moment, and should reflect your class, rehearsal, and performance commitments, as well as your current levels of fatigue or health challenges. Sticking to a strict cardio program in a week when you have extra rehearsals, and perhaps also have a cold, could be damaging to your health.

If you are feeling stressed and anxious at any time, this may also be an indication that you should modify your training program. Stress, no matter whether it relates to dance or is coming from another aspect of your life, creates muscle tension. If you then work the muscles when they are already in a state of tension, at best the benefits of your training may be compromised, but at worst, you may cause an injury.

These are just a couple of examples of how psychological challenges can affect our approach to, and the outcomes of, a supplemental training program. It is key that you pay equal attention to both your physical and psychological states before embarking on your planned routine. Having strategies for exploring and managing your emotional states at any given time is an important facet of being a dancer. While it is beyond the scope of this book to outline such strategies, it is worth seeking the help of a mental health professional if you have any concerns or would just like some guidance on managing the psychological aspects of training.

Rest

Finally, a vital component of any training program (and one that is, more often than not, overlooked) is rest. Dancers often equate the concept of rest with "doing nothing" or "being lazy," but this is not the case. The most obvious example of this is sleep. While we are apparently inactive and motionless during sleep, it is actually an incredibly productive time for the body. Here are just a few of things that your body is up to during the deep stage of sleep:

Body tissues are both growing and being repaired.

Blood supply to the muscles is increased.

Hormones are being released (particularly those that affect muscle development and general growth).

Wound healing is increased.

The immune system is strengthened.

Memories are being consolidated and filed (important for technique acquisition and learning of choreography).

Appetite is balanced (when we are sleep deprived, we may want to eat more).

Energy is being restored (we wake up refreshed and ready for the day).

Typically, we need somewhere between seven and nine hours of sleep a day. For adolescents, eight to nine hours is necessary for all the extra growth activity that is taking place. There are four stages of sleep, each taking about 90 minutes, and we should rotate through these cycles about five times each night. So if you are not sleeping for long enough, or you are sleeping only intermittently, then you will not be reaping all the benefits listed above. Your motor skills, coordination, balance, memory, appetite, mood, and so much more will be affected. If you are experiencing trouble sleeping, there are many strategies—such as breathing techniques and mind-calming exercises—that can help. Talk to your doctor if this is a concern for you.

Rest is not just about sleep. The saying "a change is as good as a rest" has some validity. By stepping out of the dance studio when you can and doing something completely different, both your mind and body will take some respite from the repetitive nature of dance training. In terms of retaining information, the brain can only hold about seven to nine pieces of new information in short-term memory, and rest is an important factor in whether or not we retain that information. Wakeful resting (just closing the eyes for ten mins) has been shown to enhance our memory capacity so that we are more likely to remember new information (Dewar et al. 2012). Obviously, it is not practical to stop in the middle of a class or rehearsal to close your eyes after learning a new piece of choreography, but perhaps finding a brief window after the session when you can allow your brain to process the new work is a possibility.

The world of sports has long understood the need for rest in the run-up to big events. The concept of "tapering" is embedded in most athletic training protocols and was discussed in Chapter 4. While it is key to build up the physical strength and stamina in preparation for an event, in the final days or even weeks before, the physical activity should be reduced or "tapered" to allow for tissue recovery and to prevent muscle fatigue. This has not typically been the case in the dance world where rehearsals tend to reach fever pitch in the run-up to a performance. Dancers often become anxious that if they are not running at full capacity, they will lose stamina and muscle memory and will not retain the choreography. However, research has shown that by using *mental practice* you can still improve your motor skills at the same time as allowing the muscles to rest (Maamer et al. 2016). When we move, the brain sends a signal to the target muscles and then movement is produced. The more we fire these signals in particular combinations for specific movements, the more skilled we become. However, when we simply think about a movement, that signal from the brain to the muscles still fires, but we do not produce the end movement. Therefore we can still improve our movement skills simply by thinking about them. This means that in the final days before a performance, we can reduce our physical activity to allow the body to regenerate, rest, and be prepared for the task ahead, while using mental practice to keep our movement skills honed and ready for opening night.

These are just some of the benefits and applications of rest in a dancer's training schedule. Rest should not be correlated with laziness or weakness; it is a vital part of the life of a dancer who wants a long and healthy career. Ignore it at your peril!

23

CONDITIONING PROGRAMS

THERE ARE MANY DIFFERENT WAYS TO ORGANIZE a conditioning program based on the exercises in this book. This chapter provides suggestions on how to organize the information to benefit your individual needs. It is important to remember there is no "one size fits all" when it comes to conditioning. As discussed in earlier sections, multiple factors will contribute to your selection of exercises. You should not be aiming to complete all the exercises in this book at any one time. Making discriminate choices based on your current needs and specific goals will produce much better results than a blanket approach. This chapter contains several suggested options of how to organize exercises to best facilitate your needs. Section I presents exercise combinations based on specific aims that dancers commonly have with regard to technique training. Section II includes general exercise combinations to create a consistent conditioning plan each week. At any time you can pick and choose specific exercises that focus on areas you feel are currently neglected in your own training.

Sample plans are designed to condition muscle groups that are commonly neglected in many ballet, modern, and jazz technique classes. For example, all dance styles depend on a strong "center," yet many technique classes do not specifically condition the trunk muscles. For this reason, the sample plan in Section II provides full-body conditioning programs and options to emphasize muscle groups. As it is important to remember to warm-up before any conditioning session, tips for doing this are also included in this section.

Section I—Specific aims

The following tables are divided into general body regions with some cross-referenced exercises depending on the goal of the exercise. They are designed to help you to find specific issues that you feel you need to address. Once you define the *aim*, look to see if there are *flexibility exercises* listed as these should be completed first. These *flexibility exercises* are aimed at creating the appropriate joint range of motion that will support the effectiveness of the strength training exercises. They will typically involve the opposing muscles of the ones about to be strengthened. Your second step is to complete the recommended *strength exercises*. After completing the strengthening work, the column entitled *stretches for muscles used* provides the components needed to complete the exercise combination.

Exercise combinations: Foot and ankle

Table 23.1 Specialized exercises for foot and ankle

Aim	Flexibility Exercises	Strength Exercises	Stretches for Muscles Used
Improving your *pointe*	12.A.2	12.A.1 12.C 12.F	12.C.2
Managing ankle instability		12.D.1 12.E Balance exercise (Chapter 22)	12.D.2
Improving your *demi-plié*	12.C.2		
Improving your jump	12.A.2	12.A.1 12.C.1	12.C.2
Address tendency to sickle	12.A.2 12.B.2	12.D.1	12.D.2
Address tendency to roll	12.D.2	12.A.1 12.B.1 12.E.1 15.G.1	12.A.2 12.B.2 15.G.2
Reducing the risk of a posterior ankle impingement injury		12.A.1 12.F	12.A.2 12.C.2

The foot and ankle exercise combinations are based on the typical needs of a dancer for maintaining optimal alignment and control during technique. The feet and ankles are the foundation of the body, so improving function in this area will benefit all the structures above.

Exercise combinations: Knee and hip

Table 23.2 Specialized exercises for the knee and hip

Aim	Flexibility Exercises	Strength Exercises	Stretches for Muscles Used
Improve knee stability (reduce injury risk)		15.A.1 15.B.1 15.E.1 15.G.1 15.I.1	15.A.2 15.B.2 15.E.2 15.G.2
Manage knee hyperextension		15.A.1 15.B.1	15.A.2 15.B.2
Improve strength for knee work and knee hinges		15.A.1 15.B.1 15.C.1 15.D.1 18.A.1 (Hundred) 18.B.1 (Swimming) 18.F (Bridging)	15.A.2 15.B.2 15.C.2 15.D.2 18.A.2 18.B.2
Improve turn-out control		15.G.1	15.G.2 (Cross-legged stretch with torso)
Improve leg height in extensions (front and side)	15.A.2 15.D.2	15.C.1 15.G.1	15.C.2 15.G.2
Improve *arabesque*	15.C.2	15.D.1 15.G.1 18.B.1	15.D.2 15.G.2 18.B.2 (Back stretch)

The knee and hip need specialized work to support alignment, tracking of the knee, and turn-out. Bear in mind that the knee and hip are part of a sequential chain that includes the feet. Based on your aims, it will be beneficial to look at the other exercise combination tables and pick related exercises.

Exercise combinations: Trunk and neck

Table 23.3 Specialized exercises for the trunk and neck

Aim	Flexibility Exercises	Strength Exercises	Stretches for Muscles Used
Stabilize the core		18.A.1 18.C.1	18.A.2
Improve *arabesque* line	18.B.2 (Cat/ Cow)	18.B.1	18.B.2 (Back stretch)
Improve spinal flexibility	18.B.2 18.F		
Address anterior pelvic tilt (arched back)	18.B.2 (Back stretch) 15.C.2	18.A.1	18.A.2
Address posterior pelvic tilt (tuck)	18.A.2	15.D.1 18.C.1	15.D.2 18.C.2
Address neck stiffness	18.E.2	21.A.1	21.A.2
Stabilize a hypermobile neck		18.E.1	18.E.2

Once you have built a strong foundation and stabilized the chain through the knees and hips, the muscles involved with spinal movement need to be addressed. As you see, in the table there are cross-referenced exercises included.

Exercise combinations: Shoulder and arm

Table 23.4 Specialized exercises for the shoulder and arm

Aim	Flexibility Exercises	Strength Exercises	Stretches for muscles used
Improve scapular stability for upper-body weight-bearing and partner work	21.B.2 21.I.2	21.A.1	21.A.2
Improve control for a hypermobile shoulder (*glenohumeral*) joint		21.D.1 21.E.1 21.F.1 21.G.1	21.D.2 21.E.2 21.F.2 21.I.2
Address round shoulder alignment	21.B.2 21.I.2 18.E.2 (*Anterior fascia* and *platysma* stretch)	21.A.1 21.H (Arm openings)	21.A.2
Improve arm support in second position		21.A.1 21.C.1 21.D.1 21.I.1 21.L.1 21.M.1	21.A.2 21.C.2 21.D.2 21.B.2 21.L.2 21.M.2

Upper-body strength and mobility are essential, especially considering the physical demands of today's dance world. Placement of the *scapula* and alignment are key elements in shoulder work.

Section II—Comprehensive Conditioning

Here optional workouts have been provided to use and to assist you in creating your own program. In choosing or creating your own conditioning plan, a few things need to be taken into account. These include the amount of time that you have available, your dance load for the day, your weekly goals, whether you are using the workout for conditioning or warm-up, any injuries you may be working with, and your performance demands. See Chapter 4 for more information on timing and structuring of exercise programs.

Dancers tend to have a variable schedule, so it is helpful to look ahead to see what the next few weeks entail for you. In order to be consistent, it is recommended that you outline your conditioning plans for each month. Not only does this provide you with a consistent schedule for each week, but it also allows for the repetition necessary to make the appropriate strength and flexibility changes. After a month you need to reevaluate your exercise plan, make adjustments by increasing or decreasing the intensity of exercises or swapping exercises, and, depending on the upcoming demands, possibly change the focus of the conditioning to another area of the body. Whatever the goal of the plan, always remember to include days of rest!

Quick warm-up for class, rehearsal, or performance

Dancers don't always have the luxury of having a comprehensive class or warm-up before a rehearsal or performance. In the concert dance realm, there may be a company class given, or in the musical theater world, dance captains may lead a structured warm-up, but these may or may not deal with the individual needs of each dancer. Lack of time or space for warm-up can be an issue in the world of commercial dance, where you are expected to be ready to go as soon as you walk into the studio. This group of exercises is designed for a quick warm-up in a limited space.

1. Elevate the heart rate: based on your available space, begin with general movements that encourage an increase in blood circulation. You want these to be low impact but intense enough to get your breathing rate to increase and for you to begin to sweat a little. You can start by articulating the feet: from a parallel position move one foot from *demi-pointe* to full *pointe* off the floor,

Table 23.5 Quick warm-up

Steps 1–5	Activity
Elevate your heart rate	Articulate the feet Walking / running / jumping jacks Arm/shoulder reaches and circles
Find your mobility	18.B.2 Cat/Cow
Activate your muscles	18.A.1 The Hundred 18.C.1 Single-leg stretch with twist 18.D.1 Side lifts 15.E.1 Parallel leg raise 18.B.1 Swimming
Full-body engagement	12.A.1 Planks
Stretch to your needs—short duration stretches only	12.C.2 Calf stretch 15.C.2 Active hip flexor stretch 15.B.2 Quad stretch 15.G.2 Cross-legged stretch 18.D.2 Quadratus lumborum stretch

then reverse to *demi-pointe*, then flat. Repeat with the other foot and gradually build up the speed until this becomes a smooth trot with alternating feet. You can then build to running in place, brisk walking around the studio, and on to jumping jacks. If space allows, try to incorporate arms, shoulder, and neck movements. You can include reaches, shoulder/arm circles, and self massage to the often stiff *upper trapezius* muscles between the shoulder and the neck.

2. Find some mobility: most likely you will have been traveling or sitting prior to your dance activity. Now that you have your blood circulating, it is important to mobilize the spine in order to maximize core exercises. Be sure to include some neck range-of-motion exercises to explore the boundaries of any stiffness.

3.   Activate your muscles: engaging the core assists you in finding your balance and bringing your attention into the body. This is not a time to push to the max, but you want to feel that you have activated the full trunk. This includes specific abdominals, sides, hip, and back exercises.

4.   Full-body engagement: dance requires full-body integration. After activating specific muscle groups, engage in a final plank to encourage the body to work as an integrated unit.

5.   Stretch to your needs: stretching during a warm-up should not be aimed at reaching a maximum or new ranges of motion. Choose individual stretches specific to your needs to release tension and prepare you for dance. Stretches should only be held for short bursts of up to 15 seconds in the warm-up phase in order not to fall into the trap of muscle deactivation.

Full-body training—beginning, intermediate/advanced

This program includes a standard full-body workout to include most muscle groups at the appropriate intensity level. Table 23.6 identifies entry level exercises that are a good starting point. You can make great improvements with these beginning exercises if you pay attention to the details. After you develop clean technique with the exercises presented in Table 23.6 and you feel the need to increase the intensity of your workout, proceed to Table 23.7, which provides intermediate/advanced versions of the previous exercises. Each level follows the same full-body exercise format, followed by additional exercises for specific body regions. It is important to rotate and alternate the specific muscle groups being worked in order to maximize the conditioning benefits. This program should be scheduled for when you have recovery time available before returning to dance. As you rotate through the various body areas, you may highlight an issue of weakness or stiffness on which you want to focus. You could then choose a tailored program from the "specific aims" section to address this.

1.   Elevate your heart rate: you have the option of following the process described in the quick warm-up above, or if you have access to equipment such as a stationary bike or elliptical

Table 23.6 Full body training—beginning

Steps	Exercises
Elevate your heart rate	Quick warm-up Bicycle or elliptical machine
Strength: Abdominals	18.F Bridging 18.A.1 Chest lift 18.C.1 Oblique reach
Flexibility: Abdominals	18.A.2 Abdominal muscle stretch
Strength: Hips	15.C Supine hip flexor 15.E Parallel leg raise 15.G.1 Clam shell 15.F.1 Side lying with chair 15.D.1 Prone leg lifts 18.D.1 Side lifts 21.A.1 Wall planks with scapular press 21.H Arm openings 21.I.1 Resisted bicep curl 21.J. Resisted triceps extension 18.B.1 Basic back extension

machine, these can also be used to warm up the body at a low intensity for about ten minutes.

2. Generalized conditioning: the focus is to make sure the majority of the body is either directly or indirectly involved in the exercise plan and you are also balanced between flexion and extension exercises. In making your own plan, think of following the sample order: spinal articulation, abdominals, hips, sides/waist, scapular stabilization, arms, and, finally, a back extension. Flexibility exercises can be interspersed as required, with further attention to stretching at the end.

Table 23.7 Full body training—intermediate/advanced

Steps	Strength Activities
Elevate your heart rate	Quick warm up Bicycle or elliptical machine
Generalized conditioning	18.F Bridging, roll ups 18.A.1 The Hundred, single-leg stretch 18.C.1 Single-leg stretch with twist 15.C.1 Iliopsoas training 15.D.1 Kneeling hamstring and gluteal muscle work 15.G.1 Side leg lifts in turn-out 15.F.1 Supine with a wall 18.D.1 Side planks 21.A.1 Planks 21.H Dips 18.B.1 Swimming

3. Additional emphasis: once you have completed the general conditioning, choose the body region to which you plan to give extra attention that day. The idea is to emphasize specific muscle groups, such as those in the feet or arms, on alternating days. Once you have cycled through all the body regions over several days, you can begin again.

Table 23.8 Body region emphasis

Emphasis foot and ankle	12.A.1 Foot articulation
	12.B.1 Resisted dorsiflexion
	12.C.1 Resisted plantar flexion
	12.D.1 Resisted ankle eversion
	12.E.1 Resisted ankle inversion
	12.F Pointing without the calf
Emphasis knee and hip	15.A.1 Single-leg kicks
	15.B.1 Knee extensions
	15.F.1 Supine knees bent with ball or cushion
	15.H.1 Side leg lifts with internal rotation
	15.I.1 Single-leg knee bend
Emphasis trunk and neck	18.A.1 Single-straight-leg stretch, double-straight-leg stretch
	18.E.1 deep neck flexors, extensors
Emphasis shoulder and arm	21.B.1 Resisted shoulder flexion
	21.C.1 Latissimus dorsi pull
	21.D.1 Resisted side arm raise
	21.E.1 Resisted arm adduction
	21.F.1 Resisted external rotation
	21.G.1 Resisted internal rotation
	21.H Reverse plank
	22.K.1 Palms up / palms down
	21.L.1 Wrist curls with hand weights
	21.M.1 Wrist extension with hand weights

24

MOVING BEYOND and NEXT STEPS

AS MENTIONED BACK IN PART I, our society is inundated with exercise books, online fitness programs, 24-hour fitness cable channels, blogs, and websites that all promise to help you to achieve your fitness dreams. This multimillion-dollar industry is ever evolving and we are now seeing the rise of wearable technology, such as smart watches and fitness trackers. Everywhere you look you will find fitness centers sporting the latest trends in exercise training in an attempt to draw in new customers. If you are new to the world of fitness, it can be a daunting task to find which type of exercise system is right for you.

According to the American College of Sports Medicine (ACSM) Worldwide Fitness Trends for 2016, some of the most popular trends include body weight training, HIIT (high intensity interval training), strength training, working with a personal trainer, yoga, group training classes, sports-specific training, and flexibility and mobility rollers (Thompson 2015). Additionally, group class systems like Pure Barre, Cross-Fit, Orangetheory, and SoulCycle continue to be popular workout programs. With so many fads and trends out there, how do dancers decide where to go next for their specific physical and aesthetic training needs beyond this book?

The exercises presented in this book were chosen for their ease of application with minimal equipment and are focused on training using the body weight. You may reach the point where you are ready to branch out and challenge yourself with additional fitness training—when time, finances, and access to fitness facilities allow. When looking for additional training, you should consider your personal goals, your training needs, and your own individual anatomy. Each exercise system will have its own unique benefits and limitations, so it is important to choose wisely.

Personal trainers

As dancers, we are conditioned to receive feedback on our form, placement, and performance. Working with a personal trainer can provide a similar level of feedback that can be beneficial for motivation and assisting in identifying areas of weakness. However, personal trainers are not equal in their experience, training, and perspective on what constitutes a workout. There are more than 250 third-party organizations that provide personal training certificates and this can prove confusing when trying to evaluate the quality and standard of an individual's training. Three of the most trusted certification programs are from the American College of Sports Medicine (ACSM), National Academy of Sports Medicine (NASM), and Certified Strength and Conditioning Specialist (CSCS).

Communication is a key factor in working with any personal trainer. You need to be able to discuss the demands of your specific dance style with someone who can then customize the program to those needs. A great trainer will help you to translate conditioning movements into the dance studio. It is good practice to reevaluate the results of your training after a few weeks to see if you and your trainer are still on the same page.

Alternative training modalities

There are many modalities for conditioning the body. In addition to traditional gyms, such as 24 Hour Fitness or similar facilities found on college campuses, there are alternative modalities such as Pilates, Gyrotonics, and yoga. Not all modalities will provide you with the same results, so understanding the pros and cons of each can be helpful when deciding where to put your time and money.

At a traditional gym you will have the option of using weight machines, free weights, and cardio equipment. Weight machines are designed to strengthen the large muscle groups used in various movements. They can be used to enhance some, but not all, dance movements. Nevertheless, dancers can benefit from strength training on weight machines. Dancers are understandably concerned about developing bulky, tight muscles. It has been well-documented that conditioning can support dance performance, but there is a point at which overzealous training programs can be detrimental to the dancing body. Machines can offer moderate resistance exercises that work the muscle groups discussed in this book. Most of the machines have guides providing you with specific information on execution and the muscles being trained. By using low to moderate resistance and increasing repetitions, gains in strength can be achieved with little muscle bulking. Machines used with high levels of resistance will create more bulk and can place strain on the muscles and joints.

Other modalities common in the dance community are Pilates, Gyrotonics, and yoga. Dancers tend to gravitate toward these programs due to the mind-body focus of the programs and the embedded balance between strength and flexibility exercises. If taught by a qualified instructor, dancers will develop strength and tone in their muscles without the excess bulk of traditional weight lifting. Just as discussed in the personal training section, it is important to evaluate the background of your instructor and find out if they understand the demands of dance. For example Pilates instructors with comprehensive training from programs such as Balanced Body, BASI, Stott, and the Classical Method, to name a few, truly understand the Pilates principles and see the work as not just a series of exercises. Ask questions about the studio and the individual teachers' backgrounds, and take a few classes to get a sense of the dynamics and training focus before making a larger financial commitment.

Lastly, in the process of choosing the type of classes to take as a complement to your dance training, look closely at where you excel and where you need some work. For example, a hypermobile dancer may love to take yoga as this modality has a strong focus on flexibility. However, if you are hypermobile, then it is likely that what you really need is strength conditioning, as you are probably already flexible enough. This is where Pilates or Gyrotonics may be more beneficial as, although they do work on flexibility, they also have a strong dynamic strengthening component when using their specialized equipment.

You don't need to be exclusive to one type of training. We already specialize enough in our dance training. It may be helpful to spend one day in the gym working on your cardiovascular needs and then alternate other days with Pilates or yoga to focus on the body in a different way.

The best part of being a dancer in today's world is that there are some well-developed programs of training available, excellent trainers to be found, and a growing scientific evidence base to support safe and effective training for dancers. It is now up to you to make decisions on what you need the most and to continuously reevaluate throughout your career.

Cooling down and wrapping up

While it is essential to warm up before you begin any dance or exercise activity, it is equally important that you cool down afterward. Most dance activities increase in intensity toward the end of the session. When circulation and respiration rates are elevated, it is key to allow them to reduce gradually rather than coming to a sudden stop. Blood that has been directed toward the muscles during activity needs to be returned to the brain in order to prevent dizziness, and the waste products produced during exercise need to be distributed rather than being allowed to pool in the muscles. If left latent in the muscles, these waste products can contribute to post-exercise muscle soreness and stiffness. Carrying this over into your next activity or the next day can increase your risk of injury. Your cool-down period should last approximately ten minutes and should focus on gradually reducing the pulse rate and bringing your breathing under control, while allowing your body temperature to return to normal. The joints you have been using in the preceding activity should be gently mobilized through their normal range of motion as this is thought to support the health of the joint capsule (Quin, Rafferty, and Tomlinson 2015). You should then incorporate passive stretches that are held for at least 30 seconds. If you are going to be dancing again that day, keep the stretches shorter (around 15 seconds) to avoid deactivating the muscles before your next activity.

You should also incorporate time for rehydrating during your cool down and if possible change into dry clothing. Be aware of the risks of going out of a warm studio in damp clothes into a colder environment. This can cause contraction of the muscles that can lead to stiffness and an increased risk of injury. The cool-down phase is often neglected by dancers who are running to the next activity or who just want to get home quickly. However, this is a vital part of maintaining your conditioning as a dancer and should be afforded the same level of importance as warming up. The cool-down phase is also important for mental recovery. This is a time to focus on yourself, check in with your body to see which areas need attention, and to let go of any stress or anxiety that may have arisen during the class, rehearsal, or performance. The majority of dancers' injuries and psychological challenges have a cumulative nature where issues become compounded through being denied or ignored. Take this time to be honest with yourself and to take the appropriate action to recover fully. Be sure only to carry forward the beneficial aspects of your training, such as technique and strength gains, and clean the slate of any unwanted issues.

So we have now reached the cool-down phase of this book and it is time for wrapping up. The information provided may seem overwhelming at first pass, but take the time to reread the chapters as you become more familiar with the material. A second read-through will clarify many points as you will have the benefit of the overall context and content of the book. The brain is much more able to absorb new information when it has a clearer context to which it can hook the new ideas.

To sustain a long and healthy dance career takes an intelligent and analytical approach. Honesty is key as you begin to appraise your strengths and weaknesses. When you have developed a true picture of your current fitness status, you can begin to construct a comprehensive program that will support you in achieving your training goals. Your conditioning program can come to represent a friend and ally in your quest to be the best you can be. If you find yourself struggling in class, rehearsal, or performance, you can comfort yourself in the knowledge that these issues can be addressed by finding the appropriate exercise combination to help you to navigate any technique hurdles. While you may sometimes feel that the time in the studio is about meeting the goals of a teacher or choreographer, the time spent in supplemental training is entirely in your hands. Taking the wheel of responsibility for your training needs can be both an empowering and a liberating experience for a dancer. Knowing that you have the control to develop the dynamic stability to keep you safe and strong in your movements allows you to release and free your mind to explore the expressive and artistic aspects of your performance. The focused attention on your supplemental training needs will reward you with the freedom of expressive movement, allowing you to dance longer, stronger, and with a true sense of joy.

APPENDIX: INTERVIEWS WITH DANCERS

THE AIM OF THIS BOOK IS TO PROVIDE YOU with a variety of dance-related training protocols that will serve as a firm foundation for reaching out to other training disciplines. In this section, key figures from many disciplines of dance—Leanne Cope, Julio Agustin, Amy Yakima, Ricardo Cervera and Allison Burke have all generously shared their thoughts on, and experiences of, supplemental training. They discuss the various different modalities of cross-training that they have found useful and how these have contributed to career longevity. (Some of the supplemental training they talk about exists outside the realm of dance.)

Interview with Leanne Cope

Leanne began her training at the Dorothy Coleborn School of Dancing (in Bath, England) and went on to The Royal Ballet School (London), graduating into the company in 2003. As a First Artist, Leanne danced in all the major Royal Ballet classics and created several roles with Liam Scarlett, The Royal Ballet's Artist in Residence. These included Emily Dimmock and Annie E Crook in *Sweet Violets* and Gretel in *Hansel and Gretel*. In 2015, Leanne made her Broadway debut, originating the role of Lise Dassin in *An American in Paris*. For this role, she was nominated for a Tony Award, Drama Desk Award, and several other awards for Best Leading Actress in a Musical. She won the Astaire Award for Best Dancer in 2015 and was awarded the Dorothy Loudon Award for Excellence in the Theatre.

Leanne Cope

Have you ever used supplemental training in addition to regular dance class? Was this during the recovery phase from an injury or as a core part of your regular training (or both)?

Yes. I've used Pilates, swimming, and yoga.

Pilates has always been part of my routine since I became a professional dancer at The Royal Ballet. But when I got the part of Lise in *An American in Paris*, my body maintenance other than regular ballet class became a lot more specific. I saw my Pilates teacher, one-on-one, twice a week. After assessing my body and watching the show, our main aim was to even out my body from doing the same choreography eight shows a week. Swimming was a great way to build stamina for the show without the strains of gravity on the body, and yoga was a great way to counteract always working in turn-out. It also helped me feel more grounded, which helped with the singing and acting aspect of the role.

What aspects did you find helpful or not helpful?

I found it all helpful, even when I made the mistake of overexerting myself. It's a continuing lesson of how to do the best for your body without exhausting yourself before the most important part of the day, the show. I found what I needed on a Monday to get myself ready for the show was very different to what I needed on a Friday. Monday, I had the energy for strength building exercise, whereas Friday, my Pilates class was based more on stretching tired muscles.

Did anyone ever explain the benefits of supplemental training to you, either as a student or a professional?

Pilates was introduced to us at school; mainly when recovering from injuries, you tend to learn more about your body. I have learned most from other dancers and performers by talking to them about what has helped them. I believe cross-training is now involved with most people's training.

What role do you think supplemental training should play in the life of a dancer?

I think it's something that should be introduced as early as possible to anyone considering a career in dance, both for general body health and hopefully a longer career.

Interview with Julio Agustin

Julio Agustin is assistant professor of acting at the University of Miami. To date, he has performed in six Broadway shows (including *Chicago, Fosse, Steel Pier,* and *Women on the Verge of a Nervous Breakdown*) and runs a monthly audition studio in New York City, The Transition Workshop (JulioAgustin.com). Award nominations include the AUDELCO (Audience Development Committee) Award for Best Direction (*Sweet Charity*, at the New Haarlem Arts Theatre, New York) and Syracuse Area Live Theater Award for Best Choreography (*In the Heights* at the Hangar Theatre). His book, *The Professional Actor's Handbook*, was released in February 2017.

Julio Agustin

Have you ever used supplemental training in addition to regular dance class? Was this during the recovery phase from an injury or as a core part of your regular training (or both)?

After completing my college degree, I returned home to Miami to continue training while working locally. During that time, the ballet instructor at a well-known and reputable studio who was nurturing my early career told me that I had to start lifting weights in order to balance my larger lower half. Okay, what he really said was that I had a big butt and I should try to fix the proportions. Really! He mentioned that a proportioned body would do wonders for my dance technique. That is when I began to develop a gym routine of cardio and weights that I have maintained throughout my professional career and continue even today. I also discovered Pilates during a hip injury while in the Broadway company of *Fosse* and continue to use many of the exercises within the system to maintain core strength and a healthy alignment.

Weight training and cardio routine have been a regular part of my conditioning (warming up, improving flexibility and alignment, strength training for partnering). The Pilates work started as part of the recovery from an injury and has continued as part of sustaining a dance career into my 40s—when I had to dance smarter and not harder.

What aspects did you find helpful or not helpful?

I wish that I could afford to do one-to-one Pilates work every day! Although it is hard and grueling, each and every aspect of working on a Pilates Reformer is super helpful in both conditioning and injury prevention. I also find that including the gym as part of the whole in sustaining a dance career is essential, especially for men like myself who are often asked to partner the female dancers in Broadway musicals.

Did anyone ever explain the benefits of supplemental training to you, either as a student or a professional?

Training as an undergraduate was about technique; this included learning how to dance preventatively. Focus was not only on learning the skills for each genre of dance (contemporary, ballet, jazz, tap, musical theater), but proper alignment and technical skills were also a focus of the training in my program at the Florida State University under Kate Gelabert, Head of Music Theatre (dance area).

What role do you think supplemental training should play in the life of a dancer?

My opinion: the body is a machine and every machine has a shelf life. That said, the better the parts, the stronger the materials, the more attention given to its care and maintenance, the longer and stronger it will work for you. Supplemental training is a must for any dancer wishing to sustain a long-term career as a performer, choreographer, and teacher.

Amy Yakima

Interview with Amy Yakima

Amy Yakima grew up dancing at Noretta Dunworth School of Dance in Dearborn, Michigan. While training, she was cast in the *Radio City Christmas Spectacular* as Clara for three years at the Fox Theatre in Detroit, Michigan, and one year at the Radio City Music Hall in New York. She is most notably known for winning season ten of Fox's hit TV show *So You Think You Can Dance* and continuing to tour nationwide that fall with the top ten contestants of that season. She toured with Travis Wall's Shaping Sound dance company and was a performer in Lindsey Stirling's "Shatter Me" national/international tour. She was a dancer in Carrie Underwood's "Something in the Water" music video and came back to SYTYCD as an all-star performer. Yakima trained on scholarship for one year at Marymount Manhattan College and was on the faculty at the Velocity Dance Convention and the West Coast Dance Convention. She recently made her Broadway debut as Peter Pan in *Finding Neverland*, a role she performed for more than a year.

Have you ever used supplemental training in addition to regular dance class? Was this during the recovery phase from an injury or as a core part of your regular training (or both)?

Yes, I have used supplemental training in addition to regular dance class. I like to take yoga, Pilates, gym time, and boxing, in addition to my other dance classes every week.

I have used supplemental training for my everyday training as well as during the times I have had an injury. I usually will have an hour or two dancing per day, either class or renting a studio to create in. I really just love moving in general, so taking a boxing or yoga and/or Pilates class during the week helps with keeping up stamina, as well as targeting certain muscles that are harder to work on. When I have an injury, I consult my doctor and we pinpoint the cause of the injury. It is usually a move or moves based on the job or rehearsal that I am currently working on. After we determine the cause, I will be realigned and given certain exercises that will help basically "wake up" those weak muscles in order to relieve the injury and make my body work properly and effectively.

What aspects did you find helpful or not helpful?

I find all of it helpful! I am continuously learning how my body works and always open and willing to add new training methods to my regimen. With that being said, I understand that everyone has a different body type and certain exercises or training methods may not benefit others as much as it does me. During the recovery process, I find the most help with the exercises that are specifically given to me to help strengthen my weak muscles, as this weakness causes other muscles to become overworked or injured. I also appreciate the dance knowledge that my doctor acquired in addition to his medical knowledge. He understands the importance of my continuous training and helps me avoid as many injuries as possible by explaining my specific anatomical composition—and teaching me how to adjust certain exercises in order to benefit me in minimizing injuries.

Did anyone ever explain the benefits of supplemental training to you, either as a student or a professional?

I first saw the benefits of adding supplemental training to my dance training when I was a student. After enjoying the results of adding supplemental training, I would consult other respected dancers and professionals to discover the type of training regimen they put their bodies through. Being part of the dance community, we are always talking to each other and learning about new training techniques to help our bodies grow in order to perfect our craft.

What role do you think supplemental training should play in the life of a dancer?

Supplemental training is an essential part of our lives in order to keep our bodies active and healthy throughout our careers. With that being said, overdoing it can also affect our career negatively, so finding that nice balance between supplemental training and dance training is what will help benefit a dancer most.

Interview with Ricardo Cervera

Ricardo Cervera

Spanish dancer Ricardo Cervera is Ballet Master of The Royal Ballet. He trained at The Royal Ballet Upper School and joined the company in 1993, promoted to First Artist in 1996; Soloist in 1999; and First Soloist in 2002. He was appointed Assistant Ballet Master in 2014 and Ballet Master in 2016, and retired as a dancer in 2015. His repertory with the company included Mercutio (*Romeo and Juliet*), Lescaut (*Manon Lescaut*), Bratfisch (*Mayerling*), Hans-Peter/Nutcracker (*The Nutcracker*), Arthur Troyte Griffith (*Enigma Variations*), Colas and Alain (*La Fille Mal Gardée*), Jester (*Cinderella*), Hilarion and *pas de six* (*Giselle*), Antigonus (*The Winter's Tale*), and Monkey (*"Still Life" at the Penguin Café*). Cervera trained as a *répétiteur* on the Frederick Ashton Foundation's mentoring scheme and has worked as assistant choreographer with Liam Scarlett on several works, including *Hansel and Gretel*. He has taught ballet in Japan, Spain, and around the world.

Have you ever used supplemental training in addition to regular dance class? Was this during the recovery phase from an injury or as a core part of your regular training (or both)?

Yes, I have always supplemented my dance training and career with both Pilates and Gyrotonics. They became tools to maintain my body at its optimum condition and to correct body alignment, as well as preventing any future injuries due to faulty technique.

When I first started doing Pilates it was viewed more as part of the recovery treatment from an injury. But I soon discovered it would be an important part of injury prevention throughout my career.

What aspects did you find helpful or not helpful?

I personally found both Pilates and Gyrotonics extremely helpful for my career as a dancer. I have a strong, muscular body type that has a tendency to be tight and compact, which is not ideal for a classical ballet line. So the extracurricular training helped me to lengthen and to find hip rotation from the correct muscles. It also helped me to strengthen the smaller muscle groups, which are otherwise overridden by the bigger and stronger muscles. The only thing it didn't provide was cardio training, but that wasn't much of an issue for me personally.

Did anyone ever explain the benefits of supplemental training to you, either as a student or a professional?

Yes. Both at the Royal Ballet School and at the company there was an emphasis on Pilates as an ideal form of training that it is directly applicable to dance.

What role do you think supplemental training should play in the life of a dancer?

In my opinion, it plays a crucial role in a dancer's life, in terms of both longevity and a healthy career. More often than not the work a dancer has to perform favors one side of the body much more than the other. Therefore, there is a need to find the right supplemental activity to iron out this imbalance and help reestablish the body's equal balance.

Interview with Allison Burke

Originally from Dallas, Texas, Allison began her training at various preprofessional competitive-dance studios across the Dallas–Fort Worth area. She earned various performance awards and scholarships, including the opportunity to travel across the United States as a teacher's assistant at Co. Dance Convention. Allison also assisted choreographer Kim McSwain at JUMP Dance Conventions. She graduated from Chapman University in 2014 earning a bachelor's degree in dance as well as a bachelor's degree in advertising with a minor in film studies. After graduation, she performed at the Divadlo Kolowrat National Theater in Prague, Czech Republic. Allison signed with MSA Talent Agency

Allison Burke

and has booked various jobs including a Garnier commercial, New York City Times Square TruFusion Print Ad Campaign, Soul Clap Fitness DVD, a Myke Terry music video, Aria New Year's Eve Gala, and the iHeartRADIO Party at Light Nightclub. She was recently an ensemble dancer in Cirque du Soleil's "The Beatles LOVE" show in Las Vegas, Nevada.

Have you ever used supplemental training in addition to regular dance class? Was this during the recovery phase from an injury or as a core part of your regular training (or both)?

Ever since I was a teenager I have been incorporating fitness into my daily regimen to supplement my dance career goals. This included gym cardio sessions and light weight lifting. However, post-college, I became more aware of my body's need for Pilates and alignment work, as well as more mindful, varied, and balanced workouts.

This awareness really took flight when I suffered a labral tear in my left hip while performing in a rigorous show. The frequency of shows (ten per week) took its toll on my body. It was clear I was not meeting my body's warm-up/cooldown and conditioning needs, therefore my hip responded with a severe injury. I had surgery to repair the tissue, and during the rehabilitation process, Pilates and alignment work were very important in my recovery. Discovering alignment and compensation issues and correcting them allowed me to rehab my hip fully and become more knowledgeable about injury prevention. Now, I use Pilates, cardio, and weight lifting to condition my body to perform safely and at peak performance.

What aspects did you find helpful or not helpful?

As a professional dancer, it is important to vary workouts in order to prepare the body for dynamic movements. It's not helpful to do the same workout every day. For cardio specifically, treadmill intervals and Tabata training (high-intensity interval training) has helped me to condition my cardio needs for the high intensity show I perform. Weight lifting helps my muscles to remain strong and protect my joints. Lifting weights that are too heavy is not helpful, however, as it can lead to injury or bulkiness.

Did anyone ever explain the benefits of supplemental training to you, either as a student or a professional?

The benefits of supplemental training were especially emphasized during my time at Chapman University by my professors. However, I had never experienced a major injury or issue with training, therefore I thought my body was invincible and I did not implement a lot of the valuable advice and expertise given to me at that time. Post–hip injury, I realized retrospectively that I should have listened to my professors about body care and conditioning. You live and you learn!

What role do you think supplemental training should play in the life of a dancer?

I believe supplemental training should always be incorporated into a dancer's daily regimen. Whether that means yoga, stretching, running, weight training, Pilates, or walking your dog—all safe supplemental activities should be celebrated.

My advice to young dancers wanting to have a long and healthy career would be to listen to your body and honor that voice. Train hard, then rest hard: balance is key. Listen carefully to professors and mentors in their offering of expertise about body health and supplemental training. Lastly, feed, nourish, and care for your body, because you only get one and it happens to be the vessel in which you express yourself and create art.

REFERENCES

Batson, Glenna. 2008. "Proprioception—What Is It?" Resource Paper: Proprioception—International Association for Dance Medicine & Science, October 4. https://www.iadms.org/page/210.

Bronner, Shaw, and S. Rakov. 2014. "An Accelerated Step Test to Assess Dancer Pre-Season Aerobic Fitness." *Journal of Dance Medicine & Science* 18 (1): 12–21.

Challis, Jasmine, Adrienne Stevens, and Margaret Wilson. 2016. "Nutrition Resource Paper 2016." Resource Paper: Nutrition—International Association for Dance Medicine & Science. https://www.iadms. org/?page=RPnutrition.

Clippenger-Robertson, Karen S. 1985. "The Snapping Hip Phenomenon." *Kinesiology for Dance* 7 (4): 12–13.

Critchfield, Brenda. 2011. Resource Paper: Stretching for Dancers— International Association for Dance Medicine & Science. Accessed September 12, 2017. http://www.iadms.org/?353.

Deighan, Martine A. 2005. "Flexibility in Dance." *Journal of Dance Medicine & Science* 9 (1): 13–17.

Dewar, Michaela, Jessica Alber, Christopher Butler, Nelson Cowan, and Sergio Della Sala. 2012. "Brief Wakeful Resting Boosts New Memories Over the Long Term." *Psychological Science* 23 (9): 955–60. doi:10.1177/0956797612441220.

Esco, Michael R. 2013. "Resistance Training for Health and Fitness." American College of Sports Medicine. Accessed September 12, 2017. https://www. prescriptiontogetactive.com/app/uploads/resistance-training-ACSM.pdf.

Fitt, Sally S. 2001. *Dance Kinesiology.* New York: Schirmer Books.

Grossman, G., K. N. Waninger, A. Voloshin, W. R. Reinus, R. Ross, J. Stoltzfus, and K. Bibalo. 2008. "Reliability and Validity of Goniometric Turnout Measurements Compared with MRI and Retro-Reflective Markers." *Journal of Dance Medicine & Science* 12 (4): 142–52.

Howse, Justin, and Shirley Hancock. 2014. *Dance Technique and Injury Prevention*. London: Routledge.

Laible, Catherine, David Swanson, Garret Garofolo, and Donald J. Rose. 2013. "Iliopsoas Syndrome in Dancers." *Orthopaedic Journal of Sports Medicine* 1 (3): 232596711350063. doi:10.1177/2325967113500638.

Luttgens, Kathryn, and Katharine F. Wells. 1982. *Kinesiology: Scientific Basis of Human Motion*. Philadelphia: W. B. Saunders.

Maamer, Slimani, David Tod, Helmi Chaabene, Bianca Miarka, and Karim Chamari. September 2016. "Effects of Mental Imagery on Muscular Strength in Healthy and Patient Participants: A Systematic Review." *Journal of Sports Science and Medicine* 15 (3): 434–50.

McCormack, A., J. Briggs, A. Hakim, and R. Grahame. 2004. "Joint Laxity and the Benign Joint Hypermobility Syndrome in Student and Professional Ballet Dancers." *The Journal of Rheumatology* 31 (1): 173–78.

Park, Rachel J., Henry Tsao, Andrew Claus, Andrew Cresswell, and Paul Hodges. February 2013. "Changes in Regional Activity of the Psoas Major and Quadratus Lumborum with Voluntary Trunk and Hip Tasks and Different Spinal Curvatures in Sitting." *Journal of Orthopaedic & Sports Physical Therapy* 43 (2): 74–82. http://www.jospt.org/doi/pdf/10.2519/jospt.2013.4292?code=jospt-site.

Quin, Edel, Sonia Rafferty, and Charlotte Tomlinson. 2015. *Safe Dance Practice*. Champaign, IL: Human Kinetics.

Rafferty, S. 2010. "Considerations for Integrating Fitness into Dance Training." *Journal of Dance Medicine & Science* 14 (2): 45–9.

Rodrigues-Krause, Josianne, Mauricio Krause, and Álvaro Reischak-Oliveira. 2015. "Cardiorespiratory Considerations in Dance: From Classes to Performances." *Journal of Dance Medicine & Science* 19 (3): 91–102. doi:10.12678/1089-313x.19.3.91.

Thompson, Walter R. November and December 2015. "Worldwide Survey of Fitness Trends for 2016: 10th Anniversary Edition." *ACSM'S Health & Fitness Journal* 19 (6): 9–18. doi: 10.1249/FIT.0000000000000164.

Weber, Alexander E., Asheesh Bedi, Lisa M. Tibor, Ira Zaltz, and Christopher M. Larson. July 2015. "The Hyperflexible Hip: Managing Hip Pain in the Dancer and Gymnast." Sports Health. Accessed September 13, 2017. https://www.ncbi.nlm.nih.gov/pmc/articles/PMC4481673/.

Wyon, Matthew. 2005. "Cardiorespiratory Training for Dancers." *Journal of Dance Medicine & Science* 9 (1): 7–12.

Wyon, Matthew. 2010. "Preparing to Perform. Periodization and Dance." *Journal of Dance Medicine & Science* 14 (2): 73–74.

RESOURCES

This list has been compiled to provide you with current resources available online and in print. The resources include information on further health education, accessing healthcare providers and trainers, dance medicine research, and ideas for further reading.

Performing Arts Healthcare Organizations

International

International Association for Dance Medicine & Science (IADMS)
> www.iadms.org
> (Healthcare professionals. Health education.)

Performing Arts Medicine Association (PAMA)
> www.artsmed.org
> (Healthcare professionals. Health education.)

North America

Dance/USA: Task Force on Dancer Health
> https://www.danceusa.org/dancerhealth
> (Health education.)

Dance Resource Center (DRC), Los Angeles
> www.danceresourcecenter.org
> (Healthcare professionals. Health education.)

Harkness Center for Dance Injuries, New York City
> https://med.nyu.edu/hjd/harkness/quality-healthcare-dance-community
> (Healthcare professionals. Health education.)

Healthy Dancer Canada
    www.healthydancercanada.org
    (Healthcare professionals. Health education.)

United Kingdom

British Association for Performing Arts Medicine (BAPAM)
    www.bapam.org.uk
    (Healthcare professionals. Health education.)

One Dance UK: Dance in Health and Wellbeing
    https://www.danceinhealthandwellbeing.uk
    (Healthcare professionals. Health education.)

National Institute of Dance Medicine and Science (NIDMS) UK
    www.nidms.co.uk
    (Healthcare professionals. Health education.)

Other Countries

Australian Society for Performing Arts Healthcare (ASPAH)
    www.aspah.org.au
    (Healthcare professionals. Health education.)

The Dutch Performing Arts Medicine Association (NVDMG)
    www.nvdmg.org
    (Healthcare professionals. Health education.)

Other Healthcare Organizations

American College of Sports Medicine (ACSM)
    www.acsm.org
    (Healthcare professionals. Health education.)

Athletes and the Arts (AATA)
    www.athletesandthearts.com
    (Health education.)

The Actors Fund
    www.actorsfund.org
    (Healthcare professionals. Health education.)

Books

The Anatomy of Exercise and Movement for the Study of Dance, Pilates, Sports, and Yoga
    Jo Ann Staugaard-Jones. North Atlantic Books (2011).

The Authentic Performer: Wearing a Mask and the Effect on Health
    Jennie Morton. Compton Publishing (2015).

Conditioning for Dance
    Eric Franklin. Human Kinetics (2003).

Conditioning for Dancers
    Tom Welsh. University Press of Florida (2009).

Conditioning with Imagery for Dancers
    Donna Krasnow. Thompson Educational Publishing (2010).

Dance Anatomy
    Jacqui Greene Haas. Human Kinetics (2010).

Dance Anatomy and Kinesiology (Second edition)
    Karen Clippenger. Human Kinetics (2016).

Dance Science: Anatomy, Movement Analysis, Conditioning
    Gayanne Grossman. Princeton Book Company (2015).

Dancer Wellness
    M. Virginia Wilmerding and Donna H. Krasnow. IADMS/Human Kinetics (2017).

The Healthy Dancer: ABT Guidelines for Dancer Health
    American Ballet Theatre National Training Curriculum (2008).

Pilates
    Rael Isacowitz. Human Kinetics (2006).

Pilates Anatomy
> Rael Isacowitz and Karen Clippenger. Human Kinetics (2011).

Safe Dance Practice: An Applied Dance Perspective
> Edel Quin, Sonia Rafferty, and Charlotte Tomlinson. Human Kinetics (2015).

Journals

Journal of Dance Education
> www.ndeo.org/jode
> Official publication of the National Dance Educators Organization.
> (Dance education.)

Journal of Dance Medicine & Science
> www.iadms.org/jdms
> Official publication of the International Association for Dance Medicine & Science.
> (Dance medicine research. Health education.)

Medical Problems of Performing Artists
> www.sciandmed.com/MPPA
> Official publication of the Performing Arts Medicine Association
> (Dance medicine research. Health education.)

Training Organizations

Personal Trainers

American College of Sports Medicine (ACSM)
> https://certification2.acsm.org/profinder

National Academy of Sports Medicine (NASM)
> https://www.nasm.org/about-nasm

National Strength and Conditioning Association (Certified Strength and Conditioning Specialist)
> https://www.nsca.com/Certification/CSCS/

Franklin Method
> https://franklinmethod.com

Pilates Instructors

Balanced Body
> https://www.pilates.com/BBAPP/V/pilates/index.html

BASI Pilates
> https://www.basipilates.com/about/

Classical Method Pilates
> https://classicalpilates.net/about-pilates-health.php

Pilates Method Alliance
> https://pilatesmethodalliance.org

Stott Pilates
> https://www.merrithew.com/stott-pilates/method

Dance Education Organizations

National Association of Schools of Dance
> https://nasd.arts-accredit.org
> (Dance education.)

National Dance Education Organization
> http://www.ndeo.org
> (Dance education.)

4Dancers
> 4dancers.org
> (Dance education. Health education)

Nutrition

Academy of Nutrition and Dietetics
    Finding a Practitioner
        http://www.eatright.org/find-an-expert
    Education Resources
        http://www.eatright.org
    (Healthcare professionals. Nutritional health education.)

Psychology

American Psychological Association (APA)
    www.apa.org
    (Psychological health education. Psychological support.)

INDEX

abdominal muscles, 32, 57–58, 104, 134, 136, 145, 157, 199–201, 219, 231, 266, 283, 312–313
  four layers of, 175–177
  exercises for, 193, and Chapter 17 (185–198)
  in Pilates (The Hundred), 203
abduction, 253, 255, 264, 273–274, 279
  defined, 11
  in the hip, 102–103, 106–107, 128
  in the shoulder girdle, 237, 238, 241
  of the arms, 246, 248
  of the wrist, 253
  strength exercises, 148, 157, 165
acetabulum, 21, 101, 125, 126
Achilles tendon, 46, 50, 53, 61, 65, 67, 90–91
acromioclavicular joint, 236
acromion, 235–236, 239, 241
adduction, 153, 248, 264, 274–275, 279, 315
  defined, 11
  in the hip, 102, 106–107, 128
  in the shoulder girdle, 237–242, 244, 246
  of the arms, 246, 248
  of the wrist, 253, 256
  strength exercise, 274–275
adductor brevis, 105–107

adductor longus, 106–107
adductor magnus, 105–107
aerobic fitness, 6, 19, 295, 330
agonist, 22–23
alignment,
  en pointe, 55
  foot and ankle, 41–42, 47, 52, 53–57, 110–112
  knee, 110, 114, 116–117, 307–309
  misalignment, 42, 53–54, 195
  neutral, 110, 13–15, 110–112, 183, 256
  pelvic, 83
  shoulder, 256
  spinal, 185, 188, 196
  torso (trunk), 183
  while dancing in heels, 60
anconeus, 249, 251
ankle, 39–46, 70–93
  dorsiflexion, 43, 50, 70, 84
  eversion (pronation), 43, 84–85, 315
  inversion (supination), 43, 88–89, 315
  muscle actions (Table 10.1), 44
  plantar flexion, 43, 59, 70
  sprain, 61, 62, 84, 88
  strength exercises, 84, 88
  supination, 43
  weights, 18, 37
antagonist, 22–23

anterior deltoid, 241–242, 247–248

anterior tilt of the pelvis, 62, 186

arabesque, 11, 64, 98, 102, 106, 122–123, 145, 157, 192, 194–195, 209, 307–308

arch of the foot, 41–43, 48, 53,

   flexibility exercise, 75–76

   strength exercises, 71–75

arch of the spine, 161–162, 189–190, 206

arms, 13, 233, 236–238, 240, 243–248, 257–258, 313

attitude, 98, 102, 106, 122, 145, 192, 194

attitude, psychological, 301

back extension, 209–210, 212, 313

back hinge fall, 116

back pain, 139, 194–196

balance, 15, 33, 41, 63, 97, 119, 127, 129, 146, 184

   defined, 24–25

   in inversions, 261

   and proprioceptive training (exercise), 300

Balanced Body, 318

biceps brachii, 240, 242–243, 249–252, 271, 283–285

biceps femoris, 96–98, 100, 104, 108–109

big toe, 41, 43, 49–50, 52, 54, 56, 72–73

bones,

   calcaneus, 41, 43, 46–47, 51, 52, 57, 61, 65, 90–92

   carpals (wrist bones), 253, 262

      illustrated, 236

   cervical spine, 169, 171–173, 184, 189, 198, 221, 239–240

      illustrated, 172

   clavicle, 239, 241, 242

      illustrated, 236, 238

coccyx, 171–172

femur, 46, 97, 98, 99, 102, 104, 106, 107, 112, 118, 120, 121, 122, 124, 126, 148, 150

   illustrated, 95, 101, 115, 125

fibula, 42–44, 46, 49–50, 95, 97

   illustrated, 95

humerus, 235, 237, 241, 242, 244, 246–248, 250–252, 255, 273, 275

   illustrated, 236, 250

ilium, 101–109, 173, 176, 177, 191, 195, 221, 244

   illustrated, 101

ischium, 101–102, 107, 109

   illustrated, 101

lumbar spine, 15, 62, 135, 169, 171–175, 177, 1854–188, 189–190, 191–194, 206, 244

   illustrated, 172

metacarpals, 254

metatarsals, 254

   illustrated, 41, 42

patella, 95, 99, 104, 110, 114, 117, 121–122, 134

   illustrated, 95

pelvis, 11, 57, 62, 65, 83, 101–101, 103–105, 110–111, 125, 130–132, 136, 139–140, 154–155, 159–161, 165, 169, 171–175, 189, 196, 201, 203, 207

phalanges, 41, 262

   illustrated, 41

pubis (pubic), 101, 102, 173, 184, 191

   illustrated, 101

radius, 236, 248–250, 252–253

   illustrated, 236

sacral spine, 171, 177, 184, 186, 189

sacrum 15, 101, 106, 109, 171–172, 184, 186, 194–195, 244

    illustrated, 101

scapula, 235–243, 256, 259, 264, 313

    illustrated, 236

sternum, 176, 183, 208, 210, 235, 236, 242

    illustrated, 236

talus, 41–43, 52, 57, 61

    illustrated, 41

tarsals, 41–42

    illustrated 41

thoracic, 15, 169, 171, 172, 177, 179, 180, 183, 186–190, 225, 236, 239, 244

    illustrated, 172

tibia, 42–44, 46, 49, 52, 55, 61, 68, 95–99, 101, 105, 112, 117

    illustrated, 95

ulna, 236, 244, 248–253

    illustrated, 236

vertebrae, 103, 171–172, 177, 179, 182–185, 189–190, 194–196, 199, 208, 210, 239, 244

    illustrated, 172

bow legs, 120

brachialis, 249–251, 283

brachioradialis, 249–250

breathing (breath), 31, 32, 35, 196, 200, 261, 297, 303, 319

bridging, 200, 229, 313

bunions, 59, 64, 66–67

bursa, 117

bursitis, 125

calcaneus, *see* bones, calcaneus

cardiovascular fitness, 24, 293, 295, 297

cardiovascular system, 295

carpal bones, *see* bones, carpals

cartilage, 12, 96, 113, 116, 117, 121, 124–125, 172, 176, 242

cervical spine, *see* bones, cervical

chondromalacia, 121

circumduction, 237, 253

clavicle, 182, 235–236, 239, 241–242

closed system, 15

coccyx, 171–172

collateral ligament, 95, 113, 116

concentric muscle action, 13

conditioning, 6–9, 23, 26–27, 117–118, 122, 169, 190, 192, 194, 197, 208, 233, 305, 310, 312–313, 314, 317–320, 323–324, 328–329, 335–336

condyle, 97–98, 105, 121

connective tissue, 21–22, 104, 106, 176, 244

cool down, 33, 319, 320, 339

coracoid process, 235–236, 239, 242

core, 5, 136, 175, 193, 199–200, 203, 219–220, 222, 260–261, 267, 308, 311–312, 328

core exercise, "The Hundred," 203

cruciate ligament, 95

curling the toes, 71, 80, 118

dance movement, 18, 169, 233, 279

demi-plié, 44, 47, 54, 58, 65, 67–68, 82, 167, 188, 306

developpé, 8, 99, 110, 139, 301

dorsiflexion, 43–44, 50, 61, 70, 76–78, 84, 315

eccentric muscle action, 13, 189–190

elbow (joint), 242, 244, 248–249, 257, 264

elbow, movements at,

    extension, 11, 249, 251, 285

    flexion, 10, 249, 282

hyperextension, 244, 261, 262

inward rotation of forearm (pronation), 249, 250, 264, 288, 339

outward rotation of forearm (supination), 249, 250, 264, 283, 288

elevation of the scapulae, 237

elastic resistance bands, 29, 37, 76, 77, 81, 84, 88, 89, 138, 149, 158, 167, 268, 274, 277, 279, 284, 285

    illustrated, 284

en pointe, see pointe

eversion of the foot, 43–44, 47, 57, 70, 84–86, 87, 90, 315

extension, 5, 11, 49–50, 57, 95–97, 99, 102, 104, 106, 124, 128, 133, 135, 139, 142, 145, 171–177, 179, 181–182, 187, 189, 194, 199–200, 205–206, 209–210, 212, 236, 241–244, 249, 251, 253, 255, 264, 270–271, 282, 285–286, 291, 313, 315

extensor carpi radialis, 251, 253, 255

extensor carpi ulnaris, 251, 253, 255–256

extensor digitorum brevis, 49

extensor digitorum longus, 44–45, 47, 49

extensor hallucis longus, 44–45, 49–50

external obliques, 174–177, 179–180

external rotation, 11, 54, 57, 110, 128, 157, 241, 264, 275–277, 315

fascia, 3, 12, 51–52, 176–177, 228–229, 244, 309

    defined, 21

fatigue, 16–17, 19–20, 27–29, 32–34, 75, 78, 133–134, 143, 197, 257, 277, 295, 297, 302, 304

femur, *see* bones, femur

fibula, *see* bones, fibula

flexibility exercises,

    ankle dorsiflexion, 44, 78

ankle eversion, 70, 86

ankle inversion, 70, 86,

ankle plantar flexion, 81

elbow extension, 285

elbow flexion, 264, 283–284

foot articulation, 70, 75

hip adduction, 128, 155

hip abduction, 128, 160, 166, 167

hip extension, 128, 139, 147

hip external rotation, 110, 128, 160–164

hip flexion, 139–142

hip internal rotation, 128, 166–168

knee extension, 128, 134

knee flexion, 131

neck muscles (deep), 200, 224–225

scapular stabilization, 264, 267

shoulder abduction, 264, 279–283

shoulder adduction, 264, 271–272, 279

shoulder extension, 271–272

shoulder flexion, 269–270

shoulder internal rotation, 279–280

trunk extension, 212

trunk flexion, 208

trunk rotation, 217

trunk side-bending, 220

wrist extension, 291

wrist flexion, 289

flexion, 10–11, 49–51, 56, 59–62, 70, 118, 121, 124, 172–175, 194, 200, 219, 236, 264, 268–269, 313

    See also plantar flexion, flexion of the arms, flexion of the elbow, flexion of the hip, flexion of the knee, flexion of the neck, flexion of the shoulder, flexion of the spine, flexion of the wrist

flexor carpi radialis, 250, 253–255

flexor carpi ulnaris, 250, 253–254, 256

flexor digitorum brevis, 49–50

flexor digitorum longus, 49–50, 68

flexor hallucis longus, 49–50, 67

foot and ankle alignment, 120

foot articulation, 70–71, 315

foot pronation, 68

full body training, 313–314

gastrocnemius, 22–23, 44, 46–47, 65,
    81–83, 90–91, 96–97, 132, 143

glenohumeral joint, 235–236, 247, 264, 279

glenoid fossa, 235–237, 242, 246

gluteus maximus, 98, 104, 106–109, 124

gluteus medius, 98, 106–109, 151–152

gluteus minimus, 98, 106–108

gracilis, 96–99, 107–109

grand battement, 102, 105–106, 123

grand plié, 114, 116

gravity, 13–14, 25, 54–55, 57, 114, 117,
    161, 177, 184, 290, 292, 322

greater trochanter, 101, 107, 109, 124, 158

gyms, 9, 216, 296, 317

Gyrotonics, 9, 293, 317–318, 327

hamstring, 34, 62, 96, 98, 100, 104, 106,
    122–123, 129–132, 134, 144, 147, 314

hamstring strain, 122–123

head alignment, 14, 169, 183–184,
    186–189, 260

head rolls, 198

hip,
    bones, 101, 145, 148, 157, 159, 184,
        191, 230
    socket 57, 101–102, 122, 124, 126, 141,
        165–166
    snapping, 125

pain, 332

hip, movement at,
    abduction, 103, 107, 128, 148
    adduction, 128, 153, vii
    extension, 11, 106, 128, 139, 142, 145
    external rotation, 110, 128
    flexion, 11, 102–103, 124, 128, 135, 138
    hyperextension, 102
    internal rotation, 128

horizontal abduction, 237, 246, 248, 279

horizontal adduction, 237, 242, 248

humerus, *see* bones, humerus

hurdle position, 115

hyperextend, hyperextended,
    hyperextending, hyperextension of,
    back, 62, 173, 174, 177–179, 187,
        189–190, 192, 194, 196, 230
    elbow, 244, 261
    knees, 62, 65, 119, 133–135, 261, 307

hypermobility, 21–22, 119, 198, 331

hypertrophy, 17

iliac crest, 101, 179

iliacus, 103–104

iliofemoral ligament, 101–102, 187

iliopsoas, 99, 103–104, 124, 135–140, 142,
    174, 176, 314, 331

iliotibial band, 99, 104–106, 124

ilium, *see* bones, ilium

infraspinatus, 241, 245, 247–248, 275

intercondylar groove, 121

internal obliques, 174–177

internal rotation, 11, 128, 165–166, 241,
    264, 277–279, 315

intervertebral discs, 172, 184–185, 196

intrinsic muscles, 51, 56, 69, 71, 199

inversion, 43–44, 47–48, 57, 62–63, 70, 86, 88–90, 261, 315

inversions (dance movements), 7, 260

inward rotation, 96, 100, 108–109, 112, 165, 237, 242, 244, 247, 249, 252

ischial tuberosity, 101, 158

ischium, *see* bones, ischium

isometric muscle action, 13

joints, 11–12, 14–15, 21–22, 24–25, 55, 59–60, 63, 65–66, 93, 95, 99, 117–118, 126, 163, 196, 198, 212, 248, 257, 261–262, 285, 288, 296, 318–319, 329

  acromioclavicular, 236

  elbow, 248, 251

  foot and ankle, 41, 42

  glenohumeral, 236, 247

  hip, 98

  knee, 97

  lumbosacral, 186, 189

  shoulder, 236

  shoulder girdle, 236

  sternoclavicular, 236

  wrist, 253

jump, 8, 39, 47, 54, 58, 61, 67, 120, 169, 306, 328

jumps, 15, 35, 41, 52, 54, 68, 83, 86, 90, 124, 142, 147

knee,

  Osgood Schlatter's disease, 117

  pads, 118

  pain, 114–116, 121

  work, 117, 307

knee alignment, 111, 229

knee hinge, 116

knee hyperextension, 307

knee, movements at,

  extension, 95, 99, 121–122, 128, 133

  flexion, 97, 118, 128–129, 145

kyphosis, 184, 187

lateral flexion, 173–174, 179, 181, 183, 219

lateral tilt of the pelvis, 173

latissimus dorsi, 241, 243–244, 246–247, 258, 270–272, 315

leg extension, 5, 135, 187, 206

leg extension, 5, 8, 96, 124, 155–162, 187
  See also developpé

lesser trochanter, 101, 104

levator scapulae, 181–183, 222, 224, 227–228, 238–240, 246

ligament,

  collateral, knee, 95, 96, 113

  cruciate, knee, 95, 96, 113

  iliofemoral, 101

  pubofemoral, 101

longitudinal arch, 41–42, 48, 52–53, 57, 82

longus capitis, 181, 223–224

longus colli, 181, 223

lordosis and hyperlordosis, 184, 186–187, 221

lower back, 32, 60, 62, 64–65, 83, 122, 136, 138, 140–141, 143–145, 149, 154, 159–160, 162, 175, 177, 180, 184, 189–190, 193, 197, 201, 203, 205–208, 210–211, 219, 230, 284

lumbar curves, 62, 189

    illustrated, 184

lumbar erector spinae, 174–175, 180

lumbar lordosis, 187

lumbosacral joint, *see* joints, lumbosacral

metacarpals, *see* bones, metacarpal

metatarsals, *see* bones, metatarsal

misalignment, 42, 53–54, 195

movements of the ankle, 44

movements of the foot and ankle, 43

multifidus, 174

muscles,

    adductor magnus, 105

    adductor longus, 105

    adductor brevis, 105

    anconeus, 251

    biceps femoris, 97–98

    biceps brachii, 242

    brachialis, 250

    brachioradialis, 250

    coracobrachialis, 243

    deltoid (anterior, posterior), 242

    erector spinae (lumbar, thoracic), 178

    extensor hallucis longus, 45

    extensor digitorum longus, 45

    extensor digitorum brevis, 49

    extensor carpi radialis longus, 251

    extensor carpi radialis brevis, 251

    extensor carpi ulnaris, 251

    external obliques, 176

    flexor hallucis longus, 49

    flexor digitorum brevis, 49

    flexor carpi ulnaris, 250

    flexor carpi radialis, 250

    flexor digitorum longus, 48

    gastrocnemius, 46

    gluteus minimus, 98

    gluteus medius, 98

    gluteus maximus, 98

    gracilis, 98

    hamstrings, 97

iliacus, 104

iliopsoas, 104

infraspinatus, 245

internal obliques, 176

intrinsic muscles of foot (arch), 42, 51

latissimus dorsi, 244

levator scapulae, 240

longus capitis, 181, 223, 224

longus colli, 181, 223

multifidus, 174

outward rotators of the hip (deep six), 98

palmaris longus, 250

pectineus, 104, 105

pectoralis major, 242

pectoralis minor, 239

peroneus longus, 48

peroneus brevis, 48

popliteus, 98

pronator quadratus, 250

pronator teres, 250

quadratus lumborum, 179

quadriceps group, 95

rectus femoris, 99

rectus abdominis, 176

rhomboid major, 240

rhomboid minor, 240

rotators, 98

sartorius, 99

scalenus anterior, posterior, and
    medius, 182

semimembranosus, 97

semispinalis capitis, 178

semispinalis cervicis, 178

semispinalis thoracis, 178

semitendinosus, 97

serratus anterior, 239

soleus, 46

splenius capitis, 176

splenius cervicis, 176

sternocleidomastoid, 182

subclavius, 239

suboccipital, 181–183

subscapularis, 245

supinator, 245

supraspinatus, 244

tensor fascia latae, 99

teres major, 244

teres minor, 245

tibialis anterior, 45

tibialis posterior, 48

transversus abdominis, 32, 196

trapezius, 240

triceps brachii, 245

vastus medialis, 99

vastus intermedius, 99

vastus lateralis, 99

muscles of the trunk and neck, 181

muscle action, 13, 189–190

muscle actions of the ankle, 44

muscle actions of the toes, 49

muscle fiber, 21

muscle size, 17

muscles of the foot and ankle, 39, 43, 54

muscle soreness, 27, 319

muscle spasms, 186

muscle strain, 194

muscle tone, 17

muscular imbalance, 33, 68, 121, 124, 256

neck, movements at, 198, 311

extension, 172, 181

flexion, 181

lateral flexion, 181, 183

rotation, 181, 183

neck muscles, 169, 179, 182, 198, 200, 222–223, 225

neck rotation, 183

nervous system, 3, 17–18

neutral alignment, 13–15, 52–53, 60, 62, 75, 110, 133, 183, 217, 224, 256

nutrition, 296, 330, 338

Osgood Schlatter's disease, see knee, Osgood Schlatter's disease

optimal breathing, 31

osteoarthritis, 126–127

outward rotation, 96–97, 100, 102, 106, 108–109, 113, 159, 166, 237, 242, 247–249, 252

outward rotators of the hip, 98, 122

overload principle, 16

overstretch, 54, 57, 113

palmaris longus, 250, 253–254

partnering, 186, 196–197, 233, 242, 323

patella, see bones, patella

pectineus, 103–105, 174

pectoralis major, 150, 240–243, 246–248, 258, 269–270, 284

pectoralis minor, 238–239, 243, 246–248, 258, 279, 284

pelvic alignment, 131, 135, 142, 185

pelvis, see bones, pelvis

pelvis, anterior tilt, 62, 173, 174, 188, 230

pelvis, lateral tilt, 173, 174

pelvis, posterior tilt, 173, 174, 175, 187

periodization, 19–20, 332

peroneus brevis, 44, 47–48, 86

peroneus longus, 44, 47–48, 86

personal trainer, 316–317

phalanges, *see* bones, phalanges

Pilates exercises, 9, 26, 37, 129, 199–200, 203, 293, 317–318, 322–325, 327–329, 335–337

Pilates Method, 318, 325, 337

plantar fascia, 51–52

plantar flexion, 43–44, 46–47, 50–51, 56, 59–62, 70, 79–81, 90, 118, 315

plié, 44, 47, 54, 58, 65, 67–68, 82, 96, 113–114, 116, 122, 148, 157, 167, 188, 221, 306

pointe (en pointe), 35, 39, 43, 46–47, 50–52, 55–56, 61, 63–64, 66–67, 71, 79–80, 83, 118–119, 306, 310–311

pointe shoe, 55–56, 66, 118

pointing without the calf, 70, 90, 315

popliteus, 96–98

port de bras, 189, 243, 245

posterior ankle impingement, 47, 90, 306

posterior deltoid, 241–243, 245–248

posterior tilt of the pelvis, 187

principle of specificity, 18

pronation, 43, 56, 68, 82, 249–250, 264, 288

   See also elbow, pronation

pronator quadratus, 249–250, 252

pronator teres, 249–250, 252

proprioception, 24, 120, 330

proprioceptive neuromuscular facilitation, 36

psoas, 103–104, 175–176, 331

psychological health, 301, 338

puberty, 17

pubic bones, *see* bones, pubis (pubic)

pubofemoral ligament, 101–102

quadratus lumborum, 174, 179–180, 220–221, 311, 331

quadriceps, 95–96, 99–100, 114, 117–118, 121, 123, 129–131, 133–134149, 160, 166

radius, 236, 248–250, 252–253

rectus abdominis, 174–177, 179

rectus femoris, 96, 99, 103–105, 124, 142

relevé, 51, 65, 67, 120

repetitions, 5, 17, 26–29, 30, 80–81, 193, 317–318

resistance, 5, 9, 17–18, 27–32, 37, 76–77, 81, 84, 88–89, 106, 108, 138, 149, 158, 160, 167–168, 177, 182–183, 242, 244, 246–247, 254, 268, 274, 277, 279, 284–285, 317–318, 330

respiratory system, 3

rest, 12, 20, 28, 51, 67, 69, 101, 117, 123, 133, 137, 148, 152, 155–157, 159, 194, 208, 212–213, 223–226, 228, 233, 236, 267–268, 270, 272, 277, 285, 287–288, 297–298, 302–304, 310, 329

rhomboid minor, 238–239, 258

rib cage, 169, 171, 185–187, 189, 191, 195, 217, 221, 228, 259, 265, 281

rolling in, foot, 43, 52–53, 56, 66–67, 72

   See also pronation

rolling out, foot, 37, 43, 52–53, 56, 67, 72

   See also supination

rond de jambe, 301

sacrum, *see* bones, sacrum

   See also sacral spine

sartorius, 96–99, 103–105, 108–109

scalenus anterior, 181–182

scalenus medius, 181–182

scalenus posterior, 181–182

scapula, *see* bones, scapula

scapular stabilization, 260, 263–264, 313

scoliosis, 184, 194–195, 256

second position, arms, 13, 237, 257, 258, 281

semimembranosus, 96–97, 100, 104, 108–109

semispinalis capitis, 178

semispinalis cervicis, 174, 178

semispinalis thoracis, 174, 178–179

semitendinosus, 96–97, 100, 104, 108–109

serratus anterior, 238–240, 246–248, 259, 265

shin splints, 56–58, 65, 68–69

shoes, 58–62, 66, 125, 298

shoulder alignment, 258, 309

shoulder blades, winging, 259

shoulder extension, 270–271

shoulder flexion, 268–269, 283, 315

shoulder girdle, movements at,
   abduction of the scapulae, 237, 238, 239–240, 264, 279
   adduction of the scapulae, 237, 238, 239– 240, 264, 279
   depression of the scapulae, 237, 238, 239–240
   elevation of the scapulae, 237, 238
   upward rotation of the scapulae, 237, 238
   downward rotation of the scapulae, 237, 238

shoulder girdle muscles, 237–240, 243, 247

shoulder joint, 184, 219–220, 235–237, 240–242, 244, 246–248, 257, 268, 277, 279, 285

shoulder joint, movements of the arms,

abduction, 11, 241, 248

adduction, 11, 241, 242, 244, 248

circumduction, 237, 253

extension, 241, 242, 243, 270–271

flexion, 241, 249, 264, 268–269

horizontal adduction, 237, 242

horizontal abduction, 246, 248, 279

internal (inward) rotation, 237, 241, 264

external (outward) rotation, 241, 264

shoulders,
   rounded, 256, 258
   tension, 225, 238, 268, 290, 292

sickle, 48, 62–63, 77, 79, 306

sickling, 43–44, 62–63, 67

sitting bones, 102, 132, 162, 213–214, 217

sit-up, 175, 193

soleus, 44, 46–47, 65, 68, 81–83, 90, 143

specificity principle, 18

spinal alignment, 134, 147–148, 157, 159, 161, 188–189, 195

spinal curves, 184–186, 189, 195
   cervical, 184–186
   lumbar, 184–186
   sacral, 184–186
   thoracic, 184–186

spine, 13–15, 101–102, 110, 135–136, 169, 171–180, 182–196, 212–213, 229–230, 260, 311

spine, movements at,
   extension, 171, 175–177, 182–183, 184–185, 189, 200
   flexion, 171, 174, 179, 182, 200
   hyperextension, 171, 174, 177, 182–183, 189–190, 196
   lateral flexion, 174, 179, 183
   rotation, 171, 173–174, 180, 183, 198, 200

splenius capitis, 176, 181–183

splenius cervicis, 176, 181, 183

spondylolisthesis, 194

spondylolysis, 194

step test, 297–299, 330

sternoclavicular joint, 236

sternocleidomastoid, 181–183, 221, 223

sternum, *see* bones, sternum

stress fracture, 194

stretch,
  intensity, 35
  passive, 139, 141, 142, 156, 319
  timing, 34

subclavius, 238–239, 243

suboccipital, 181–183

subscapularis, 241, 245, 247, 258, 277, 279

supination, 43, 249–250, 264, 283, 288

supinator, 245, 249, 252

supplemental conditioning, 1, 4–5, 6–9, 20, 31

supraspinatus, 241, 244, 246, 273

swayback knees, 119

symphysis pubis, 184, 191

tarsals, 41

temperature, 21, 34, 319

tendon, 12, 44, 46, 50, 53, 58, 61, 65, 67–68, 90–91, 95, 97, 99–100, 114, 117–118, 121, 124, 126, 254

tendonitis, 51, 56–58, 67–68, 125

tendu, 45, 75, 102, 106, 143, 145, 155, 301

teres major, 241, 243–247

teres minor, 241, 245, 247–248

testosterone, 17

TheraBand®, 37

thoracic erector spinae, 174, 179

tibia, *see* bones, tibia

tibialis anterior, 22–23, 44–45, 48, 58, 65, 68, 78–79, 90

tibialis posterior, 44, 47–48, 68, 90

tibial torsion, 54, 112–113, 188

tight muscles, 84, 317

timing,
  patterns and tempos (of exercises), 29–30
  stretches, 34

toe box, 56

toes, curling, 49, 51, 71, 80, 118

toe extension, 57

toes, movements at,
  extension, 49–50
  flexion, 50–51

toes, muscle actions of, 49

torso alignment, 188

transverse arch, 41–42

transversus abdominis muscle, 32, 196

trapezius, 26, 222, 224, 227–228, 238–240, 243, 246–248, 265, 311

triceps brachii, 244, 249, 251–252, 271–272, 285, 287–288

trunk extension, 200

trunk flexion, 200

trunk rotation, 200, 217

trunk side-bending, 200, 218

turning, 11, 15, 42, 96, 102, 108, 110, 181, 249

turn-out, 6, 11, 52–54, 57, 66–69, 96, 108–109, 112–114, 121–123, 126, 143, 145, 153, 155, 157, 159–160, 165, 187, 194, 307–308, 314, 322

turn out, 82, 102, 130, 156

turns, 18, 59–61, 233

two-joint muscle, 99, 242, 244

ulna, 236, 244, 248–253

valsalva maneuver, 31–32
vastus intermedius, 96, 99
vastus lateralis, 96, 99, 121–122
vastus medialis, 96, 99, 121–122, 134
vertebrae, *see* bones, vertebrae
vertebral subluxation, 186, 194

warm-up, 18, 26, 32, 114, 169, 197, 203, 296, 305, 310–313, 328
weight-bearing movements, 166, 261, 289
weight machines, 317

weights, 9, 16–18, 37, 288–289, 291, 315, 317, 323, 329
wing, 44, 61, 63, 256, 259
winging, 43, 63–64, 259
wrist bones, 254
wrist, movements at,
    abduction, 253, 255
    adduction, 253, 256, 315
    circumduction, 253
    extension, 253, 255, 291–292, 315
    flexion, 253, 254, 262, 264, 289
    hyperextension, 253, 255, 262

Yoga, 7, 9, 37, 293, 316–318, 322, 325, 329, 335